THE

ORDEAL OF FREE LABOR

IN

THE BRITISH WEST INDIES.

BY WM. G. SEWELL.

NEW YORK:
HARPER & BROTHERS, PUBLISHERS,
FRANKLIN SQUARE.
1861.

THIS WORK,

ON THE

RESULTS OF EMANCIPATION IN THE BRITISH WEST INDIES,

IS

Dedicated,

WITH THE TRUE REGARDS OF THE AUTHOR,

TO

HIS EXCELLENCY, FRANCIS HINCKS, ESQUIRE,

GOVERNOR-IN-CHIEF OF THE WINDWARD ISLANDS.

PREFACE.

Letters on Free Labor in the British West Indies, originally written for the New York Times, and, since their publication in that journal, revised and enlarged, make up the volume now offered to the public. It is not designed, in this work, to draw from the results of British Emancipation any inference or to point any conclusion favorable or unfavorable to slave labor in the United States; and for the reason that a great territorial disparity between the islands on the one hand, and the southern section of the Union on the other, forbids even a comparison of their social and political institutions. The writer's aim has been to give, as free from comment as possible, such statistical and other information concerning the West Indian populations, their habits and customs, their industry, their commerce, and their government, as he has been able to procure from reliable sources, or to gain by personal observation. The writer does not know how far his views on the West India labor question coincide with those of the governor of the Windward Islands; and it is, therefore, proper to say that the dedication is prompted altogether by personal esteem for a valued friend, and by sentiments of high regard for a public officer who has successfully defended the West India colonies from misrepresentation, and whose liberal and impartial rule has revived a confidence in West India enterprises.

New York, November, 1860.

CONTENTS.

THE

ORDEAL OF FREE LABOR

IN THE

BRITISH WEST INDIES.

THE WINDWARD ISLANDS.

CHAPTER I.

FIRST IMPRESSIONS.

Bridgetown, Barbados, 1859.

No greater contrast could possibly be imagined than that between New York in the month of January and this beautiful Barbados. The one, as I left it in the middle of a cold snap, like some mighty floe in the Arctic Ocean, frigid and repulsive; the other, as I approached it, like an emerald gem, curiously and exquisitely set in a sea of the deepest blue, glowing with summer beauties most alluring.

The cry of "Land ho!" was not more welcome to the Portuguese discoverers of Barbados, about three centuries ago, than it was to me—passenger in a vessel familiarly known as a "horse-jockey." Let me describe the article for the benefit of all wanderers from Yankeedom who seek among these islands health or recreation during the winter months. I am informed, and the information has every appearance of truth, that the Barbadians use up their horses much more effectually and much more rapidly than Broadway omnibus-drivers, and that the trade in this domestic animal, carried on exclusively between the United States and the island, is large and profitable to all parties concerned. The *Flying Jack*, for example, leaves New York with a deck-load of threescore horses. When in the latitude of Bermuda a stiff breeze is felt from the far-famed onion-tops—perhaps, as happened to our bark, a violent head-wind for a week, making the little vessel rock and reel as she struggled on under double-reefed topsails. The unfortunate quadruped passengers—from whom the unfortunate biped passengers are only separated by a wooden partition—can not be said to enjoy the motion of the ship. They are tied by the head, so that they are unable to lie down; but, their legs being free, they kick up a devil's delight during the storm, and sharpen the sensations of their sea-sick neighbors. They snort, and neigh, and groan with terror, as each succeeding wave sweeps over them; they trample the deck as though they would tear it into a thousand pieces. All this noise and the confusion attendant thereon, the cries of Jack, as, in his vernacular, he vainly roars out "Steady," or calls to his companion on the watch to "haul taut the main-brace" of this or that animal; the confusion worse confounded when a horse tumbles down, and, as he hangs suspended by his head, all hands are summoned to his assistance; the rolling of the ship, the roaring of the tempest, and the occasional wash of a wave down the cabin stairs, are a combination of unpleasant circumstances which a sane man would naturally wish to avoid. The evils may be met singly, but concurrent they are overwhelming. Imagine a man of sense selecting a stable as a sleeping apartment, and having his victuals cooked at the other end of the same room! Nor is this all the inconvenience. When the tropical region is approached the heat becomes oppressive, and, as in our case, the distemper sometimes breaks out among the animals. The excitement of a day at sea is then varied by the death on an average of two horse passengers per diem; and as our skipper, faithful to the owner's interest, would not consign them to the deep until after they had given their last kick and a looking-glass had been held to their noses, we were often spectators of a prolonged death-scene. Poor brutes! They made no confessions. The insurance companies will not guarantee their lives; but the risk of importing horses from America being readily accepted by speculators, it follows that the trade is a profitable one. The survivors, diseased and wounded, are generally all sold twenty-four hours after their arrival, at an advance on New York prices of one hundred and fifty to two hundred per cent. Many Americans visit this island, and are compelled to take passage in sailing-ships, and they would do well to learn before they embark whether their vessel is a "horse-jockey."

Cheerily, then, most cheerily, sounded the cry of "Land ho!" It was a misty day—not such a mist as beclouds a northern sky, but a light, fleecy, vapory, refreshing mist, that sufficed to dampen the fiery ardor of the sun. We approached the Barbadian shore within fifteen miles, and could only then discern the loom of the land. It seemed much higher than geographical authorities allow. We were within a mile of the coast before it became distinctly visible. Suddenly the sun burst through the mist, like magic dispelled every cloud, and revealed a picture of most enticing beauty. There lay the island, bathed in the rich light of a tropic evening. The sun, fast sinking in the opposite horizon, was dripping with liquid gold, and its rays penetrated every nook and corner of Barbados, from the white, distinctive line which separated the water from the land up to its highest elevation. It was but a bank of gently-sloping verdure as compared with our extended landscape views; but so deliciously soft, so fresh, so fair, so varied in its minute scenery and in the delicate tints of its coloring, that it seemed more like a piece of fairy mechanism than a famous sugar-producing colony. The island, I was told, was parched for want of rain; but it looked to me far otherwise—like a New York clover-field in early summer, variegated with green of every possible hue, divided and subdivided into hill and valley, crowned with a golden wreath by the setting sun, and luxuriating in the blessings of an eternal spring.

Bridgetown, the capital of Barbados, is situated in the Bay of Carlisle, and is surrounded by an amphitheatre of minute hills, which gently rise around and beyond it. In this bay there are generally at anchor some fifty vessels, many of which are from Northern ports in the United States. The trade-winds blow continuously from the shore, and the harbor is considered a safe one, though in the open sea, from any ordinary storm.

Directly a ship drops her anchor in the Bay of Carlisle she is surrounded by a swarm of boats, and colored youths of from ten to twenty years of age scramble up her sides and darken the deck. These are held to be the worst portion of the negro population of the island, and, judging from actual investigation, I should certainly say that almost all of them were ready to lie or steal, as suited their convenience. I believe the eighth and ninth commandments are excluded from their moral code. They give a stranger a bad and most mistaken impression of the place. They are intolerable bores, by whom threats and entreaties are alike disregarded. I was going to compare them to New York cabmen at a railway station, but I would be doing a gross injustice to that important body of our independent fellow-citizens. In this class there are Creoles of every shade of color, from the bronzed quadroon to the jet-black negro. The negroes, however, predominate. They are sharp, active, and wonderfully alive to the importance of having a passenger to convey ashore. Perhaps a dozen boats will congregate where the services of only one will suffice. The owners of the boats—there are usually four boys to each—will throng the deck, or, climbing the rigging, will hang by their legs from a rope as they abuse each other and advertise the superior accommodations they have to offer. The jabber is infernal. It is impossible for the uninitiated to comprehend a dialect that sounds more like French *patois* than any possible contortion of the English tongue. But English it is, if that can be called English which finds no place in Johnson or in Webster. By the merest accident I caught the sound of an English oath; but beyond this, I no more understood the conversation than if it had been conducted in ancient Caribbee. These watermen were all well and many of them neatly dressed, with cotton shirts and trowsers, straw hats or white linen caps, and bare feet; they looked cleaner, more lithe and active, more intelligent, and more impudent than any indiscriminate body of Irish laborers that could be selected in an American city or upon an American railroad. The class of which I am speaking throng the bay and the pier at Bridgetown, and must not be taken as a type of the colored population of the island. Their chances of remuneration are small, for passengers who arrive are few in number, and, therefore, I was the more surprised that these proverbially indolent people should exhibit so much energy in the prosecution of their business. The spirit of rivalry and emulation was never more fully displayed than by them, and I was soon sensible that prejudice alone prevented me from regarding these people as quite equal in what a Yankee would call smartness to youths of their own standing in any large American or European city.

These remarks must be received as the first impressions of a stranger. To arrive at correct conclusions on the free-labor system of the island requires more research than an American would imagine. The people seem averse to statistics, and even the census has been neglected for several years past. No statistics, such as every village in the United States will possess, can be obtained in Barbados; and I am at a loss to understand the cause of such an important omission of duty on the part of the authorities. The inference of a stranger naturally is, that figures would demonstrate decay instead of progress; but the contrary is stoutly maintained by those who have the best opportunity of judging. In support of their argument they point to facts which can not be controverted, and which are so plain that he who runs may read. Whatever may be the consequences of emancipation in other West India islands, they hold that, in Barbados, it has been an undoubted success—a success established in the broad face of day, and of which every one who seeks for truth may be fully convinced.

A stranger in Barbados can not fail to be impressed at the outset by the neatness and tidiness of the homes of the poor. Humble as they are, the very worst locality that can be selected in Bridgetown is clean, and offers a favorable contrast to a New York Mulberry Street. The people are talkative and noisy after their fashion, but they are orderly and industrious, without any rowdyism, fighting, or open drunkenness of any kind whatsoever. They are most unquestionably above the level of their brethren in the United States. I marveled much as I saw them on the Sabbath-day dressed as respectably as any people in the world, and thronging their churches—intelligent, God-fearing citizens, loyal to their faith, loyal to themselves, and loyal to the government of that great empire which could afford to pour out gold like water and desolate, for a time, some of its fairest provinces in order to unloose bonds which the slaves themselves scarcely felt, and from which at first they had no desire to be released. The moral grandeur of the act may not be questioned. You feel its force as you mark the change it has wrought in the Barbadian negro, and hear him boast, with all the pride and pomposity of a down-east Yankee, that he is free.

But the elevation of the negro, if it can be proved,

does not embrace the whole argument of emancipation, for the condition and prosperity of the white inhabitants of the West India islands enter as largely into its merits as the condition and prosperity of the blacks. Have the West India proprietary been ruined by that one great grant of freedom, or did they help to bring down destruction on their own heads? Widely, wildly as this subject has been discussed for a quarter of a century, it has too often been discussed from a purely partisan point of view. There is much that is true in West Indian history, and much that will sound novel to the world still unrecorded. I dare not hope to be able to say one half of what can be said or what ought to be said, but I do hope to be a faithful reporter of existing facts and realities. I care not whither they may lead, what they may prove or what they may disprove. I have no cherished theory of my own to demonstrate. My only aim is, if possible, to throw light upon a subject never more important than at the present time, but about which, until I came here, I knew nothing and could learn nothing. The people of Great Britain and of the United States, for it is of deep interest to both, have watched these many years the contest between philanthropy run mad on the one side, and the incarnation of selfishness on the other. One party finds in the negro nothing but perfection; the other, affecting to believe in his organic inferiority, would debar him the privileges and rights of a reasonable being, and would exclude him forever from the possibility of self-culture and self-improvement. While the fanaticism of the day asserts that, if the negro will not labor in the field, it is wrong to find a substitute that will, those wedded to the traditions of slavery obstinately refuse to look beyond the length of its chain or profit by their own experience. They learn no practical lesson from the prosperity of Barbados. Though Demarara and Trinidad, with less natural advantages than Jamaica, have rallied from their depression and recovered from their embarrassments, there are some who will trace the desolation of Jamaica to no other cause than emancipation. But while extremists are fighting over abstractions, the West Indian problem is slowly and surely working itself out, confounding, in its issues, the predictions of one party, and disproving the assertions of the other.

CHAPTER II.

BARBADOS AND ITS CAPITAL.

Bridgetown, Barbados, 1859.

I DO not propose to enter into any description of this island, except in so far as it will tend to elucidate my subject—the Results of Emancipation. Elaborate and minute particulars of Barbados and her beauties may be found in the works of Schomberg, Edwards, or Martin. I can not, however, consistently pass by Bridgetown, or fail to notice its peculiarities. A stranger, and most especially an American, upon first landing, would hasten to proclaim it an exhausted city, once, possibly, the centre of a flourishing business and the emporium of great wealth, but now almost abandoned to ruin and decay. This impression would be formed from various reasons, and from none more than the contrast which the capital of Barbados presents to what we should call a rising place. To illustrate this assertion from my own experience, I might say that I was first struck with the narrow streets and the ruined appearance of the houses. It seemed as though no attempt had been made to repair their dilapidated condition within half a century. The paint was worn away from roof and wood-work, and the mortar which had fallen from the walls had never been replaced, except in very few cases. Around each dwelling of more than ordinary Barbadian pretensions there was generally an unfinished-looking wall, with broken pieces of glass bottles on the top to protect the property from the trespass of the wicked. In going to my lodging-house, a quarter of a mile distant from the wharf, I was obliged to traverse several acres of vacant lots, which were overgrown with wild cactuses and studded with moss-covered ruins. They lay in the very heart of the city—the "burnt district," as it is called, of twenty years' standing. Picturesque it was, but it gave very little indication of industry or enterprise. I passed up Broad Street, a combination of Wall Street and Broadway; but though it was the busiest time of day, I saw few signs of the enormous trade that this island carries on, and nothing to remind me of an American city with a population, as Bridgetown has, equal to that of New Haven. The lounging gait of pedestrians looked lazy to a traveler fresh from the United States, and the groups of idlers along the pier seemed to confirm the popular idea of African indolence. But first impressions are not always correct impressions. I soon discovered that the climate was a formidable enemy to paint and mortar, and that a moist temperature rendered any architectural ornamentation a piece of useless extravagance; that "the burnt district" was the site selected for new and commodious public buildings; that business was transacted with much less ostentation than in America, and that the idlers on the wharf were idle because crop-time had not come. I learnt, too, to make allowances for the enervating influences of a tropical climate and for the penalties of exposure to a burning sun.

The town seemed to me to possess peculiarities at

once African, European, and West Indian. The swarms of chattering negroes in the streets keep the African aspect of Bridgetown constantly before your eyes. The market-place—about an acre of ground inclosed with a neat row of butchers' stalls—reminds one of New Orleans. There the clatter of tongues extolling the virtue of divers fruits and vegetables offered for sale is Sambo all the world over. The centre of the market inclosure is filled with splendid evergreens, and beneath their shade several scores of negro women, with pairs of scales and piles of yams, sugar-cane, sweet potatoes, oranges, grape-fruit, mangoes, etc., before them, earn their daily bread. The fish-market—a solitary shed erected on the beach—is in full blast about nightfall, after the fishermen have returned well laden with flying-fish; and at the confused noise in this focus of business even a London Billingsgate would be compelled to hide its diminished head. It is characteristic of Sambo throughout; his untiring tongue never stops for a moment to take rest. A cab-stand presents another vivid picture of Sambo. In the midst of Trafalgar Square, near the statue of Nelson, and beneath a gigantic evergreen, the cabmen find it convenient and profitable to assemble. Woe unto the stranger whom they espy and who may be in search of a one-horse chaise; and when he has selected his vehicle, and has made his escape from the crowd, it is amusing to hear the successful driver denounce the "unperlite b'havior of dem niggers," and deplore the city as the "awfulest he never see'd."

I think I was most struck with the European aspect of Bridgetown. There is, it is true, an absence of that stern look of labor and endurance which characterize a purely Anglo-Saxon city; but there is no slight similarity between the Barbadian capital and some inferior town in the south of France. I was almost startled every now and then as I came across a banana, a cocoa, or a cabbage-palm-tree. Their tropical look seemed out of place, and, for a moment, I wondered how they existed there. A traveler from the north will be most liable to forget that, in Bridgetown, he is far down in the tropics, within eight hundred miles of the equator. The climate is not tropical; it is to be imagined and felt, for it can not be described. Select the most perfect day that September ever presented to New York, and I should do injustice to a Barbadian sun and Barbadian breezes if I compared Barbadian with American weather. The sun necessarily gives out a great heat, but it is always tempered by incessant winds and by intermittent showers. Night or day, in winter or in summer, the temperature knows no change. The inconveniences of heat are seldom felt; the penalties of cold are never known. There are no thunder-storms like those which desolate more elevated regions within the torrid zones; no poisonous reptiles of any kind; no annoying insects like those which in summer months will make known their presence even in the latitude of New York. The appearance of the houses, which are of one story and built solidly of stone, may perhaps remind you that you are in a country where the severities of winter are not even imagined, and, after you have entered them, you will no longer fancy yourself in a European or a North American dwelling. The spacious rooms, with polished pine floors, the contrivances to make every thing about you look cool, as well as to make you feel cool—the huge pitchers of ice-water on the side-boards and the comfortable cane chairs, placed so as to catch the never-ending breezes —are luxuries here which one might look for as necessities in other tropical countries. The inside of a house in Bridgetown is very different from what its outside appearance would lead a stranger to infer; and this disregard of outward appearance is only one of a thousand English idiosyncrasies to be encountered. A few scattered purely tropical trees are about the only outward indications that Bridgetown possesses of being a tropical city. You may be puzzled every now and then by the sight of a black soldier in Zouave costume, or a black policeman in a London uniform, but they are anomalies. They do not belong to the picture.

Bridgetown, in fact, is European, though somewhat behind the age of European progress. It is, perhaps, necessarily behind the age, owing to its insulated position. Its shops remind you of an inferior English town, and it is only after you have entered them that you discover how well and with what first-rate articles they are supplied. The streets are macadamized with the native calcareous rock, and are light-colored and perfectly smooth. The white population have wonderfully preserved their English manners and customs. You find here none of the indolent and luxurious habits of the tropics. Though a vast amount of business is transacted before breakfast, the lazy noonday siesta is not indulged in, but work is steadily performed until four o'clock in the afternoon. The churches are similar in their architecture to those that may be seen in any English village; the forms and ceremonies of English society are preserved even to the farce of wearing a stove-pipe hat whenever you wish to appear in full dress; in spite of yams and mangoes the dinner you eat is as nearly English as circumstances will admit; and the bed you lie upon is unmistakably of English make and fashion. Perhaps the British officers, military and naval, help to keep alive the peculiar customs of the mother-land; but it is undoubtedly a fact that the Barbadians take a pride in preserving as close a resemblance to the old country as the differences of position will allow, and I am not prepared to say that in so doing they act an unwise part. The few Americans who have emigrated here, though they have brought with them the spirit of American invention and enterprise, have lost their peculiarities, and have succumbed to prevailing custom. But Yankee clocks, Yankee buggies, and that famous Yankee establishment to which all Bridgetown daily resorts—the ice-house—have brought fortunes to their proprietors and delight to the hearts of the Creole population.

Directly you leave the precincts of the capital the European phase of the island vanishes. You may be reminded of the fair scenery of Old England, to which, indeed, these lovely hills and valleys are likened; but you can never for a moment forget that you are looking upon productions which no English soil could bring forth, and which no English sun could ripen. The landscape scenery is necessarily on a small scale, but in variety it is complete, and occasionally it approaches the sublime. One of the grandest spectacles I ever witnessed was the view from Hackleton's Cliff—a bold bluff on the eastern coast of the island, rising

1000 feet above the level of the sea. Looking north, you see in the far distance a range of hills running parallel with the one upon which you are standing, and in the intermediate valley, which gradually slopes toward the sea, the productions of all the Indies are gathered together. Here and there, upon some projection of coral rock which the cactuses carefully conceal, a palm-tree towers like a land-mark on the horizon, or a gigantic sentinel at his post. Cottages are thickly scattered over the picture; the red wheel of the sugar-mill, unchanged for a century, may be seen at every point, and you may strain your eyes in vain to look for a single spot which has not been cultivated even beyond what we should call perfection. The surf, as it crawls up the long line of white sand that lies extended far beneath you, and the ocean beyond, complete a picture of what may well be termed the Eden of Barbados. You look down upon a valley which burns and blazes with all the heat of the tropics, but you are standing upon a spot ever open to the fresh and invigorating breezes of the temperate zones.

What I have said here in regard to cultivation is equally applicable to the entire island, from the estate of the richest planter to the plot of the poorest negro. I have traveled over the whole of Barbados, and have seen scarcely a single acre of uncultivated land. The highways impassable forty years ago except for horsemen, are now perfect models of cleanliness and smoothness, and the cane-fields, more luxuriant than those of Louisiana or Texas, are without inclosure, and extend to the very edge of the roads, which, for want of space, appear to have been reduced to the narrowest limits. Barbados is essentially a sugar-island, and you do not meet in it the abundance of fruit-trees that are to be seen in St. Vincent or Grenada. The cocoanut-trees, which were once valued at a pound sterling each per annum, were destroyed some years ago by a plague of insects, and the few that remain are more ornamental than profitable. Orange-trees, lemons, grape-fruit, mangoes, and bananas are abundant in Barbados, but they are not reared in such large groves here as in other islands. The cabbage-palm, of gigantic stature, is one of the most beautiful of its class, and is best calculated to adorn the peculiarities of the landscape. A planter's house is generally surrounded with these stately trees, which make it an object of attraction for miles around.

I have said enough, perhaps, in regard to the general appearance of Barbados, to give an idea such as I wish to convey of its great natural beauty and high cultivation. I shall proceed, therefore, forthwith to examine the political and social condition of the colony, and compare it now with what it was before the abolition of slavery. The question has many ramifications, and each of the West India islands—I might almost say each plantation—must stand upon its own merits, for I know that causes which might ruin one would not affect another. Arguments that may apply to overcrowded Barbados might with equal justice be used in regard to Kansas and Dacotah as to the rich virgin soil and sparsely-settled island of Trinidad. The subject, indeed, is not to be approached hastily; but I hope that the information which I have procured only from authentic sources I shall succeed in giving with unbiased faithfulness.

CHAPTER III.

THE GOVERNING CLASSES OF BARBADOS.

Bridgetown, Barbados, 1859.

In comparing the commerce of the British West India colonies under freedom with their commerce under slavery, it has been broadly stated that, in 1831, the sugar exports amounted to four million cwt., and in 1857 to three million cwt.; and upon this ground the deterioration of all the colonies is asserted. While I do not deny the fact of a diminished exportation of the staple product, I must dispute the conclusion to which it has given rise. It is altogether unfair to group the islands for any such purpose—as unfair as it would be to class half a dozen Mexican departments with Texas, and judge of the condition of Texas by the average prosperity of the whole. The West India islands differ essentially one from another. Evils which combined to injure one have not existed in another; and while some, under the emancipation *régime*, have notoriously fallen off in their trade, others have as notoriously progressed. We have given due credit to the alleged disastrous effects of emancipation without attempting to account for the phenomenon that Barbados, for example, is infinitely more prosperous now than she ever was in the palmiest days of slavery. This fact—for a fact I expect to prove it—has induced me to look more closely than I otherwise should have done into the past and present condition of this island; to examine the relations of her landed aristocracy and her people as landlord and tenant, master and servant, planter and laborer; to compare slave labor with free labor, and the civil and social condition of the island under one system with its civil and social condition under the other; and to explain, if possible, the causes that have increased Barbadian resources, and have contributed so greatly to Barbadian wealth.

I will admit at the outset that I have no sympathy with the argument of the Abolitionists, that the question of emancipation is one in which the black race are to be only considered, or that "depreciation of property is as nothing compared with a depreciation of morality." I deem the question a commercial one, to be judged favorably or unfavorably by commercial rules; for whatever philanthropists may say to the contrary, it seems to me very evident that a system which would bring inevitable ruin on that portion of a population which controls the elements of civilization can not contribute to the moral or material progress of a country.

Those who have searched for the truth, and have patiently and with unbiased judgment unraveled the thread of West Indian difficulties, can not fail to have remarked that, long before the Emancipation Act was passed, the sugar estates had reached the *acmé* of their prosperity, and had commenced steadily to decline. The embarrassments of the proprietary in those days were owing to heavy incumbrances, to want of capital, to extravagance, mismanagement, and absenteeism. But whatever the cause, in whole or in part, it is sufficient to establish the fact; and scores of Parliamentary blue-books will furnish particulars to those who are curious in such matters of the chronic distress of West India planters. We find, for instance, that in 1792, before the abolition of the slave-trade, the Jamaica House of Representatives reported that within twenty years 177 estates had been sold for debt. Again, in 1807, the same body reported that in the five years preceding the abolition of the slave-trade 65 estates had been abandoned. The complaint of the planters then was that the old islands were unable to compete with the new colonies which, by conquest, had recently become dependencies of the British Crown, and they endeavored to secure a protective tariff in the British market. Another grievance was the abolition of the slave-trade. On this account the planters were unable, as they said, to compete with the foreign colonies, and we find them again before Parliament pleading "that the West Indies are now and have been for some time past laboring under multiplied difficulties and embarrassments." In 1831 a convention of delegates from all the West India colonies met in this very island upon the basis "that a unanimous expression of the sentiments of the colonists on the present alarming and depressed state of the West Indies would tend to impress more strongly on his majesty's government and the Parliament of England the very urgent necessity which exists for immediate and substantial relief to save them from impending ruin." It was the policy of the planters at this time to prove the expense of slave labor, and to show that, without the slave-trade, they could not produce sugar as cheaply as it was produced in those islands where the traffic was not prohibited. In the

Parliamentary blue-books of the day we find the most elaborate statistics (alarming to contemplate) of the cost of slave labor, and, among other items of this expensive system, one which fixed the average number of non-effective slaves on an estate at 30 and 40 per cent. was strenuously urged. A few years afterward, when the emancipation excitement was at its height, and the planter again came before Parliament with his grievance, his policy was changed. He had now to demonstrate the cheapness of slave labor as compared with the extravagant cost of free labor; and it is curious and amusing to compare the statements before the Commons Committee of the same men who sought in 1831 to place slave labor at the highest, and in 1837 at the lowest possible figures, and to note their glaring inconsistencies.

In proper historical order, emancipation was the third grievance of which the planter complained, and over this he brooded for many years. He did not hesitate to ascribe all his misfortunes to this, the latest act of injustice, carried through the British Parliament in a moment of hasty enthusiasm, and made a law without the consent or advice, and against the interests of those whom it most deeply and most vitally concerned. The act well-nigh produced as great a political as it did a social revolution in the islands; and it may naturally be supposed that many years would elapse before the planter would become reconciled to the change. Yet he *did* become reconciled; he believes now that the system under which his estate is worked is cheaper and more profitable to himself than that of the old *régime*. With what reason I shall hereafter have occasion to show; but I assert, without the fear of a single contradiction, that no Barbadian planter would hesitate in 1859 to select free labor in preference to slave labor, as in his belief the more economical system of the two. But the old spirit of the plantocracy still lives. When that fabric of barbaric times, Monopoly, was swept away, the West India proprietary once more lifted their voice in complaint. "What," said they to the British people, "after all your professions of philanthropy, are you going to admit slave-grown sugar on a par with free-grown sugar? are you going to place a premium on slavery after you have crippled your own colonies with abolition?" But alas! for the selfishness of human nature, the British of to-day are a practical people; and, whatever the philanthropy of their fathers may have been, or whatever their own may still be, they are determined to have their sugar at the lowest possible figure. They want to place this emancipation bugbear upon a broader basis than the one on which it has hitherto stood. They no longer favor their pet scheme, but have left it to fight its own battle with slave labor, and whatever be the result they will be the gainers. The argument of the planter that free trade in sugar places a premium upon slavery is certainly a home-thrust for the Abolitionist, who contends that this question of emancipation should only be considered from a moral point of view. But it is like all other pleas for relief advanced by the West India proprietary. They have represented themselves as the victims of profound distress under the slave-trade, under slavery, and under emancipation, omitting only to state that this distress was aggravated, if not caused, by their own extravagance, and by the monstrous debts with which their estates were heavily burdened.

If the planters admit, as they all unquestionably do, that free labor is cheaper than slave labor, they do not agree that, under the former system, the necessary force can be as readily and as regularly obtained as under the latter. This, in fact, is the great grievance of the present day—not of Barbadian planters, but of those in the other islands. It must be borne in mind that, protected by her small area and dense population—a population larger to the square mile than that of China—Barbados since emancipation has not suffered from the want of labor like other colonies. To this cause more, perhaps, than to any other, she owes her present wonderful prosperity. It is usually urged, as the very strongest argument against emancipation, that the negroes, no longer compelled to work, abandoned the estates, which, as a natural consequence, fell into ruin and decay. I am not going to deny that many and many estates were abandoned, but the causes of their being abandoned should be rightly understood. If the indolence of the negro be one cause, a second may be found, as history proves, in the mortgages with which the estates were burdened; and a third, as practical observation will demonstrate, in the uncertain and impolitic relations that have existed since emancipation between landlord and tenant.

At the time of emancipation the slaves were left in possession of their houses and allotment-lands, which they continued to occupy after their term of apprenticeship had expired. In Barbados the tenant worked for the landlord at 20 per cent. below the common market rate, and his service was taken as an equivalent for rent. But the practice produced endless difficulties and disagreements; the law did not bear out the planter, and another system was introduced. Under the new practice, still in force, a laborer has a house and land allotment on an estate for which he pays a stipulated rent; but he is under an engagement besides, *as a condition of renting*, to give to the estate a certain number of days' labor at certain stipulated wages, varying from one sixth to one third less than the market price. The rate of wages for field labor in Barbados is about 24 cents per day; but the laborer, fettered by the system of tenancy-at-will, is compelled to work for his landlord at 20 cents per day. He is, therefore, virtually a slave; for if he resists the conditions of his bond he is ejected by summary process, and loses the profit he hoped to reap on his little stock. This remnant of coercion must be abolished wherever it exists—and it prevails, with some exceptions, in all the West India colonies—before it can be said that emancipation has been thoroughly tested. A free tenancy on an equitable system—a yearly instead of the present monthly tenure—are reforms most urgently needed, and a movement in this direction has been already undertaken. Last autumn an association was formed in Barbados to improve the social and moral condition of the laboring population; and, in the preamble to the resolutions adopted at the first meeting, it was asserted—a fact too patent to deny—that one of the main barriers to social progress arose from "a want of confidence between the employer and the employed." But the proprietary body have so set their faces against the movement that its chances of success for the present are very unpromising. The planters, tenacious of their privileges, and, like aristocracies all the world over, anxious to retain their power over the masses, met to counteract the new movement. They denounced the society "for attempting to arouse unjust suspicions in the minds of the ignorant touching their rights;" they viewed "with alarm" and "as a political movement" the desire for a more liberal tenure, and as "an endeavor to jeopardize the successful system of plantation management as now adopted;" they maintained that "the best of feeling" existed between them and their tenants, and, finally, they declared their "inherent right" to adopt such measures as they might think fit for the good government, safety, and well-doing of their properties. The absurdity of these pretensions in a professedly free country need not be pointed out; and I only introduce them in order to show the illiberal nature of the tenure which the planters still resolutely uphold. They hope by stringent measures to retain the liberated peasantry on their estates, but their laws produce the very opposite effect; and in spite of the warnings of experience and the dictates of common sense, they obstinately stick to a policy which has ruined many a fair West India property.

I must again repeat that Barbados offers a solitary exception to the general argument. The population here, as I have said, is extremely dense, averaging 800 persons to the square mile, and partly from an aversion of the negro to leave his home, partly from his fear, still easily excited, of being sold into slavery, no material emigration from the island has ever taken place. In Barbados, therefore, labor has been always abundant, and the island, which out of 106,000 acres has 100,000 under cultivation, presents the appearance of a perfect garden. Land, as I shall hereafter show, averages $500 an acre; and when it is added that the land which brings such a price is purchased for agricultural purposes only, we have, in the fact, conclusive evidence of most remarkable prosperity. All this, practically considered, is owing in a greater degree to an adequate laboring population than to the special benefits of abolition, as illustrated in an Anti-slavery Society's annual report. But no credit is due to the Barbadian plantocracy for retaining that adequate laboring population in their employ. To the latter it was the option of work at low wages, and on most illiberal terms, or starvation. But in other colonies, as in Trinidad or British Guiana, where the same illiberal tenure prevailed, the result was very different. There, where land was cheap and abundant and the population sparse, the laborer soon discovered that a path to independence lay open before him; and as the planter became more stubborn in his system of coercion, and more rigid in exacting the requirements of an obnoxious tenure law, he discovered too late that, for want of labor, lost through his own mistaken policy, he was compelled to abandon his estate. And yet it is surprising how the negro, in spite of all disadvantages, has clung to the soil upon which he was born. So true is this, that after having closely examined the causes of estates being deserted, I find that they are debt, incumbrance, and want of capital, far more than want of labor. We in the United States have heard of abandoned properties in the West Indies, and, without much investigation, have listened to the planters' excuse—the indolence of the negro, who refuses to work except under compulsion; but I shall be able to show that, in those colonies where estates have been abandoned, the laboring classes, instead of passing from servitude to indolence and idleness, have set up for themselves, and that small proprietors since emancipation have increased a hundred-fold. I shall also show that in those islands, as in St. Lucia, where a more liberal tenure prevails, the industry of the laboring population is not to be questioned. It was only the other day that I read an extract from a Tobago paper in the planting interest, in which the writer deplores "the perverse selfishness of the laborers." He complains that the laborers have large patches of land in cultivation, and hire help *at higher wages than the estates can afford to pay*, and suggests "as the only remedy for these serious evils" a fresh importation of coolies. The planter can indeed point to Barbadian estates as having been successfully worked under his peculiar tenure system; but they are exceptions, not the rule; and that they *have* been successfully worked is owing to an overcrowded laboring population, and not to any merit whatsoever in the tenure itself.

But there is a more general view to be taken of the question—a more general cause than the specific one which I have explained, to which the abandonment of the sugar-estates may be assigned. It is a truism that where land is cheap there labor is dear; and where land is dear there labor is cheap. In the overcrowded districts of England land is dear and labor cheap; in the sparsely-settled states of Western America land is cheap and labor dear. This became the case in the West Indies as soon as the people were released from bondage. The examples are precisely parallel, the reasoning and deductions exactly similar. In the old and thickly-settled island of Barbados land was dear, the people could not purchase, and labor has remained to this day cheap and plentiful. In Trinidad or in British Guiana land was cheap and plentiful; the people could purchase, and have purchased in surprising numbers, and labor is, consequently, both scarce and dear. In Barbados, through their overcrowded condition and the policy of the planter, the people have been kept in a subservient position. In Trinidad or British Guiana the people have been able to exchange a condition of servitude for one of independence—in other words, to leave the estates upon which they were laborers; and they are, as a natural consequence, more enlightened, better educated, and more wealthy than their brethren in Barbados. Compare, again, a thickly-populated European district with a sparsely-settled county in Western America. In the one case the vast majority are toiling for their daily pittance, and, whatever the wealth of the place may be, it is in the hands of the few. In the other case there is a population of freeholders, every man independent, and wealth is evenly distributed among all. Though the European district should export a hundred-fold more than the American county, no one will pretend that the American farmer is not much more elevated in the social scale than the European laborer. This is exactly the distinction that should be made between the negroes in Trinidad and in the other islands where they have been able to leave the estates and work for themselves, and those in Barbados, where, by force of circumstances, they have been compelled to remain on the estates and work for others. It is the instinct of human nature to aspire to independence, and, in this respect, the arguments applicable to a white man may with equal propriety be applied to the negro.

I have considered the planter as a lord of the soil and as a landlord; but before I leave this branch of my subject I have a few words to say of him as a legislator. Politically considered, the population of Barbados may be divided into three classes—the aristocracy, who are the planters; the middle class, composed alike of white and colored mechanics, and the lower orders, which are the black laborers. The first alone is represented in the Legislature; and the government, like the old Venetian republic, is a pure oligarchy. The influence of the governor is the only protection for the masses against plantocratic legislation. In the present representative of her majesty people of all classes have found an impartial chief and a statesman of profound and practical experience. He has made the labor question, as a question of political and social economy, the subject of the closest investigation within the limits of his government, which includes Barbados, St. Vincent, Tobago, Grenada, and St. Lucia. Mr. Hincks has neither forgotten nor forsaken the enlightened and liberal views which placed him for so many years at the head of the Canadian administration, and we find him in Barbados earnestly advocating whenever he can an extension of the franchise. But, by his very position, a colonial governor is deprived of any active political influence, and the Barbadian franchise remains as it stood a century ago. It gives a vote to every freeholder with a rental of $60 per annum, to a leaseholder who pays $320 per annum, and to a possessor of a town occupancy of $160 per annum. This franchise utterly excludes the middle class from the polls, and places legislation under the complete control of the planting interest. I will not, therefore, be deemed far wrong when I call this government an oligarchy, especially when it is known that, at the last election for the "popular branch" of the Legislature, the whole number of votes polled in Barbados amounted to one hundred and forty-seven, out of a population of one hundred and fifty thousand souls!

The planting interest of these islands may be characterized as one of unqualified selfishness. But it has not the merit of being a prudent, sagacious, or far-seeing selfishness. Extravagant in all that pertained to their own ease and luxury; penurious when the improvement, moral, social, or political, of the people was in question; tenacious of their aristocratic privileges, opposed to reform, and behind the age in political, agricultural, and mechanical science, the planters themselves have done all they could to retard the progress of the West India colonies, and to aggravate the evils which an ill-planned and untimely scheme of emancipation entailed upon the islands. Theirs was not the broad, grasping selfishness of a powerful oligarchy wise enough to combine their own aggrandizement with that of the nation at large; but it has been from first to last a narrow-minded selfishness that pursued crooked paths to accumulate gain at the expense of the public weal, and to the infinite detriment of the colonial credit.

CHAPTER IV.

THE BLACK AND COLORED POPULATION OF BARBADOS.

Bridgetown, Barbados, 1859.

WHILE the over-crowded condition of Barbados has tended to keep her laboring population in a subservient position, a deficient system of education has done much to prevent the circulation of general intelligence. There would be nothing surprising, and no ground for argument against emancipation in the fact, if fact it could be proved, that the laboring classes are still as ignorant and unlettered as they were in the days of slavery. But, in spite of all obstacles, I find that after the lapse of twenty years they have made decided progress in the social scale, and, though their natural vices are often shocking to witness, they are not so abundant or so extravagant as a theorist would suppose them to be after the restrictions of slavery had been suddenly removed.

It is a fact which speaks volumes, that within the last fifteen years, in spite of the extraordinary price of land and the low rate of wages, the small proprietors of Barbados holding less than five acres have increased from 1100 to 3537. A great majority of these proprietors were formerly slaves, subsequently free laborers, and finally landholders. This is certainly an evidence of industrious habits, and a remarkable contradiction to the prevailing idea that the negro will only work under compulsion. That idea was formed and fostered from the habits of the negro as a slave; his habits as a freeman, developed under a wholesome stimulus and settled by time, are in striking contrast to his habits as a slave. I am simply stating a truth in regard to the Barbadian Creole which here, at least, will not be denied. I have conversed on the subject with all classes and conditions of people, and none are more ready to admit than the planters themselves that the free laborer in Barbados is a better, more cheerful, and more industrious workman than the slave ever was under a system of compulsion. These are the opinions of men who themselves were once violently opposed to freedom, and who still strive to keep the laboring classes in complete dependence; and they are opinions so universal that I have sought dilgently, but in vain, to hear them contradicted. The negro will not work with the steadiness of a white man, nor can it be expected that he should, with all the disadvantages of a tropical climate against him. But from my own observations, which I purposely made as extended as possible, I can assert that the crowds of laborers, male and female, whom I frequently met in the cane-fields, were as diligent in the performance of their duties as any other class of Africans I ever saw either in freedom or in slavery; and actual comparisons have proved that the free laborer gets through more work in a specified time than ever a slave did under the old system.

I can not speak as highly of the morality of the laboring population of Barbados as I can of their industry. The clergy may publish church and school statistics, which, I admit, go to show that scholars and churchmen multiply. But statistics on such subjects are not of much importance when they run counter to common every-day experience. To prove that the vicious put on a religious demeanor with their Sunday coat, and will listen patiently to a tedious, incomprehensible sermon, only makes the case worse. It is shown that since emancipation the higher crimes are less frequently committed than they were before. Crimes of violence are almost unknown, and in the streets, thanks to efficient police regulations, the most perfect order is preserved; but crimes of calculation, thieving, swindling, and the minor vices have apparently increased. I speak from prison statistics, and it must be borne in mind that over a large number, if not all, of these offenses the planter formerly had exclusive jurisdiction, and they were never known beyond the precincts of his own estate. It is, therefore, unfair to make any deductions from the criminal records of the present day and compare them with those of the past, when no just comparison can be instituted. But I have seen exhibitions of unrestrained passion, of cruelty, and of vice, to which, in a state of slavery, the negro would never be permitted to give vent. I have seen parents beat their children in such an inhuman manner as to make me feel that liberty to them was a curse to all over whom they were allowed to exercise any authority or control. I am speaking now of what is the rule rather than the exception among the lowest class of the negro population. Among their other vices, immorality and promiscuous intercourse of the sexes are almost universal. From the last census it appears that more than half of the children born in Barbados are illegitimate.

The clergy, and with some show of reason, claim that the immorality of the people under freedom is not so bad as it was under slavery, where marriage was not even allowed. But I can not think the argument sound. It may show that the new civil and social *régime* is an improvement on the old one; but *quoad* those who, at their own election, prefer vice to virtue, it does not present them in a very favorable light.

Against the middle class—as a class—the imputation of unfaithfulness to the marriage vow could not be maintained; but among the laboring people morality, not now through ignorance or compulsion, but from choice, remains at the lowest ebb. I leave the reader to draw what inference he pleases from such a state of things. I simply report facts. But it seems to me that the moral grounds of the Abolitionist for removing the restrictions of slavery are, in Barbados at least, the very worst that could be selected. Morality has not kept pace with material progress. Making every allowance for the influence of climate, there is still no palliation for such a superabundance of vice.

Observing the wide distinction that exists between the colored people of the middle and those of the laboring classes, I have no hesitation in saying that it is chiefly due to an imperfect and erroneous system of education. That education is not based upon the broad democratic principle that it is the province of the state to see that the children of the state possess sufficient intelligence and information to perform their duties as freemen. Education in Barbados is confined to those who have the means to pay for the luxury of knowledge, and though statistics show a marked progress since the date of emancipation, it is rather the progress of a class than of the whole population. Of the daily primary schools in connection with the Church of England, which in Barbados is the established Church, there were in 1834 twenty-seven, with an average of 1574 scholars; in 1858, twenty-two years afterward, the schools had increased to 70 and the scholars to 6180, besides the establishment of an infant school, with an average attendance of 1140 children. The Sunday-schools, which, in 1834, numbered 19, with an attendance of 1679, now number 24, with an attendance of 2071. On the other hand it must be observed that what were called estate schools under slavery exist no longer. The schools enumerated above are all in connection with the Church of England; those attached to the Moravian and Wesleyan persuasions, of which I have been unable to procure statistics, may number about half as many more. But all the schools are under church influence, and are necessarily imbued with church prejudices; and were education on such a system much more extended than it really is, one would scarcely look for any wholesome diffusion of popular instruction. If we are to judge of the capacities of the negro population by those who have been fortunate enough to receive a tolerable education, we must believe that knowledge here, as elsewhere, will elevate the laboring classes, and will greatly diminish prevailing vice. The large increase of small landed proprietors, the number of colored mechanics, merchants, clerks, and business men, in public and private establishments—all of whom make up the middle class—abundantly illustrate the industry of the African and his capacity for improvement.

I need not attempt to delineate what is so thoroughly well known as the character of the untutored negro. His degradation I do not doubt; his moral and intellectual deficiencies can not possibly excite surprise. But what I do protest against is, that this photograph of the enslaved African should be held up as the likeness of the same man after he has been twenty years free. All who have witnessed African slavery will be ready to recognize the careless, reckless, thoughtless nature of the bondsman, as exhibited during passing moments of relief from the eye of a taskmaster. Would any white people in the world, born and bred in slavery, uneducated, untaught, ignorant even of the fact that they were responsible beings, act differently? Would any white people in the world similarly situated fail to act as the blacks acted when they found themselves suddenly freed from the restraints of a rigorous and vindictive code? I think the wonder is, that in all this Western Archipelago there was a solitary freeman on the morning of emancipation willing to remain in the same position that he filled as a slave if it were possible for him to earn his bread in any other way. Twenty years ago! Let the reader reflect that it was only twenty years ago that these people were degraded, despised, besotted in ignorance; that they were in the same abject condition that the Africans of Cuba occupy to-day; and if he marvel not at the change and the contrast he will marvel at nothing. Where are the people in the world who, in the same space of time, have made the same progress in civilization? It is not fair to select those, be they numerous or be they few, who have been unable as yet to shake off the traditions of their servitude, and who remain the thriftless, idle creatures that they were in times forever gone by. How, in the name of all that is reasonable, does this affect the argument? how does it prove that the African is incapable of being brought up to the level of the white race? When we wish to illustrate the power and capacity of the great Anglo-Saxon race we do not look for our subjects in the coal-pits of England, but we point to her statesmen, her orators, her men of science, her men of art. I protest, then, against the criticism which consigns to utter worthlessness the West Indian Africans because a dozen, or twenty, or a hundred good-for-nothing fellows lounge about the streets of Bridgetown, or because a planter or a dozen planters are annoyed that one or a dozen of their laborers have deserted them in their time of need. The same inconveniences are suffered in every free country where labor is scarce; and many a New England farmer loses his crop because he can not obtain timely assistance to reap it. The only philosophical way to determine the capabilities of the African race is to look at those, and their number exceeds all belief, who have emerged from serfdom, in spite of serious obstacles and downright opposition, to become most intelligent and cultivated men—men of wealth and position, fully able to appreciate their independence and their rights of citizenship. The colored mechanics and artisans of Barbados, I most unhesitatingly assert, are equal in general intelligence to the artisans and mechanics of any race in any part of the world equally remote from the great centres of civilization. They are now what the peasantry will be as soon as education is more generally diffused. It is impossible to produce a single man of color in Barbados, if he can boast of any education at all, who will answer to the popular idea of the negro character. That character, as I said before, is the character of a slave, or of a free man before he has *learned to work* or understand his moral responsibilities. There are many, doubtless, in such a condition to-day, but let the blame be laid on those who merit the censure. Let the planting interest, which includes the legislators, the guardians, and the absolute rulers of this island, be condemned for their folly and selfishness, in that they have made no effort to second the work of emancipation, but rather have stood as a stumbling-block in the way, no effort to instruct the negro or teach him his duties as a freeman, no effort to conciliate his affections or command his allegiance, no effort to elevate him socially, politically, or morally, but—most fatal error!—have actually striven to keep him in ignorance and servile dependence. What wonder that, with such a power arrayed against his progress, many a peasant born a slave should live a freeman without appreciating the blessings purchased for him at an unparalleled cost? What wonder if he be thriftless, thoughtless, indifferent about the future, and only concerned in the enjoyment of the present moment? Is the course that ought to have been pursued from the very first any longer to be doubted? Emancipate these people from ignorance, give them power to understand their duties and their rights as freemen, and we shall hear no more drivel about organic defects in their mental capacity. As far as their numbers go, greatly deficient as I believe these numbers to be for the wants of the colonies, they will form an intelligent, peaceable, and industrious portion of the laboring classes. I am sick of the statement so constantly and so thoughtlessly repeated that the African won't work. This, of course, is not said of Barbados, for its labor market is overstocked; but it is said of other islands where land is plentiful and labor scarce. Won't work? Why should they work for the planter, and bind themselves to a new tyranny? Where is the moral obligation that chains them forever to the serfdom of estate labor? Why should they work for a master when they can work more profitably for themselves, and enjoy at the same time a perfect independence? Why should they work for any one who does not take the trouble to point out a single advantage to be gained in his service? Would an American work for another on any such terms? I have shown that the negro has grave faults of character—faults which, unchecked, must affect the prosperity of a country in which the laboring population are of African descent; but I do believe that, under a wiser system of plantation management than that practiced in most of the colonies, and with more extended education, these faults would be speedily eradicated. I can not doubt that, if the governing classes in the West Indies had pursued a more liberal policy than they have done, if they had consulted in some degree the interest and the welfare of the people upon whom their own prosperity largely depended, the success of emancipation at the present day would be so securely and so widely established that no misrepresentation could possibly conceal it.

The condition of the colored population of Barbados demonstrates, on the whole, that they lack neither industry nor natural intelligence. The habit of labor, after all, is an acquired one; and no man, white or black, will really work where necessity does not exist. I have watched with great interest Barbadian laborers going to work, and their light, elastic step and cheerful faces indicate the very opposite of lazy dispositions. If their moral progress falls short of what the Abolitionist would ask us to believe, it is, doubtless, owing as much to the want of properly directed educational efforts as to any other cause. The masses are certainly no worse than they were under slavery; while those who had the intelligence, industry, and energy to rise, *have* risen to positions of competence, independence, and wealth which they never could have attained and enjoyed under any other than a free system.

CHAPTER V.

EXPERIENCES OF FREE AND SLAVE LABOR IN BARBADOS.

Bridgetown, Barbados, 1859.

I HAVE argued that the question of emancipation in the British West Indies, or in Barbados, which is under special consideration, is a commercial question, and must be determined by a commercial standard. If this be true, and if, as I maintain, all other issues are involved in this, it is plain that a faithful comparison between the relative cost of free and slave labor, as found in Barbados, will exhibit which of the two systems is best suited to that island. If it be cheaper to raise sugar in Barbados with free labor than with slave labor, then emancipation in Barbados has been a success. If not, not. Among a multitude of estimates that I have obtained on the subject I select one presented by the governor of these islands. In a letter, written for publication and very widely circulated, his excellency says:

"As to the relative cost of slave and free labor in this colony, I can supply facts on which the most implicit reliance can be placed. They have been furnished to me by the proprietor of an estate containing 300 acres of land, and situated at a distance of about 12 miles from the shipping port. The estate referred to produced during slavery an annual average of 140 hogsheads of sugar of the present weight, and required 230 slaves. It is now worked by 90 free laborers—60 adults, and 30 under 16 years of age. Its average product during the last seven years has been 194 hhds. The total cost of labor has been £770 16*s.*, or £3 19*s.* 2*d.* per hogshead of 1700 pounds. The average of pounds of sugar to each laborer during slavery was 1043 pounds, and during freedom 3660 pounds. To estimate the cost of slave labor the value of 230 slaves must be ascertained; and I place them at what would have been a low average—£50 sterling each—which would make the entire stock amount to £11,500. This at 6 per cent. interest, which, on such property, is much too low an estimate, would give £690; cost of clothing, food, and medical attendance, I estimate at £3 10*s.*, making £805. Total cost £1495, or £10 12*s.* per hogshead, while the cost of free labor on the same estate is under £4."

This, it must be remembered, is a practical comparison between free and slave labor, and not an abstract estimate of the expenses of the two systems, to be varied by time, place, or circumstance. It is also a reasonable average of similar comparisons that might be instituted on all the estates of the island. I might easily multiply examples; but those who would doubt the fairness of the one I have selected would doubt a hundred others. I can only say, on the assurance of the governor himself, that his statistics come from a source of unquestioned reliability, and, if their application as an average representation be denied, it must be on the ground that the expenses of slavery have been under-estimated. What Cuban slaveholder would place the average value of his slaves at $250, and the cost of clothing, maintenance, medical attendance, and depreciation at only $17 per annum? James M'Queen, in his "Statistics of the British Empire," gives the actual cost of maintaining a slave in Barbados before emancipation, with interest on his value, as £9 10*s.* sterling, considerably more than the governor's estimate, and yet, according to the latter, field labor in Barbados during slavery was two hundred and fifty per cent. more expensive than it is now under freedom!

The question, I think, *quoad* Barbados, does not admit of an argument. Among the expenses of a slave there must be included his food, clothing, medical attendance, house-rent, depreciation at 10 per cent., and interest on the capital sum invested, all of which must be paid for every man, woman, and child on an estate, in fair weather or in foul, in sickness or in health; and I have before me a variety of statistics which show that at least thirty per cent. of the slaves must, on an average, be regarded as non-effective. The West India planters themselves, long before emancipation, claimed protection for their sugar on the ground that it could only be produced at an extravagant cost, and they represented as one of their heaviest burdens that 30 and even 40 per cent. must be allowed for non-effective slaves. Their evidence is upon record, and can be seen on reference to the Parliamentary blue-books of the day. Under the free system every laborer employed is necessarily an effective one, and his cost, according to the prevailing rate of wages in Barbados, is less than 25 cents a day. In the estimate that I have quoted above, it is demonstrated that the Barbadian laborer who works by the task, which he can complete in six hours, does as much in that space of time as the slave did in his twelve hours' forced work; but admitting, for the sake of argument, and against direct evidence to the contrary, that they worked alike, or even that the slave under compulsion worked better than the free man in his independence, there would still be a large margin in favor of freedom, as the more economical system of the two. This the Barbadian planter has learnt by experience. He admits it readily, and if he did not admit it there is practical evidence of its truth in the fact that agricultural land in Barbados will bring at this moment double what it brought under slavery, and infinitely more than land brings in Cuba. Is it common sense to suppose that every acre of Barbadian ground—confessedly poor in comparison with the rich virgin soil of Cuba—that every available acre would be occupied (as it is), and would estates be greedily purchased at extravagant prices (as they are), if the production of sugar with free labor was an unprofitable business? I have stated it as a fact, of which any one may convince himself, that of the 106,000 acres in Barbados 100,000 are under cultivation. Schomberg, who wrote in 1845, says that there were 40,000 acres planted in sugar-cane; and Davy, who wrote in 1854, has evidently borrowed his predecessor's figures. I think that they are an exaggeration. According to the best estimates that I have been able to procure, there are not more than 25,000 acres of cane reaped annually in Barbados, and the *Agricultural Reporter*, a monthly periodical published in Bridgetown, placed the number in 1853 at 23,333. But we may suppose that 25,000 acres are as near the truth as it is possible to get. Keeping this in view, we find, upon examination, that the average yearly importation of guano during the past five years has amounted in round numbers to $250,000, which would allow, for foreign manuring alone, about $10 an acre. This certainly does not indicate that the land is naturally very rich, and yet the price it brings is most astonishing. Governor Hincks, in the letter from which I have already quoted, has selected an estate which, he says, gives a fair idea of the increased value of land on the island. The property in question, composed of 300 acres, was worth £50 an acre during slavery, or a total of £15,000 sterling. The value of the slaves is estimated at £11,500—the sum that the proprietor received for them at the time of emancipation. *After* compensation had been given this very estate was sold for £15,000, and was purchased by the present proprietor a few years ago for £30,000, or about $500 an acre. This, I can certify, is by no means an unusual price for land; for only recently an estate of 110 acres was bought for £14,000 sterling, which the purchaser himself had sold three years before for £9000. It must be remembered that this land was not bought on a speculation, but purely and simply for agricultural purposes. After informing himself of these prices, and of the further great expense of manuring before the cane can be successfully cultivated in Barbados, a stranger naturally asks why capitalists are so ready to purchase. There is only one answer. The profits of sugar-growing with free labor are amply remunerative, and were never more so than they are at present.

This brings me to the consideration of an important argument, used by those very few British West

Indians who still fancy that slave labor in Barbados would be cheaper than free. It is urged, and truly, that when the duties were removed by the imperial Parliament from Cuban and other slave-grown sugars, the Barbadian planter complained that he was unable to compete with the foreign producer. I think that a simple quotation of late sales of real estate in Barbados is, of itself, a pretty strong proof that the complaints of the Barbadian planter were unfounded, and that, in reality, he *could* compete, and *does* compete, on equal terms with the foreign producer in the British market. But allowing the complaint to be just and the representation true—supposing that the Cuban *does* raise sugar cheaper than the Barbadian can—it is an erroneous inference that slave labor should, therefore, be more economical than free labor. Labor is not the *only* expense in the growth of sugar. There are the expenses of management, manure, machinery, and the interest on the value of the land, as well as the expense of labor. Now it is a fact which needs no demonstration, that while land in Barbados costs $500 an acre, land in Cuba costs only $100; that while manure in Barbados costs $10 an acre, in Cuba none is required; that while, in Barbados, the canes must be planted every season, the land in Cuba is so rich that the process of ratooning can be carried on for many years in succession with the smallest amount of work. These, and not the superior economy of his slave labor, have enabled the Cuban planter to undersell his Barbadian rival in the British market. In the richness of his soil the Cuban planter has an advantage that enables him to pay an extravagant price for labor, and that he does pay an extravagant price we know full well. It is a matter of common report that the average life of a field laborer on a Cuban estate is not over ten years; but this is not regarded by the planter as any great misfortune, with the slave-trade in full operation. Supposing the value of a Cuban slave to be $1000, his depreciation under the terrible work to which he is subjected will amount to ten per cent., or $100 per annum; add to this the interest of capital, the expenses of maintenance, and the loss by non-effective laborers, and the cost to the Cuban proprietor for each of his slaves will be found to average, at the very lowest estimate, $180 per annum. If we take another mode of arriving at the same conclusion, we find this figure to be considerably under the mark. Those planters, for instance, who hire slaves, have to pay $25 a month to their owners, and to feed and clothe the laborers besides. The amount paid for hire will then be $300 per annum, and, estimating the cost of maintenance at $35 more, we arrive at a total of $335 a year as the actual expense per man to the Cuban planter who hires labor for his estate. Now, the cost of a Barbadian free laborer is only $75 a year. He receives in this island 25 cents a day, or rather a task, and he finds that ample in such a climate to supply all his wants. If he is unusually ambitious and industrious, as I have shown in a former letter that many of them are, he will often perform his two tasks per diem, and in the course of time will rise, as many have done, to positions of wealth, influence, and independence.

The most formidable cry that the West India proprietary have raised under emancipation is want of labor. The evil never existed in Barbados, and this, perhaps, may be regarded as the first cause of her unchecked prosperity. But in the other islands where negroes have left the estates, I am perfectly convinced and can prove that, in nine cases out of ten, want of capital, heavy encumbrances incurred during slavery, and a mistaken policy which obstinately refused any inducement to the laborer to remain on the soil, are the prime causes of desertion. In these islands, where land is cheap and abundant, the negroes, acting as Englishmen or Americans similarly situated would, have become small proprietors whenever and wherever they could, preferring an independent to a servile position, diminishing thereby, it is true, the supply of labor, but exhibiting themselves to be an industrious rather than an indolent people. While, therefore, many an old estate has been abandoned, we find at the same time a vast increase of small proprietors; and insufficiency of labor, the want in all new countries, follows as a matter of course. I do not doubt that there has been a want of labor in all the colonies except Barbados; I do not doubt that that want explains, in some degree, the diminution of sugar exports; but the fault and the folly lie at the door of the planter, and may be traced to his blindness and his extravagance. But, whatever the cause, if there be in reality a deficiency of labor, if labor is all that is necessary to raise the West India colonies to a loftier position than any they have hitherto occupied, I do not think that the regulation of a proper demand and supply should be left to time or to chance. Governor Hincks is of opinion that there *is* a sufficiency of labor in many of the colonies, and that the resort to indiscriminate Coolie immigration is unnecessary and uncalled for. He thinks that this, next to slavery, is the most expensive kind of labor; one which it is impolitic to encourage when Creole labor can be procured by the inducements of higher wages and a more liberal tenure. The governor advises that the labor question in the islands should be left to work itself out, which he believes it would in one of the three following ways: first, that the planter would be obliged to increase the laborer's rate of wages, which he could afford to do in all the colonies except Barbados; or, secondly, that the planter would have to adopt the *Metairie* system, that is, to divide the profits with his laborer—a system that has been successfully worked in St. Lucia and Tobago, and is not unknown in the United States; or, thirdly, that the planter, who is now both agriculturist and manufacturer, would have to confine himself to manufacturing, for which he is better fitted by education and experience. These opinions, coming from such a source, must not be thrown aside as mere speculations, for they are the result of a very extended experience. As, however, they have no reference to Barbados, but only to those colonies which have imported large quantities of Asiatic Coolies under government supervision, they have only a general bearing on the subject which I have undertaken in this chapter to discuss.

I have instituted a comparison between free and slave labor in Barbados, where, under both systems, labor was necessarily abundant, and I deem it established that free labor is the cheaper of the two. But it would be unfair and illogical, from these premises, to draw any conclusions as to the cost of free and slave labor in the United States. The island of Barbados, with its overstocked and imprisoned population, compelled to work on such terms as the planters may dictate, has nothing in common with the slave states of the American Union, and an unbounded territory adjoining, to which the liberated classes, were their liberation within the bounds of possibility, would immediately resort. With as little prejudice as possible I have endeavored to explain, in a summary way, what I have learned during a residence on the island; and while it appears, after comparing the two systems, that free labor in Barbados is cheaper than slave labor, the same result can, with still greater force, be shown by the improvement since emancipation in Barbadian commerce, and in all other branches of material prosperity.

CHAPTER VI.

COMMERCE AND PROSPERITY OF BARBADOS.

Bridgetown, Barbados, 1859.

It requires no deep scrutiny to discover that the commerce of Barbados is much more extensive and much more flourishing under free labor than it was under slave labor, and as any general statistical work will demonstrate this fact, I need not occupy much space with particulars. I am not going to assert that the increased prosperity of Barbados is solely due to emancipation; some credit must undoubtedly be given to improvements in agricultural science and economy of labor. But these improvements are very inferior to those which have marked the progress of the planting interest in the United States during the past thirty years. The Barbadian, after long hesitation, has at length introduced the plow, though some few fogies, as fossiliferous as their own rock, still question the safety of the innovation. Out of some five or six thousand mills on the island there are not over a dozen propelled by steam; and when it is remembered that steam power, from its greater certainty, makes a favorable difference in a sugar crop of ten or fifteen per cent., it can not be said that science has lent all her aid to the increase of Barbadian products. Nor can it be urged that there is a larger extent of land under cultivation, for, in this respect, Barbados has undergone no material change within the past half century. The number of acres in sugar-cane is probably less than it was thirty years ago. I have estimated them, upon good authority, at 25,000; and though I can obtain no statistics on the subject, there is reason to believe that when the island was owned exclusively by large proprietors, whose sole object was to make money with the great staple product, there were more cane-fields in cultivation than there are now, when small proprietors, holding less than five acres, and who grow their own articles of consumption, have increased three hundred per cent.

Again, it can not be argued that an increased population has been the cause of an increased production of sugar. The last census of the island, taken in 1851, gives the population of Barbados as 135,939, of whom 15,824 were whites, 30,059 were colored or half-castes, and 90,056 were negroes. Of this number, 20,000, nearly all blacks or colored, are supposed to have died of cholera in 1854, and, making an allowance for this and for a slight emigration to adjacent islands, it is fair to estimate the present population of Barbados at 140,000 souls. For all purposes of statistical science the census of 1844 and that of 1851 are deplorably deficient. In the former, for fear of giving offense, there was no distinction made between the whites and blacks; in the latter there are no distinctions of trade, profession, or pursuit. I am unable, therefore, to ascertain accurately what it is important to know—the exact laboring force of the island. The census of 1844 puts down laborers above 18, male and female, at 30,005; persons above 18, male and female, and employed in trade, 28,125; persons above 18, and having no employment, 8956, and children under 18 years 55,112. Making these figures the basis of an estimate for the present year, I should say that there are, in round numbers, 124,000 black and colored people in Barbados who may thus be classified: 55,000 under the age of 18; 25,000 employed in trade, 22,000 field laborers, and about as many engaged in domestic and other subordinate occupations—leaving a white population of some 16,000 souls. There has been a great increase since 1838 of persons engaged in trade and mechanical arts, causing a large deficiency of field labor, which, under slavery, was estimated at 77,000 in 1817, 78,000 in 1823, 80,000 in 1830, and 81,000 in 1832. These figures included children, who, in the estimate of a planter's expenses, had to be ranked at so much per capita with adults; but, deducting them from the laboring population for the purpose of this argument, it will be seen that there is a very material difference between the available field force of Barbados to-day and its field force before emancipation. If, then, Barbados, with a diminished laboring force and the same amount of land under cultivation, produces more now than she ever did before, what is the cause of the improvement? In spite of all drawbacks this island exported last year twice as much as she did in any year from the period of her first settlement down to the day of emancipation. Judging Barbados by herself, without reference to any other island or country whatsoever, I can imagine, or conceive, or give no other explanation of her increased and increasing resources than the adoption of a cheaper system of labor in the production of her great staple. And if it be urged that the negro in Barbados has been driven by force of circumstances to work for his daily bread (though the statement is only partly true, it may be admitted for the sake of argument), practical observation as well as statistical returns alike show that, under emancipation, his labor is far more valuable to the proprietor and the country than it was under slavery.

In the year 1830 Barbados exported 22,769 hhds. of sugar, and in 1834—the year of abolition—she exported 27,318 hhds., the largest crop ever recorded under slavery. But in an island like Barbados, where trade, owing to hurricanes, and unfavorable weather for crops, has fluctuated very much, it is scarcely fair to judge of its improvement by a comparison of particular seasons. I prefer to take an average of sugar exportations, which from 1720 to 1800 was 23,000 hhds. per annum, and from 1800 to 1830 was 20,000 hhds., showing a decline under slavery of 3000 hhds., a decline apparent at the time in most of the West India colonies, and to be attributed, as I have explained in a former chapter, to the large hypothecation on landed property.

Let us now look at the Barbados sugar exportations of the present day, premising with the observation that from 1826 to 1830 the average weight of a hogshead of sugar was 12 cwt.; from 1830 to 1850, 14 cwt., and is now from 15 to 16 and even 17 cwt. With this difference of weight *against* her, Barbados exported, in 1852, 48,610 hhds.; in 1853, 38,316 hhds.; in 1854, 44,492 hhds.; in 1855, 39,692 hhds.; in 1856, 43,552 hhds.; in 1857, 38,858 hhds.; and in 1858, 50,778 hhds., or nearly double what she exported during the most favorable year of slavery! I find, upon examination, that the average of Barbadian sugar exportation from 1835 to 1850, including the wretched ordeal of apprenticeship, was 26,000 hhds., and from 1851 to 1858, 43,000 hhds., against 20,000 hhds. of an inferior weight during the first thirty years of the present century. The exportations of molasses are in the same proportion, with this difference, that while nine tenths of the sugar go to Great Britain, more than one half of the molasses now goes to the United States. It must be remembered that this immense sugar-crop comes from about one fourth of the land under cultivation. I have no statistics in regard to other productions, but the average exportation of miscellaneous articles of native growth may be valued at £20,000 sterling per annum, and the inference is that a considerable portion of the island, and especially the lots owned by the laboring population, are grown in articles of food for home consumption. I have seen large and promising fields of Guinea and Indian corn, but the pasturage is necessarily poor, and will not bear comparison with ours. Sweet potatoes, eddoes, yams, pigeon-peas, the cassava-root, and other vegetables are extensively cultivated.

Turning now to the imports, I find that their average annual value from 1822 to 1832 was about £600,000 sterling. In 1845 the imports amounted in value to £682,358, and in 1856 to £840,000, of which about £640,000 were consumed in the island. But a comparison between the value of imports now and their value when prices were very different is manifestly an unjust one. A fairer test may be found in the shipping returns. In the year 1832 the largest number of vessels entered Barbados under the slavery *régime*, and amounted in all to 689 vessels, of 79,000 tons. In 1856—I select the year at random—966 vessels, of 114,800 tons, were entered, and this may be taken as an average of the last eight years. The character of the imports deserves special consideration. About one half are articles of food, including groceries, wines, and liquors. The other half is composed of manufactured articles, lumber, and guano. For the last century, with some slight exception, Barbados has imported food for her laboring classes from the United States, and the course of trade in this respect remains unchanged. Such statistics as are within our reach, and they are scanty enough, show a remarkable increase in the different branches of Barbadian commerce with America. In 1854 Barbados imported 36,414 barrels of flour, 1500 of beef, 9438 of pork, and 49,106 of meal. In 1858 she imported 79,766 barrels of flour, 2646 of beef, 12,196 of pork, and 67,053 of meal. Other articles of food imported from the United States bear the same proportionate increase. While under slavery American importations did not exceed in value £60,000 per annum, they now average five and six times that amount. As an illustration I select again the imports of the year 1856, having the figures before me. The value of breadstuffs and food imported that year from the United States amounted to more than £200,000; of manufactured articles, to £70,000; of lumber and wood goods, to £20,000; and of horses and mules, to £6000, besides minor articles. The fact, then, that all the American importations have greatly increased, that they are required by the masses, as their nature indicates, and that they are obtained at much cheaper rates than if brought from Europe, as they formerly were, are so many arguments in favor of the prosperity of Barbados, and of the improved condition of her laboring population.

Before I leave this subject, there is an existing anomaly in the trade with the United States which requires explanation. It is a matter of complaint that American merchants, who export so largely to Barbados, receive money, and not the staple of the country, in return. Their ships have to leave the island in ballast and look elsewhere for a cargo on the home voyage; and so true is this that, out of an average of 200 American vessels which annually enter the port of Bridgetown, not more than forty clear with cargoes for the United States. I have before me a dispatch from the governor of these islands to the colonial secretary, in which this anomaly is explained; and it is shown conclusively that the Americans are compelled by the Barbadians themselves to take money for their goods, and to purchase their sugars in Porto Rico or Cuba. The sugar-producers in Barbados are divided into three classes: First, non-resident proprietors with unencumbered estates, who have sole control of their produce; second, resident and non-resident proprietors whose estates are encumbered, and their produce shipped through mortgagees; and third, resident proprietors whose estates are free. The first class, which is very small, never offer their sugars for sale in Barbados. The produce is shipped to agents in England, and it is very clear that these proprietors can not complain that Americans do not purchase what they themselves will not sell. The second class, which is by far the largest of the three, can not sell in Barbados if they would, for their crops must be delivered to the mortgagees, and are also sold in England. The third class, which is the smallest of all, are indeed at liberty to sell to whom they please; but even they are reluctant to offer their staple in the Barbados market, especially when there is the slightest chance of a rise in price. So far from Americans being indisposed to take Barbados sugar, it is a fact that they *will* take it, and *do* take it, whenever they can get it. There is only one class of proprietors from whom they can possibly purchase—the resident proprietors with unencumbered estates—and this class bears a small proportion to the whole. Yet a commencement has been made in this branch of trade with the United States. Prior to 1855 the value of Barbadian sugar exported to the United States was insignificant, but in that year it amounted to £8865; in 1856 it amounted to £46,000; in 1857 to £55,000, and in 1858 to over £60,000 sterling.

There is very little doubt, and it can not be intelligently questioned, that Barbados, under the *régime* of slavery, never approached her present prosperous condition; and, in comparing the present with the past, whether that comparison be made in her commercial, mechanical, agricultural, industrial, or educational status, I can come to no other conclusion than that the island offers a striking example of the superior economy of the free system.

CHAPTER VII.

SOCIAL DISTINCTIONS IN BARBADOS.

Bridgetown, Barbados, 1859.

THERE are peculiarities in the social condition of the Barbadian people, which, in discussing the results of emancipation, merit some consideration. I have spoken, in a former chapter, of three classes—the white, the half-caste, and the black—and while the first and the last, the lords of the soil and the serfs, have practically retained the positions they always occupied, the half-castes, or middle class—the progeny of the other two—have multiplied and strengthened under freedom, and promise to secure for themselves, sooner or later, the political preponderance now so jealously guarded by the dominant race. The mulatto people are wonderfully suited to the climate. Being endowed with an energy that white people do not possess in tropical countries, and with an intelligence capable of the very highest development, I believe that their ultimate ascendency is only a question of time.

The distinctions of caste are more strictly observed in Barbados than in any other British West India colony. No person, male or female, with the slightest taint of African blood, is admitted to white society. No matter what the standing of a father, his influence can not secure for his colored offspring the social *status* that he himself occupies; and the rule is more rigidly carried out among women than it is among men. The amalgamation of the two races is nevertheless very general, and illicit intercourse is sanctioned, or at least winked at, by a society which utterly condemns and abhors a marriage between two people of different color. There are cases, it is true, where white people have intermarried with mulattoes, but they are rare, and I know of none where the white is a born Barbadian. A white man who marries a half-caste is nearly always an Englishman, who comes to the West Indies with little or no prejudice against the race, and is ignorant of the unanimous feeling that, on this subject, secretly pervades the whole of Barbadian society. But it is not color alone that creates the line of demarkation—the gulf, impassable to those whose judgment and personal actions are swayed and guided by public opinion. The lineage of every person on the island is known, and remote descent from an African ancestor makes some unhappy creature a pariah from the little world of Barbados. It would, of course, be improper to illustrate the assertion by example; but instances are not wanting where people of both sexes, without the faintest trace of color, with the Saxon form and features of one parent strikingly predominant, and with all the advantages that a most liberal education can bestow, are still shut out from the society of those who belong exclusively to the superior race.

The amalgamation of the African and Anglo-Saxon, and the exclusiveness of the latter, have thus combined to build up the half-castes, and make them somewhat of a distinct people—a people neither African nor European, but more properly West Indian. This class—the middle class—is already very large and intelligent, and is rapidly increasing. It is composed of small landed proprietors, of business men, clerks in public and private establishments, editors, tradesmen, and mechanics. Shut out from the whites, on the one hand, who will not admit them to their society, and from the blacks on the other, to whom they are immeasurably superior, they, nevertheless, are constantly receiving accessions from the ranks of both. Their political sympathies are, of course, with the black population; for between the mulattoes and the blacks there is not the same gulf fixed that there is between the mulattoes and the whites. In the former case, it is possible to rise from the lowest class to the middle class, but it is utterly impossible to rise from the middle to the highest. The very fact that the half-castes, with more than the sensitiveness of Europeans, have to bear all the indignities that are heaped upon the African race, makes them bitter against the dominant few; and, as they increase in numbers and acquire more and more political and moral influence in the community to direct and control, as they can even now direct and control the desires, passions, and aspirations of the entire colored population, they assume formidable proportions as a party which, sooner or later, must be conciliated and appeased. These half-castes, inheriting the intellectual power and force of the white race and the passions of the black, must eventually present a successful opposition to the existing anomalies of government; must break down the plantocratic oligarchy, and obtain for themselves political equality, if not political ascendency. It is a result of emancipation still to be worked out. It is a necessary consequence of the original grant of freedom, that these people, now that they fully understand and appreciate what freedom is, should possess all the rights of freemen, and especially the right of voting. They will insist upon being fully represented in the Legislature, and they will be satisfied with nothing less. The social problem is one more difficult of solution; and as long as it remains unsolved—as long as a colored man is made to understand that, in spite of his equal intelligence, education, refinement, and wealth, he is still regarded by the white as an inferior, the worst possible feeling must exist between the two. That feeling must gain strength as the mulattoes increase in numbers, influence, and general intelligence. It would be hard to say that, to remedy this evil, the whites, as the minority, should yield up their so-called prejudices. Those prejudices can not excite our surprise; it would be surprising, indeed, if they did not exist. Most of the white inhabitants remember the day when the people who now claim to be their equals were their slaves. We can readily imagine how offensive, under these circumstances, the union or even association of white and colored people must be considered; but, in reality, it is only after a long residence in the island that a stranger begins to appreciate the horror with which a Barbadian white will shrink from the mere mention of a matrimonial alliance with a Creole of African descent, though she were as fair to look upon as the mother of all mankind.

The question of social independence is a most delicate one to touch, and when I seem to suggest that in free Barbados social distinctions are too marked for a perfectly friendly feeling to exist between the white and black portions of the community, I do not mean to uphold the absurd pretension of social equality, in the name of which, and under the ægis of modern democracy, so many detestable abuses and so many flagrant violations of individual liberty have been practiced. Nature has drawn a line of demarkation between a man with talent and a man without; education divides the learned from the ignorant; habit the industrious from the idle; society the man of refinement from the boor; and necessity the poor man from the rich. Nothing can be more practically hopeless—nothing more destructive to personal freedom than the doctrine of social equality; nor do I for a moment pretend that the Barbadian planter should be censured because he regards his laborer, his shoemaker, or his tailor as social inferiors. But when he, and all the other white inhabitants of the island, make difference of color their only line of distinction, and parade their reasons in an offensive and obnoxious way—when white planters refuse to associate with colored planters, white merchants with colored merchants, and white mechanics with colored mechanics, simply because they *are* colored, the question ceases to be a purely social one, and assumes a dangerous political complexion. As long as the colored people were slaves, their heart-burnings and their jealousies might be disregarded with impunity or contemptuously ignored. But freedom has opened to them the way of progress and power; and if their present progress and present power have proved, as they *have* proved, that color is no insuperable barrier to intellectual development and refinement, it is but wise to make it no longer an insuperable barrier to social advancement. I know of parties in Barbados who refused to visit Government House because they met there colored persons of the very highest respectability and cultivation; and though I am ready to make every allowance for prejudices so ingrained as these of the white against the colored race in a land where they have lived as master and slave—though I come from a country where these feelings are more than cherished, and where the man in whom they are found wanting is condemned by public opinion, and can expect or look for no political preferment; yet, in the peculiar case of Barbados, I can not help regarding these self-same prejudices as the chief source of distrust between the two peoples, and as a decided obstruction to the satisfactory solution of the emancipation problem.

It certainly seems to me that this problem must, in a great measure, be worked out by the mulatto race. It is vain, perhaps, to speculate on the future, but we can not close our eyes to existing facts. The white race within the tropics loses much of its energy and force. It requires no very close scrutiny to be convinced of such a patent truth. You can see it in their habits, manners, and customs; in the conduct of their business, and in their daily life. The mulatto is as exclusively the *working-man*, in all professions and trades, as the black is the field laborer. Whites are the aristocrats—I speak of the Creole whites—who deem it their special right to legislate for the masses; and they do legislate abundantly, not for the masses, but in support of themselves, their privileges, and their order. But by-and-by their opponents, daily increasing in knowledge and numbers, will become too strong for them, and when that happens many a hobby will be mercilessly swept away. If the franchise in Barbados should ever be so extended as to allow the majority to govern, and I do not see how such a movement can be consistently prevented, I should only be able to hope that the passionate and revengeful temper of the colored people would not carry them beyond the bounds of moderation and make them dissatisfied with mere political equality. I have seen too many exhibitions of prejudice and violent feeling against the whites to permit me to believe the statements of leading men in this island that one class entertain no ill-will against the other. The mulatto, educated and enlightened as he is, feels much more acutely the inferiority of his position now than he felt it as a slave; and this feeling of social inferiority in consequence of color is calculated to excite and keep alive the animosity of a people much more readily than the sense of any other wrong. I can assert positively that it is not the prevailing opinion among the whites themselves that they are regarded with too much affection by their social inferiors. Some short time ago the British government proposed to remove the white regiment from Barbados and leave only the black, but the proposition created such general alarm that the idea was abandoned. I do not mean to say that the removal of the force would have been followed by any thing so absurd as an insurrection; I simply wish to show that an insurrection was considered, in such an event as the withdrawal of the troops, a possible occurrence, and the project created no little uneasiness. It is, moreover, a fact that this very proposition to withdraw the white troops was freely discussed among the lower classes of the people, and their notion, very generally expressed, was that they would *then* be able "to do as they liked."

While I think it established that free labor in Barbados is cheaper than slave labor, and that, therefore, it is a success, there still remain unsettled issues, social and political, flowing from emancipation which may one day create trouble. The planters have done nothing to conciliate the peasant population; on the contrary, they have done all they could to keep them on low wages and in dependent servitude. The peasant, then, is under the complete influence of the mulatto, between whom and the white there exists a feeling amounting almost to hostility. The half-caste, after he has acquired wealth and independence, does not and will not comprehend the inexorable prejudices which still keep him the inferior of the white, and he frets under the restraint. While, therefore, these prejudices remain, and I see no sign of their disappearance, and the mulatto or middle class continue to increase in strength and influence, the day must come when their interests and the prejudices of the white population will more openly conflict, and, with chances of success more nearly equal, will strive for the mastery. Both can not triumph, nor can both always exist together. Happily the colonies acknowledge the sway of a power strong enough to control them, and to prevent men's passions leading them to follow examples like those that we read of in Haytian history.

CHAPTER VIII.

ST. VINCENT SINCE EMANCIPATION.

Kingstown, St. Vincent, 1859.

I HAVE come down to see these "ruined" islands of the Windward group, and to learn why St. Vincent and her Grenadine dependencies, which, before emancipation, exported, on an average, twenty-five million pounds of sugar, should now export only sixteen or seventeen millions, and why the sugar exportations of Grenada have fallen away from twenty-two millions to something less than one half of that amount. The two islands—Grenada and St. Vincent—are about eighty miles apart, but are almost connected by the Grenadines—a chain of minute islets, which, seen from a distance, resemble fantastic clouds lying low upon the horizon. Very similar in physical formation, about equal in size, with nearly the same quantity of land under cultivation, and about the same number of inhabitants, and exhibiting the same proportionate decline in the exportation of their staple product, Grenada and St. Vincent may be classed together for the purposes of this argument. Each, at the present moment, is supposed to be in great straits for labor, and in each, as far as I have been able to judge, the causes that have led to this result are very similar.

An ardent lover of the picturesque would almost regret to see a spirit of Yankee go-a-head-ativeness kindled in St. Vincent. Here a thousand cone-shaped peaks are lifted up from their coral base until they disappear in a cloud which, like an eagle with outstretched wings, seems always to be brooding over this, the most summery of all these summer islands. The view of St. Vincent, upon entering the harbor that belongs to its only port of entry, is inconceivably grand, and the spectator finds his fancy subdued by reality. On one side a bold, lofty, sheltering promontory, on the other a fort, which, in its desolate, rugged beauty and inaccessible height, looks like another Ehrenbreitstein; in front, a mass of isolated hills, clustering round their crowned king, all clothed in green and purple from the blue sky above to the blue waters below; and at their base,buried in groves of palms and cocoas, lo! the quaint and antiquated and dilapidated "city" of Kingstown. It was impossible not to fancy, just for a passing moment, that the smoke of a steam-engine would be a blot on such a picture; it was impossible not to feel, after sober reflection and an experience of the miseries of Kingstown, that even the most enthusiastic worshiper of nature would be content to barter charms of landscape for more material comforts. Accident, design, or the fortune of travel, never led me to a place so utterly destitute of the spirit of enterprise as this lovely island of St. Vincent is.

"What is that?" said I to an intelligent youth who acted as my chaperon, pointing to a heap of classic-looking ruins.

"Houses dat am fell in, massa."

"How long ago?"

"I disremember; 'fore I is born."

There they lay in the principal street of Kingstown. Every thing that one sees in the town is more or less an indication of decay. The famed Botanic Garden, twenty years ago the pride of St. Vincent, and celebrated throughout the West Indies, can not now be distinguished; the roads in the interior of the island, never good, are now almost impassable for a horseman, and even the Souffriere sleeps in gloomy silence.

The appearance of decay which the capital of St. Vincent presents, and the fact of its diminished exportation of sugar, have brought it under the category of ruined West India islands, and its ruin is, of course, attributed to emancipation. While I fully admit its lack of enterprise and partial decline, truth obliges me to say, what I shall presently prove, that this state of things has been brought about by want of capital rather than by want of labor, and that a decrease in the growth of sugar can not be considered as the legitimate result of emancipation only, and does not constitute the "ruin" into which it is broadly asserted this island is plunged.

What I have said in a former chapter concerning the plantocracy of Barbados is applicable to the proprietary of St. Vincent. The planters of this island have made no efforts to retain the laborers on their estates. I speak generally, for there may be exceptions to the rule; indeed, I know of one or two instances where planters, in their individual capacity, have made these efforts, and have been successful. But the planters of the island, as its landed aristocracy and legislators, have not done all they might have done to reconcile the laborer to his servile position;

they have offered him no inducements to remain, as a free man, in the same inferior station of life that he occupied as a slave; and yet they bitterly complain that he has been independent enough to take the matter into his own hands and better himself. Wages here for field labor do not reach a shilling per day; and is it surprising that those who could should have left the unprofitable business of estate-service, and, having purchased lots in the interior of the island, should prefer to earn their livelihood by cultivating their own properties? The planters say that, according to the current prices of sugars, they can not afford to pay higher wages for labor. I doubt the truth of the statement, for much higher wages are successfully paid in Trinidad; but, allowing it to be correct for the sake of argument, it is an admission that the estate laborer is insufficiently paid, and a consequent justification of his quitting that kind of work for another more remunerative. I am disposed to doubt the assertion that any of the St. Vincent estates were abandoned solely because labor could not be procured at a remunerative cost. I have been unable to hear of them. Whenever I inquired about the abandonment of this or that property, I found the reason to be want of capital, or the indebtedness of the proprietor, through which the estate became mortgaged beyond its value —an indebtedness, moreover, incurred prior to emancipation. But I have already discussed this subject so fully in a former chapter that it is unnecessary for me to enter upon it again. In visiting each island, my principal object has been to make myself acquainted with the true condition of its emancipated classes, and the inquiry is all-important in colonies like St. Vincent, Grenada, Tobago, and St. Lucia, where the white population is exceedingly small.

The population of St. Vincent in 1831 amounted to 27,000, and now stands at 30,000. The census, last taken in 1851, makes no distinction between white, colored, and black, but if we estimate the first at 1500 we shall probably overrate rather than underrate their number. There will then remain 28,500 black and colored people, nearly all Creoles of the island; for immigration, as far as St. Vincent is concerned, has been very trifling.

In comparing the present occupation of the emancipated classes with their occupation under the slavery *régime*, it must be borne in mind that the effect of freedom was to abolish almost entirely the labor of women in the cane-fields. Thus, of the 13,673 field laborers for whom compensation was given by the British government to St. Vincent proprietors, one half were females, who are now engaged in domestic and more congenial duties. At present there are from 4000 to 4500 laborers on estates; and when we look for the remainder who ought to bring up the agricultural force of the island to the original figure, if the original sugar exportation is to be preserved, we find that all have bettered their condition. Many took to trade, but the great bulk remained agriculturists after they had severed themselves from the sugar estates. The returns for 1857 show that no less than 8209 persons were then living in their own houses built by themselves since emancipation—illustrating, in the most satisfactory manner, the material progress made by the Creole laborers of St. Vincent during the last twenty years. More remarkable still is the fact that, within the last twelve years, from ten to twelve thousand acres have been brought under cultivation by small proprietors, owning from one to five acres, and growing arrow-root, provisions, and minor articles for export. The statistical returns from which I gather these figures further state that there are *no paupers in the island*—quite sufficient, in my opinion, to disprove the erroneous idea that, unless compelled to work, the negro will lie all day in the sun and live on a piece of sugar-cane. I have seen nothing in the British West Indies that lends any countenance to such a supposition. The uneducated, uncivilized negro has undoubtedly many grave faults of character and defects of intellect. He will be lazy and thriftless too before he has acquired the habit or has felt the responsibility of working for his daily bread. But when he comprehends that responsibility, as he does comprehend it now in the British West Indies, he will work readily enough, and I do believe that his other faults will gradually disappear under the influence of proper educational training.

If it be considered demonstrated, from the reduced exportation of sugar, that many of the large landed proprietors of St. Vincent have withdrawn from the island, it is also apparent, from the increased and increasing growth of minor products, that the small proprietors, created by a system of freedom, are enjoying unexampled prosperity. In the one article of arrow-root alone, there was exported 1,352,250 lbs. in 1857, equal in value to about $750,000, against an average yearly export of 60,000 lbs. before abolition. The present exportation of cocoanuts is also very large. While, therefore, the decline of sugar exports from fourteen and fifteen thousand hhds. to eight and nine thousand hhds. would indicate decay, it is a decay (if the word be applicable at all) confined exclusively to the cultivation of a single article, and has been brought about partly, perhaps, by want of labor, but chiefly through the mismanagement, extravagance, and absenteeism of the proprietors themselves.

As far as statistics can be considered an authority on such a subject, the morality of the St. Vincent Creoles is of a higher standing than that of the Barbadian Creoles. Out of a population of 30,000, there is an average church attendance of 8000. There is little provision for educational purposes, and no effort was made to enlighten the people until 1857, when the Legislature established a board of education. In that year the average school attendance was about 2000. The criminal records show that there is a general obedience to law—the more remarkable as no troops are stationed in the island, and the police authorities would be utterly incapable of quelling a popular tumult if such a misfortune should occur. In 1856 there were 170 blacks convicted of thefts and misdemeanors, 4 of larceny and 4 of felony: in 1857 there were 162 convicted of minor offenses, 7 of assault and 6 of felony. This is less than the number of convictions under the *régime* of slavery, and very much less than the convictions immediately after emancipation, when the offenders of all classes during one year would average over a thousand. I do not think that any one who has visited St. Vincent will hesitate to say that, morally and materially, the Creoles of the island are infinitely superior to what they were twenty, or even ten years ago. They have the same vices and faults that their brethren in the other islands possess; but they are vices and faults which, we have reason to hope, a proper system of popular education will ultimately eradicate.

There are now encouraging prospects that, even in the cultivation of sugar, St. Vincent will soon be restored to its former prosperity. The island has already made preparations for the importation of coolie labor. In October, 1857, a law was passed authorizing the appointment of an agent-general of immigrants, and, in other respects, introducing the system so successfully practiced in Trinidad and British Guiana. To defray the expenses of this immigration a special duty is levied on sugar, rum, molasses, arrow-root, cotton, and cocoa, and a portion of the general revenue is also appropriated to the same object. Though eighteen months have passed since the immigration law was promulgated, no coolies, up to this time, have been brought to St. Vincent, and the inference is that the planters are either in want of capital or can not be in such desperate straits for labor as they ask us to believe.

But the more I see of these West India islands the more am I convinced that debt and want of capital, much more than want of labor, have led to the abandonment of so many estates. A movement in the right direction, and one already producing the most beneficial results, was the passage through the imperial Parliament, in 1854, of the West Indies Encumbered Estates Act, with similar provisions to those of the famous Irish Bill. The measure was at first regarded with suspicion, but its benefits are now generally acknowledged, and in 1856 the St. Vincent Legislature passed an act for carrying into execution the imperial law. It is already apparent that, in some cases, the difficulties created by debt and encumbrances too weighty to be borne are disappearing. One particular and remarkable example may be given—that of the Arnos Vale estate in this island, covering about 454 acres. The property passed through the Encumbered Estates Court with dispatch, and, with a free parliamentary title, was sold for $50,000, or one third more than any one believed it could possibly fetch.

There are now fifty-eight sugar estates in St. Vincent under high cultivation. Forty-six are worked with water, nine with steam, six with cattle, and six with wind-power. This, of course, is a great falling off, when compared with the sugar cultivation of the island a quarter of a century ago; but, as compared with the depression of late years, it exhibits a most decided improvement. Though St. Vincent only embraces a superficial area of 84,000 acres, there are in the island large estates yet to be rescued from ruin, and large tracts of land yet to be reclaimed from primeval forest. But, with a supply of labor such as they can now obtain, and freed from the burden of debt under which they have hitherto vainly struggled—a debt, be it always remembered, incurred before freedom was tested—the planters of St. Vincent look forward to a time of revived and redoubled prosperity. Its first fruits are already apparent.

CHAPTER IX.

GRENADA SINCE EMANCIPATION.

St. George, Grenada, 1859.

THE appearance of this town, the capital of the island of Grenada, is even more picturesque and more dilapidated than that of St. Vincent. St. George is built upon two sides of a hill, one facing the ocean, and the other the Careenage, a magnificent harbor where fifteen hundred ships could ride at anchor. The streets are overgrown with weeds; the houses look as though something much less formidable than a hurricane would level them with the ground; and there is evidence every where of former splendor, and of money lavished, thoughtlessly lavished, I should say, under the mistaken impression that these islands would one day form a great West Indian Empire. Whenever I visit a West India city, I am not so much surprised at its present condition as at the traces it bears of the exaggerated and visionary hopes of its early inhabitants. Present depression is only a comparative depression, and is a natural consequence of the fictitious value formerly placed upon property. The streets of a West India city give an unfavorable impression of the inhabitants, because the drones of all the island congregate there. But after the country districts have been visited, this impression wears off, and the impartial spectator begins to entertain serious doubts as to whether the island was more prosperous under the old *régime*, when all its wealth and all its resources were in the hands of a few landed proprietors, than it is now, when intelligence is more general, and when wealth is more equally divided among a large population. If here and there in Grenada you come across an abandoned estate, or if the houses of its ancient aristocracy have fallen into ruin because capital has left the island, there is some compensation in the fact that the humble dwellings of the peasantry have exceedingly multiplied and improved, and that villages have risen into existence with marvelous rapidity.

The decline of Grenada is no new thing; it dates back long anterior to emancipation. In 1779 the slaves of the island were rated at 35,000; and, from that period down to the day of abolition, this number continued to diminish. In 1827 the number of the slaves amounted to 24,442, and in 1837 the number for whom compensation was paid by the imperial government was only 23,641. Thus, too, in 1776, the exports greatly exceeded what they ever since attained. They amounted in that year to nearly 24,000,000 lbs. of sugar, 800,000 gallons of rum, 2,000,000 lbs. of coffee, 500,000 lbs. of cocoa, 100,000 lbs. of cotton, 28,000 lbs. of indigo, besides smaller articles; all of which together were worth, at the port of shipping, at least three millions of dollars. In 1823 the exports of sugar remained at about the same figure, but other products had so materially diminished that the entire value of the island's exportation did not reach two millions of dollars. In 1831, immediately before emancipation, the export of sugar had decreased to nineteen millions of pounds, and the value of all exports combined was a little more than one million of dollars. This deterioration can only be attributed to those evils which, as I have shown in former letters, existed then throughout the entire West Indies. Nine estates out of every ten were overburdened with debts, created partly by the expenses of the slave system and partly by the extravagance, mismanagement, and absenteeism of proprietors. But let us pass from this to the condition of the island and its inhabitants in later times.

Of the number of slaves for whom compensation was paid to Grenada proprietors by the British government, I find that 14,716 (males and females) constituted at that time the agricultural force of the island. The total population of Grenada is now about 33,000, an increase of three or four thousand over the population of 1827. Accustomed as I have lately been to the stale outcry of "want of labor," I am somewhat surprised to learn from the Grenada blue-books of 1857 that there were then nearly 14,000 Creoles (of whom a very great majority were men) engaged in agriculture. This fact alone contradicts the idea of any wholesale desertion from the estates, and it needs not that I should show in the present case—what I have all along maintained—that the abandonment of West India properties was more the fault of the masters than of the servants. In this island the majority of emancipated field laborers continued to pursue their agricultural calling, and if some have engaged in trade, or have emigrated to other islands, the only wonder is that more have not done so, when wages are as low as from five shillings to two and sixpence sterling per week. But it must not be supposed that of the 14,000 Grenadian Creoles at present engaged in agriculture, all are in a subservient position. Only 6000 are actually on the estates, and the remainder, preferring a greater independence than would be there allowed them, have rented cottages, or are living in their own houses, and may be seen traveling along the roads every morning to their daily work. That the material condition of the Creole population has improved since emancipation is as manifest in this island as it is in all others that I have visited. The small proprietors, of whom there were none prior to 1830, now number over 2000, and are greatly on the increase; nearly 7000 persons are living in villages built since emancipation, and there are 4573 persons in Grenada who pay direct taxes. In the whole island there were, last year, only sixty paupers, and these were all aged or sick. The average church attendance throughout the island was, in 1857, over 8000, against 7000 before emancipation; but the school attendance is comparatively small, being only 1600. Education among the Creoles of Grenada has been, up to this time, at a very low ebb, for it has been looked upon with jealousy and distrust. But a board of education is now in existence, and great progress in popular instruction may be anticipated. Criminal statistics for 1857 show that only eighteen persons during the year were convicted of felony, six of theft, and two of other offenses. Misdemeanors are not enumerated.

The superficial area of Grenada is about 80,000 acres, and the quantity of land now in crop and pasture goes to show that, if the island exports less sugar than it did in other days, cultivation has not proportionably diminished. The inference is that the inhabitants are not less industrious, but raise more of the minor articles of export and more food for home consumption than they did under the slavery *régime*. Thus, in 1857, there were 6372 acres in cane, 84 in coffee, 1790 in cocoa, 266 in cotton, 7262 in provisions, 975 in other cultivation, and 5284 in pasture, making a total of 43,800 cultivated acres, or an increase of 3800 over the previous year. I have no means of ascertaining the number of acres under cultivation before emancipation; but though the number of acres in cane was probably double what it is now, yet the general cultvation, I do not hesitate to say, was not nearly so large or so complete as that which the island to-day presents.

Such an inference, I think, can be drawn from a comparison, if such be instituted, between the exports of Grenada now and her exports immediately prior to emancipation. While in 1831 Grenada exported double the amount of sugar that she did in 1857, the value of all her exports in the former year was only £218,352, against £180,000, their value in the latter year, and this in spite of the very material decline in the prices of sugar. In 1832, two years prior to emancipation, the value of Grenadian exports was £153,175, considerably less than it is now. The fact is that sugar is the only article of export in which the island can be said to have suffered a decline. I do not for a moment deny the importance or significance of that decline; but it should be remembered that in minor articles, such as cocoa, the island is producing double now what it produced twenty-five years ago. The imports of Grenada also show that its colored population are not in a worse condition than they were at any period in their past history. In 1857 the imports, of which over one third were provisions from the United States, amounted to $109,000, against £78,000, £73,000, and £77,000 during the years immediately preceding emancipation.

Grenada has taken the lead of St. Vincent in the importation of coolie laborers, but want of capital is the great drawback to a proper development of the scheme. Up to the present time only three or four hundred immigrants have been introduced into the island, and it can not be expected that any remarkable benefits should be experienced by the colony from so small a supply. The Grenadian immigration laws are very liberal to the coolie. Every estate must have clean and good-sized lodging-houses for immigrants, with separate apartments for every man and wife. There must be a medical practitioner on each estate, whose duty it is to attend the coolie free of charge, and see that he is provided when sick with proper nourishment. Wages are paid in cash every month, and the employer is not permitted to deduct any thing from the sum due without the full and free consent of the coolie.

I have not heard of a case in Grenada to which the West India Encumbered Estates Act has been yet applied. But the day will come when estates now lying idle and mortgaged beyond their value will be relieved by wholesome process of law from their heavy incubus of debt, and be restored, perhaps, to their former prosperity.

CHAPTER X.

TOBAGO AND ST. LUCIA SINCE EMANCIPATION.

Bridgetown, Barbados, 1859.

THERE are two islands under the dominion of the Windward government—of all the five the smallest and most distant from each other—upon whose actual condition I must make a few remarks. I refer to Tobago and St. Lucia. The former is the most southerly of the Caribbee Islands. Like Grenada, it exhibited a gradual decline in its slave population during the fifteen years that preceded emancipation. Thus, in 1819, the number of registered slaves in Tobago was 15,470; in 1832 there were but 12,091, while the number, including non-effectives, for whom compensation was claimed by Tobago proprietors, was only 10,500. The present estimated population is 15,674, of which 160 are whites.

Of the Tobago slaves manumitted at the time of emancipation 7443 were field laborers. The latest returns show that 6440 constitute the present agricultural force of the island, the balance of the population being engaged in trade and as domestics. We find here no sufficient falling off in the agricultural force to account for the diminished production of sugar, which, in Tobago, is now three and four thousand hogsheads, against seven thousand some twenty five years ago. The decline, if it can be attributed in any degree to deficiency of labor, must have its origin in other concurrent causes. Among these causes, an important one lies in the fact that money soon found its way from Tobago to the adjacent island of Trinidad, where so many and such superior inducements were held out to capitalists. In the general argument, I do not think that sufficient weight is given to this natural transfer of capital from an old and worn-out to a recently settled and more promising island. But particularly in the case of Trinidad and Tobago—two islands only forty miles apart—it is not at all surprising that capitalists should have preferred the boundless field for enterprise of the one to the circumscribed area and limited resources of the other.

But, in spite of capital withdrawn and sugar exports diminished, I do not hesitate to say that there is as marked an improvement in the condition of the Tobagian Creoles as in that of the other colored populations of the West India colonies. The small proprietors of Tobago have greatly multiplied since emancipation. There are 2800 blacks and colored persons in the island paying direct taxation, and 2500 freeholders. Many of the common field laborers live in houses built by themselves since emancipation. The average church attendance in Tobago is large, being 41 per cent. of the entire population. There is an average school attendance of 1600. Like most of the other islands, Tobago has exhibited decided signs of revival during the past few years. The imports of 1856 amounted to £59,994 sterling, against £52,307 in 1854, and the exports in 1856 were £79,789, against £49,754 in 1854. The rainy season being very prolonged in this island, its climate can not be considered a highly favorable one for the growth of sugar. It is, however, too small an island to be brought forward (on its own merits alone) as a witness for or against the cause of free labor. Of the 62,000 acres embraced in its superficial area, 7800 are under cultivation, and of these only 2700 are in canes.

Among the smaller islands which dot the Caribbean Sea, St. Lucia presents, as far as its size will permit, a striking example of the superior advantages of free labor. The tenure of land in this island is more liberal than it is in other Windward islands. Inducements have been held out to laborers to work on the estates, and endeavors have been made, with great success, to improve their condition and elevate them in the social scale. The *Metairie* system prevails here, and tenants at will are unknown. To the wise policy that dictated such a course may be attributed the marked contrast between St. Lucia and some other West India colonies. The Creole laborers of St. Lucia are, comparatively speaking, an independent class, and the experiment of leaving them free agents, untrammeled by coercive measures of legislation, is an undoubted success. The planters of St. Lucia have made it the interest of the peasantry to work for the estates, and the result shows that they work more profitably and more willingly than ever they worked under a system of compulsion.

There was in this island, as in others, a decrease of the slave population prior to emancipation and subsequent to the suppression of the slave-trade. Of the 16,285 registered slaves in 1816 there were only 13,291 twenty years afterward. The population now is 25,307, of whom 958 are whites. Of the 13,291 slaves for whom compensation was paid to St. Lucia proprietors by the British government, 8112 were engaged in agriculture; and though I have no statistics of the fact, yet I have reason to believe that the present agricultural population of the island is about the same. The precise figures, however, it is not material to know, since we do know that the products of the island have doubled within the last twenty-five years.

Among the colored inhabitants of St. Lucia there are now 4603 persons paying direct taxes, and 2045 freeholders—become so, of course, since emancipation. Of the 37,000 acres which the island contains, 3411 are in canes, 49 in coffee, 192 in cocoa, 1013 in provisions, and 3124 in pasture. The sugar exportation of St. Lucia amounted in 1857 to 6,261,875 lbs., against an average yearly export of from three to four millions prior to emancipation; and the exportation of cocoa during 1857 was 251,347 lbs., against 91,280 lbs. in former times. The imports in 1857 were valued at £90,064 sterling, against £68,881 in 1851. St. Lucia is a very small island, and, like Tobago, may not be offered as a convincing argument in favor of free labor; but there is certainly nothing in its present condition, or in that of its population, to show that the one or the other has suffered in any respect from the effects of emancipation.

TRINIDAD.

CHAPTER XI.

CHARACTERISTICS OF THE ISLAND.

Port-of-Spain, Trinidad, 1859.

TRINIDAD has been surnamed "The Indian Paradise;" and as far as external beauty may entitle it to pre-eminence, it is magnificently pre-eminent in this Western Archipelago. In point of size—containing over 2000 square miles—Trinidad is the largest British West India island after Jamaica; and in positional importance, from its proximity to the Venezuelan coast, it is only second to Cuba.

Approaching from the north, the hills of Trinidad may be seen at an immense distance, running in a continuous ridge east and west, rising to a height of over 3000 feet, sloping almost perpendicularly to the sea, and abruptly broken at their western extremity into three entrances—the *Bocas*, or passages to the Gulf of Paria. Adventurous navigators sometimes tempt the perils of the smaller *Bocas* in order to shorten their voyage, but the *Boca grande*, formed by a solitary island rock on the left, and the Parian Cape of Peña on the right, is always selected by those wary pilots who have experienced the Scyllas and Charybdes of the "Dragon's Mouth." After a vessel has entered the passage, the storm, whatever may have been its force, is no longer felt, and the waters of the gulf, fresh from the ceaseless tides of the mighty Orinoco, are still and calm as those of the most secluded lake. And here a scene of surpassing splendor is unfolded to view. Trinidad—forest-covered from mountain-top to water's edge, its luxuriant and gigantic vegetation rich with a coloring that eternal summer alone can give—invites your approach on the one hand, while, on the other, the smoking hills of Venezuela loom through the heated atmosphere, and shrink away over the distant main. The Gulf of Paria is an extensive harbor, in which all the navies of the world might safely anchor. It is shallow near the coast of Trinidad, and is supposed to have been originally a lake formed in the delta of the Orinoco. That the island, at no very remote period, was part of the South American continent, we may now fully believe; for a geological survey, which has occupied two years and is just completed, under the auspices of the colonial government, has placed the fact beyond a doubt. The identity of the animal and vegetable productions of Trinidad with those of the neighboring Venezuelan province of Cumana—productions not found in the Antilles—long made it evident to the most unscientific that Trinidad had been detached from the continent, and the lateness of the period at which the catastrophe occurred was believed on the strength of a tradition extant among the Indians, when, in 1498, the island was discovered by Columbus, that the separation had been caused by an earthquake at no very distant date. The truth of these suppositions is now confirmed by scientific observations. It appears, from the survey-

or's report, that precious metals do not exist in Trinidad. Limestone, sandstone, and slate are the principal rock, and bitumen or fossil-pitch is to be found in great abundance. Every one has heard of that great natural phenomenon, the Pitch Lake, situated on the leeward side of the island. It is composed of bituminous scoriæ, vitrified sand and earth cemented together—a material which is now converted into valuable account. The soils of Trinidad, like its physical appearance and geological formation, are very various, and are classed under the three heads of clay, loam, and alluvial deposits. They are generally fertile, and will compare favorably with the best soils of Cuba and San Domingo.

On the west coast of Trinidad its principal town, Port-of-Spain, lies embosomed in an amphitheatre of hills. The capital has a population of over 20,000 souls, and for beauty and regularity of construction is held to be the second city in the West Indies. There is more life and business activity in Port-of-Spain than in any British Antillean town that I have seen. Extensive quays and large commodious stores give to the place, at the first glance, an air of some commercial importance. The streets are wide, are well laid out, and run parallel or at right angles with each other. The principal thoroughfare, King Street, at the head of which stands the Catholic cathedral, is nearly twice as wide as Broadway. Two rows of trees, huge in stature and magnificent in foliage, run along its centre from end to end, except where they are interrupted by a fountain—the carriage-ways being on either side, and a road for horse exercise in the middle. The stores on King Street would not disgrace a city of ten times the population of Port-of-Spain. The streets are kept clean, the drainage is good, the houses are well and solidly built; there is an immense savanna or park reserved for the recreation of the people; and the whole town, in its municipal arrangements as in its outward appearance, offers palpable evidence of increasing prosperity. No investigation is needed to ascertain the fact. As a straw to indicate the amount of business in the place, it may be interesting to know that the Trinidad branch of the Colonial Bank, after paying all expenses, makes a profit of over $100,000 per annum. A public hospital recently built in Port-of-Spain is not surpassed in America. The churches are large, elegant structures, and though the government buildings are not as commodious or as extensive as the necessities of the community require, I have seen much worse edifices of the kind in more pretentious cities. Among the estimates for the current year $83,000 are set apart for new works and repairs of public buildings, which will include the completion of the sewerage-works and a residence for the governor, who lives at present in a small country cottage. The market-place of Port-of-Spain is large, and is supplied with every convenience. It appears to best advantage on a Sunday morning, when the grounds are crowded. There is a very creditable library and news-room in the town, and, in spite of their unfriendly distance from Europe or Northern America, the inhabitants are not so much out of the world as might be supposed. No thanks, however, to the newspapers, of which there are a weekly and three semi-weekly published in the island—one at San Fernando, and the others at Port-of-Spain. The present opposition journal, whose death may be expected at any moment, is in the interest of the colored population, and is weak, coarse, and not to be relied upon; the government journal gives utterance to the opinions of a very inefficient and unpopular governor. Trinidad can not boast of an "independent press" in any form or shape.

Port-of-Spain is well supplied with water from the Maraval River. The reservoir is about three miles distant from town. Pipes varying from two to six inches in diameter are laid in all the streets, and hydrants are disposed at every 500 feet for protection against fire. This hasty sketch of the Trinidadian capital will sufficiently illustrate that the inhabitants are both able and willing to keep up with the progress of the age. A steamer runs daily to various towns along the island coast, and another, destined for the same duty, will arrive from England in the course of a few months. Land in the city, well located, is valued at 50 cents a foot, and a two-story store will rent as high as from $1200 to $2000 a year.

So much for the town: the settled country districts exhibit equal enterprise and progress. The whole island, in its physical character, is one of the most beautiful that it is possible to imagine. Lofty mountains run in parallel ranges east and west, intersected by deep valleys which contract into gorges at the centre. Nature could offer nothing more magnificent for sugar cultivation than these valleys, with their rich alluvial soil, and the hill-sides are admirably adapted to the growth of the cacao and tropical fruits and vegetables. Except at the Naparimas, where the principal sugar plantations are situated, and which present a district of uninterrupted cultivation, Trinidad has the appearance of a wild, unreclaimed, and densely-wooded country, broken up with savannas. Select any elevated point for a view, and the picturesqueness and variety of the landscape are marvelous. Here will be a hill-side smothered in the golden blossoms of the poui; there another, covered with the orange flower of the roble; beyond, a forest of gigantic cedar. Those feathery masses of light green on the left are clusters of arched bamboo, stretching over the banks of a rivulet which can just be distinguished through the luxuriant vegetation. At your feet, like a bright red carpet, extends a young cacao plantation, sheltered from the scorching heat by the motherly arms of the *bois immortel;* farther on, a savanna or a cane-field, or a grove of lofty cocoanut-trees, and in the distance the deep blue sea. Such a variety of rich, voluptuous coloring is very rarely witnessed in a single landscape-view. The birds of "northern climes abhorred" would not harmonize here, and Nature, when she filled the scene with myriads of the feathered tribes, clothed them with a brilliant plumage that none but the Great Limner could reproduce.

But I must pass from the natural aspect of Trinidad—from its woods, so valuable and multiplied, its vegetation, so luxuriant and varied, its ornithological and botanical treasures so exhaustless — to subjects more practical. I have merely wished to show that, different from Barbados and its finished cultivation, the settlement of this island and its history have but just commenced. With only a present population of 70,000 or 80,000 souls, Trinidad can sustain a million. Its soil is of exceeding richness, and of the million and a quarter acres which cover its surface, twenty-nine thirtieths are fit for cultivation. Its resources are immense; every product of the tropics, and many fruits and vegetables of temperate regions, can be grown here; and a laboring population is only wanted to develop the wealth that lies hidden in forests tenanted still by some scattered representatives of the ancient Carib. The island, as I shall hereafter show, is fast receiving that laboring population; and, since the immigration of Indian coolies commenced, it has sprung from a condition of hopeless lethargy into one of activity and life—an example and a guide to the other colonies. Within the last few years the extension of sugar cultivation has been very great, and the improvement still goes on.

But a vast work has to be done before the island can be brought under the complete dominion of man. There are now about 60,000 acres under cultivation, of which 30,000 are in cane, 7000 in cacao, and the remainder in provisions and pasture. There are about 280 sugar estates, each yielding on an average 200 hogsheads, and some as many as 800 and 1000 hogsheads. It is impossible to form a correct idea of the value of land from an average estimate when land varies in price as much as it does here; but it is fair to say that where a Trinidad estate would bring $100 per acre, one in Barbados would bring $400, and even $500. The reputation that a Barbadian Creole enjoys as a good, steady laborer, the more finished or more careful manufacture of the Barbadian sugars, and some little prejudice in favor of the older colony, make the difference, for the soil and climate of Trinidad are both superior for sugar growing to those of the sister island. Trinidad is not yet sufficiently well known to the world at large; its own inhabitants have the most brilliant hopes in its future.

The planters of this island are not very far advanced in the science of agriculture, if we measure their skill by the product of their estates, which only average one to one and a half hogsheads of sugar to the acre; but the excuse given is that, as yet, they have not been able to devote money or time to a more scientific culture of their land. They have been toiling until now for very existence. Their mills, however, are superior to those of Barbados. One hundred and thirty-five are worked with steam, and turn out six and eight hogsheads per day; about a hundred are worked with cattle, and a few with water-power. The last will soon be obsolete. Besides the regular planters, there are a very large number of small proprietors who grow their own provisions; of these I shall speak more particularly in a subsequent chapter, which I shall devote to the Creole population of the island.

The cocoa, or cacao, as it should be written, is, next to sugar, the most important article of Trinidadian growth and export. Being far less profitable than sugar, and prospering only in virgin lands, it is believed that it will ultimately go out of cultivation. These plantations cover about 7000 acres, yielding over two pounds per tree, or about 700 pounds per acre. Cotton, coffee, and tobacco can all be cultivated in Trinidad; but the first two could not, by any possibility, be made as profitable to the planter as sugar, and the cultivation of the last is not encouraged, though at the London Exhibition of 1851 a specimen of Trinidad tobacco was considered only inferior to the Havana. But, for the present, the paramount object of the Trinidad proprietary is to obtain labor and increase the cultivation of the cane; other things will follow in course of time. A move which requires early attention is the release of a portion of the lands, exceeding altogether a million of acres, locked up in the possession of the crown. Out of the entire island only 213,292 acres have been appropriated to private persons. It can not be the intention of government to monopolize these lands, but a disposition is certainly evinced to throw obstacles in the way of their settlement. It is difficult to understand the motives for such a policy now that the planters obtain labor from abroad, and no longer fear a decrease of the force through the establishment of a small proprietary body. At one time they adopted every means in their power to crush out the small proprietors. It was a foolish effort, but an apology for it existed then that does not exist now.

With the advantages that Trinidad offers to agricultural industry, it is a wonder why immigration does not set in here from the British isles. A few of the exiled Chartists came to the island some years ago, and all are doing well. The climate is glorious; essentially tropical, but tempered with pleasant breezes. The thermometer averages 80°, and seldom rises or sinks below that figure; the heat does not exceed the heat of New York in June, July, and August. In spite of occasional visitations of yellow fever, the average mortality in Port-of-Spain is not greater than that of London, and not so great as that of New York. From what I have seen of the yellow fever in the

West Indies, I am convinced that nine of its victims out of ten are people of intemperate habits. There is one disease—a fearful one—that seems to be indigenous to Trinidad: it is leprosy. There is a leper asylum a short distance from the capital, but the afflicted are not under compulsion to enter it. The consequence is that mendicant lepers may be found begging on the highways, and in the streets of Port-of-Spain, most loathsome objects to contemplate.

CHAPTER XII.

THE CREOLES OF AFRICAN DESCENT.

Port-of-Spain, Trinidad, 1859.

THE population of Trinidad, according to the census of 1851, was, in round numbers, 69,000 souls. No census has been taken since; and the great mortality by the cholera of 1854 on the one hand, and the large increase by immigration on the other—the exact figures of either being unknown—have combined to leave us in uncertainty upon this important point. I have heard the number of actual inhabitants of Trinidad estimated at 70,000, 80,000, 90,000, and even 100,000. I take a medium, and think it safe to put down the population of 1858 at 80,000 souls. The inhabitants are a curious mixture of races—European, Asiatic, African, and American. Originally settled by a few Spanish families, and deemed insignificant as compared with the gold and silver regions on the Main, Trinidad failed at first to attract the attention of the home government, and as late as 1783 we find the population only 2763, of whom 2032 were Indians. About this time an immigration from the French islands commenced, and in ten years the population increased to 17,718, including 10,009 slaves. In 1797 Trinidad became, by conquest, a British colony, and the Anglo-Saxon was added to the French, Spanish, African, and Indian elements of its population. Indeed, it is most curious to observe at the present day, in the Trinidadian Creoles of African descent, the types of the three European, as well as of the native American races. To complicate still more this amalgamation of peoples, there have been imported into the colony during the last thirteen years about 18,000 Eastern laborers—principally Indian coolies—a population which is fast giving to the island its only want, a laboring class.

The ethnological question is a most interesting one, as far as Trinidad is concerned, for in it is involved the success or failure of free labor in the island. But before attempting to form any opinion, or come to any conclusion, *pro* or *con.*, on the subject of free labor, it should be remembered that Trinidad must be judged on her own merits, and with reference to no other island or colony in these latitudes. She is as much an exception to any rule or any general idea that may be formed about the West Indies as Barbados is, though nothing can be more complete than the contrast between these two islands. Trinidad is the very opposite of Barbados in climate, soil, population, and in all that can affect a country or its inhabitants. Trinidad is a new island very recently settled—Barbados had a population of 60,000 two centuries ago. Trinidad has an area of 1,287,600 acres, of which about 60,000 only are under cultivation. Barbados, covering some 106,000 acres, is cultivated from end to end like a garden. Trinidad, even under slavery, never had any thing like an adequate laboring population. Barbados is so thickly inhabited that work or starvation is the laborer's only choice. In Trinidad land is exceedingly rich, plentiful, and cheap, while labor is scarce and extravagantly high; in Barbados land is dear and labor is comparatively cheap. So that it is impossible to make the case of Barbados applicable, in any one particular, to Trinidad, or *vice versa.* The only similarity between the two islands is that sugar forms the staple production of both, and that both have been successful, though from very different causes, under a free-labor system. I have already stated my conviction that each West India colony should be judged on its own merits, for I do believe that a departure from this rule—a classification of the whole, and an adoption of results without understanding or examining particular details—has led to much error and inconsistent argument. Upon this basis, then, and no other, I shall give the result, such as it is, of some passing observations on Trinidad and her condition since emancipation.

The majority of the people of Trinidad are negroes and half-castes. They include Creoles of this and other islands, brought here in the days of slavery and since; native Africans imported as free laborers from Sierra Leone; Africans taken from captured slavers; and a few hundred liberated slaves, who emigrated to this island about sixteen years ago from the United States. Many of these people are nearly, and some are perfectly white, and the census, probably from the fear of giving offense, does not classify the population according to color. For convenience' sake I shall speak of all the colored inhabitants of the island as Creoles of African descent. Their number, according to the best information I can obtain, is in the neighborhood of 50,000. On looking back to the period immediately preceding emancipation, we find the total number of slaves to have been about 21,000, and the free colored about 16,000. Of the former class not more than 11,000 were field laborers. To-day the number of Trinidadian Creoles attached to sugar and cacao estates is not more than 5000; and this falling off in the native and natural laboring force has been attributed here, as in other islands—and, I must add, without very much reflection—to the effect of abolition, to the indolence of the negro, and his refusal to work except under compulsion. I am unable to arrive at any such conclusion. I have taken some pains to trace the Creole laborers of Trinidad from the time of emancipation—after they left the estates and dispersed —to the present day, and the great majority of them can, I think, be followed step by step, not downward in the path of idleness and poverty, but upward in the scale of civilization to positions of greater independence.

Perhaps in no island was impending ruin, consequent upon emancipation, so glaring, so palpable, so apparently certain, as it was in Trinidad after the liberation of the slaves. Unlike other Caribbean islands, the seasons in Trinidad are purely tropical, divided into the rainy and the dry. The latter only lasts five months, and if the planter has not completed his crop operations by the first of June his loss is certain and irremediable. For this reason steady labor in Trinidad during crop season was and is of paramount importance, and the planters had every reason to be alarmed that, in this island above all others, the effect of emancipation would be to deprive them of that continuous labor with which they were already so scantily supplied. Here was a country covering 1,287,600 acres, of which over a million of acres of rich land were capable of cultivation, with only some 30,000 acres already grown in canes, cacao, coffee, and pasture. The result which the planters apprehended—namely, that the emancipated laborers would prefer cultivating their own land when land could be bought at a nominal cost—might have been apprehended with equal propriety in any other country in the world where an abundance of rich territory offered the most tempting invitation to settlers. This very result happens in all new countries where men are free to act for themselves and to advance their own interests. There labor is necessarily high—often not to be procured at any price at all. Trinidad, after emancipation, was a parallel case to most of the newly-settled American territories, with the difference—a most important one—that she had the evil of tropical seasons to contend against. The laborers, as soon as they were free, asked, and for a time received, higher wages than the planters, encumbered as their property was with debt, could afford to pay; and when this rate of wages was subsequently reduced, the majority of the emancipated deserted the estates to better their condition and to seek a more independent livelihood. A very large number purchased small tracts of land and began to plant for themselves; a few squatted on crown lands, of which the government holds an enormous proportion; while many took to trade, and, setting up as petty shopkeepers in the towns, pursued a calling more congenial with their tastes and inclinations. The planters vainly endeavored to remedy the evil; in vain they adopted most stringent measures to prevent the increase of small proprietors, and keep up, by such unnatural means, a sufficient laboring force for the estates. They imposed heavy taxes on all lands and buildings except those devoted to sugar manufacture. But their measures were futile; their policy, as I attempted to show in a former chapter on Barbados, was suicidal. Instead of endeavoring to promote a good understanding between themselves and their laborers, the planters adopted and still retain in Trinidad the odious system of tenancy at will. The laborer who lives on an estate is compelled to work for that estate, and no other, on peril of summary ejection, with consequent loss of the crop which he has raised on his little allotment. He is still in a position of virtual slavery, and it is a matter which can excite no surprise that, after emancipation, those who had means to purchase parcels of ground should have preferred to leave the estates, and either cultivate for themselves or be free to give their labor to whom they pleased, upon their own terms, and in a way which would secure for themselves and their families a greater independence. They accordingly did leave the estates; and in a few years after abolition, the majority of the entire laboring force—itself always inadequate to the wants of the large and rapidly developing colony—were lost to the proprietary. Several estates, for want of necessary labor, were deserted, and at one time it seemed probable that sugar cultivation in Trinidad would be altogether abandoned.

We have now an insight into the course pursued by those 11,000 field laborers of Trinidad who twenty years ago were released from bondage, and the knowledge leads to some important conclusions closely affecting the question of emancipation. Of the entire number about four thousand remained on the estates. These men, in spite of all drawbacks—in spite of an illiberal tenure and a lower rate of wages than they could command elsewhere, continued steadfast in their attachment to the land upon which they were born; but, like the laboring population of Barbados, which, from its density, was compelled to remain in a servile condition, the estate laborers of Trinidad have not progressed as their brethren have progressed in general intelligence and worldly prosperity. They supply labor to nearly all the cacao estates; but comparatively few are to be met with on the sugar plantations. As for that portion of the Creole laboring population which left the estates, and which I estimate at 7000, I do not hesitate to say that their material condition has been very much improved, though for a time their desertion threw the planting interest into the greatest embarrassment. Five sixths of them became proprietors of from one to ten acres, which they now own, and which they grow in provisions for themselves and families; to supply other wants they give casual labor to the estates. But they are free of the estates, and can work for whom they please, or whom they deem the best paymaster. If any one doubts that a very large—a very astonishing number of the emancipated laborers have become independent proprietors, let him look at the score of villages built up since abolition, and so thickly scattered throughout the cultivated districts of Trinidad that it would be superfluous in me to point them out. I am merely stating a fact which no one who has visited Trinidad will think of denying. The labor of these men, not being a continuous or certain labor, is lightly esteemed by the planter, and hence they are not classed as belonging to the regular working force of the island. Yet I have been assured that during crop-time as many as four or five thousand of these independent laborers and small proprietors will work on the estates; and I do not think the proportion so small when the large numbers of Creoles engaged in trade are taken into consideration.

I am astonished at the utter disregard of the first principles of economical science displayed by the West India planters. They do not seem to reflect for a moment that the interest of a proprietor is to elevate, not to degrade, his laborer. They have misjudged the negro throughout, and have put too much faith in his supposed inferiority. After the important step of emancipation was taken, little was done to turn emancipation to the best account. I deny that these people lack industry when by industry they can add to their means or advance their prosperity. Nor can I agree with the West India planter who denounces the Creole laborers as thriftless vagabonds because they have preferred independence to servitude, or the pursuit of trade to that of agriculture. Unquestionably there is a certain amount of idleness and vagabondism among the Creole laborers of Trinidad, but I see no evidence that these vices exist in a larger proportion among them than they would exist among any other class of laborers similarly situated. In leaving the estates the great majority were actuated by a desire to better their circumstances and to lead a more independent life. Land was cheap and abundant, and they preferred to have their own property rather than labor at low wages in a condition of precarious servitude. Added to this, the course of the planters contributed greatly to the very evil which they dreaded, and from which they afterward so severely suffered. Instead of endeavoring by liberal terms to induce the laborers to remain on the estates, they commenced a system shortly after emancipation of giving less wages and exacting more work; and when the laborers retired, as they did, from estate to field work, they were summarily ejected from the houses and lands they occupied on the estates, and their provision-grounds were destroyed. The emancipated laborers had, therefore, no resource left but to separate themselves from the planting interest.

In the observations I have made I have spoken principally of that portion of the emancipated class which remained agriculturists. Those who forsook field labor for trade offer also an apology for their course, though its wisdom we may be permitted to question. Work in the cane-fields was the negro's sole occupation in the days of slavery, and this species of work he is now disposed to look upon as degrading, and to fancy that it drags him back to the condition of servitude from which he has been liberated. Here we find an explanation of the large and utterly disproportionate numbers of colored people engaged in trade—from keeping a store down to selling a sixpence-worth of mangoes on the street. Not only have the tradesmen of 1830 and the free Creoles of that period continued to follow mercantile and mechanical pursuits, but the laborers after they were freed made every exertion to bring up their children as traders or mechanics, and the consequence is, that to-day these professions in Trinidad are almost entirely supplied from the colored population. If we take Port-of-Spain as an illustration, we find that four fifths of the inhabitants, Creoles of African descent, are engaged in trade, and their condition, I must add, is one of prosperity and independence. I have personal knowledge of many instances where great wealth has been accumulated by men who were slaves themselves a quarter of a century ago. Trade seems to be the destiny of the Trinidadian Creoles, for the position they once occupied as tillers of the soil is already filled by another race.

The moral condition of the people whom I have thus briefly endeavored to trace from the time of slavery down to the present day, has not kept pace with their material prosperity, and all I have said of Barbadians in a former chapter, under this particular head, may with still greater force be applied to Trinidadians. The amalgamation of the European and African races is even more general in Trinidad than in Barbados; and though marriage between whites and people of color is not opposed here with any thing like the feeling it meets with in Barbadian society, yet I find, on examination, that in Port-of-Spain the ratio of births is 100 legitimate to 136 illegitimate—an exhibition of morality considerably below that of Havana. I may say that the so-called prejudices against color are less to be observed in Trinidad than in any other island. Perhaps it is that there are more wealthy and intelligent Creoles here than in other colonies, and I can assert, from my own experience, that Trinidad can boast of many colored planters and merchants who in mind and manner are most accomplished gentlemen. But, as I said before, the great mass of the colored population do not exhibit any remarkable improvement in morality. Taking up the matter of crime, I find that the annual average of convicted offenders for the last five years is, for felony, 63; for misdemeanor, 865, and for debt, 230; against a much lower average before emancipation. It is to be observed that theft is the principal crime under the head of misdemeanor. Arson is frequent, and the perpetrators are discovered with great difficulty; more often they go unpunished. The criminal records of Trinidad show that a majority of the felonies have been committed in uncontrollable ebullitions of anger; in the minor offenses the most curious deliberation and cunning are often apparent. It is also a fact worthy of remark that the county of Victoria gives the largest proportion of offenders. This is the most important agricultural district of the colony; but while it gives the largest number of criminals, it shows at the same time the lowest proportion of small independent proprietors, as well as by far the greatest number of estate laborers. The inference is, that that portion of the emancipated class which left the estates attained a higher *status* of morality, as they undoubtedly did of material prosperity, by the course they pursued, though that course was directly hostile to the planting interest.

Trinidad, like all the other islands, is lamentably behind the age in educational science, and there is ample room to hope that when knowledge becomes more general crime will decrease. Educational statistics do not show that there is any great eagerness on the part of the Creole population to learn, or on the part of their rulers to place the means of instruction within their reach. Before emancipation, the number of children attending public and private schools was above a thousand; last year the average of children attending all the schools and seminaries was considerably under 3000, accounting for little more than the natural increase of the population. In fact, no general system of public instruction was introduced until 1851; but that system has many excellent features. The schools were made purely secular; a board of education and an inspectorship of schools were created; also, a school for training masters and mistresses, whose efficiency for office is determined by the strictest scrutiny. The estimate for educational expenses in Trinidad this year is $20,000. In regard to church statistics, I have no means of ascertaining the number of persons who attend places of Divine worship in this island; but were they in my possession I should not have much faith in them as an evidence of the moral or religious tone of the community. To judge from appearances, the Creole inhabitants of Port-of-Spain are even fonder than Barbadians of showing off their Sunday garments. More than one half of the entire population of the island are Romanists, and the superior zeal of the Catholic Church to secure proselytes may account for the outward devotion of its children.

CHAPTER XIII.

THE SCHEME OF ASIATIC IMMIGRATION.

Port-of-Spain, Trinidad, 1859.

I ENDEAVORED to show in the last chapter—what is, indeed, a matter of historical record—that within a few years after the emancipation of the slaves in Trinidad, a large proportion of Creole labor, always inadequate to the demand, was lost to the estates—not as some suppose, through the idleness of the negro, but from his natural aspirations after greater independence, and his very commendable desire to improve his circumstances. The Creoles did not leave the estates as soon as they were free; they waited until they had acquired sufficient means to purchase land; and it was not until 1844 that the planters felt in its full force the severity of the loss they had sustained. During this and several subsequent years, the gloomiest apprehensions were entertained, and it was feared that sugar cultivation would be entirely abandoned in the island. In justice to the Trinidad proprietary, it must be said that they did not yield to misfortune. They were a new race compared with the ancient proprietary of Barbados or Jamaica, and, with more life, intelligence, and energy, they made every exertion that men could make to extricate themselves from their difficulties. Inter-colonial immigration was encouraged, and captains of vessels were offered a bounty for every laborer brought to Trinidad. This immigration has been large and useful in its way, but it is at all times uncertain, and can not be depended upon. The Creoles from other islands are not bound by any contract to labor on the estates, and, like their brethren in Trinidad, they will quit the estates as soon as they have means to do so. Some may remain in Trinidad as small proprietors, but many return home. The system, moreover, has given rise to much fraud. Creoles are taken away and reintroduced to obtain the bounty, and this nefarious practice, I understand, is still successfully kept up. By the latest report of the agent general for immigrants, it appears that the number of laborers, Creoles of Trinidad, who are now working on the sugar estates, is 3832, and the number of laborers, Creoles of other islands, is 4041. Adding to these the estimated number of Creole laborers on the cacao estates, there would be a total of about 5000 Creole laborers of Trinidad, and the same number of Creole laborers from other islands actually at work during the harvest season. I say during the harvest season, because many of the Creole laborers from other islands are not permanent residents of Trinidad, but return home as soon as crop operations are over.

The planters of Trinidad have also encouraged immigration from Canada and the United States, and several hundred people of color did actually come from the Republic; but being principally tradesmen and mechanics—a class too numerous already—they were of no advantage to the planting interest. Several thousand Africans, liberated from slavery, and a few hundred voluntary emigrants from the Kroo coast, were a valuable accession to the labor force of the island; but the supply was limited and insufficient. The number of native Africans on the estates at present is 2885. The total importation of negroes, including Creoles from other islands, Africans and Americans, amounts to 20,000; and if they could have been retained, they, with the Creole laborers of Trinidad, would have sufficed at least for immediate want. But many of them returned home; others bought land for themselves, or engaged in trade or as domestics; and the remnant of this immigration, and of the native Trinidad laboring force now working on the sugar and cacao properties, does not exceed 13,000 estate and day laborers. I am of decided opinion that the tenure system of Trinidad has strengthened the dislike of the negro to perform estate work. It is true that the Trinidad planter exacts no rent from the laborer on his estate, and supplies him with medical attendance; but the laborer, in return, is compelled to work for the estate alone, and for five cents a day less than the current rate of wages. It may be urged, and with truth, that house-rent and medical attendance are worth more than five cents a day; but for these privileges the laborer is required to give up his independence, and I do not think it natural that even the negro should, of his own free choice, prefer the exchange.

It will thus be seen that the exertions made by the planters to obtain Creole labor were only partially successful, and the unremunerative outlay to which they were subjected swelled the number of encumbered estates. But desperate circumstances stimulate exertion, and the importation of foreign labor, after the successful example of the Mauritius, was finally attempted. The first ship with Chinese immigrants arrived in the harbor of Port-of-Spain in 1845. But the importation of Indian coolies was soon substituted for that of Chinese. The experiment remained for some time very doubtful. The laborers arrived for several years in small detachments, and at long intervals; and they were brought from the opposite extremity of the world at an enormous cost. They had to be instructed, and from the day on which the first convoy was landed down to the year 1853, no one could say whether the plan was a success or a failure. But, now that it has been fairly and fully tested, the advantages to the colony of this importation of Indian labor are so thoroughly established that no one who visits Trinidad in 1859, after having seen her and known her in 1846, can hesitate to believe that not only has the island been saved from impending ruin, but a prospect of future prosperity has been opened to her such as no British island in these seas ever before enjoyed under any system, slave or free. I am speaking of a fact which is apparent to every one who walks the streets of Port-of-Spain, or surveys the splendid picture of cultivation which the Naparima counties present. There, for miles and miles, you can travel over undulating land, rich with waving fields of sugar-cane. The smoke from a hundred chimneys indicates the prevalent use of steam, and strangely contrasts with the purely tropical aspect of the country, checkered as it is with dense masses of shrub or groves of mango, and fenced in with rows of gigantic palm. The story that every Naparima planter tells is, that within the last ten years he has greatly extended and improved the cultivation of his estate, and has doubled his produce. It is a story you can well believe, if, during crop season, you enter the mills and see an average of from six to eight hogsheads of sugar daily manufactured in each. This extension of culture—fully borne out by facts and statistics—is increasing every year, and the consequence is that every year the proprietary are demanding more and more labor. It is to be hoped that they will continue to be supplied through the means of a system beneficial alike to the laborer and his employer, and that the outcry raised against coolie immigration will not be allowed to prevail.

I shall endeavor in this chapter, and I hope with some success, to present such information as I have procured, and such actual observations as I have been enabled to make, on the theory and practice of Trinidad immigration. I can not consider the objections to it well founded, whether they be judged by a standard of sound colonial polity, or in the higher balance of rigid morality. The most serious of these objections is that injustice is done to the coolie, and to that I now direct attention.

The chief feature in Trinidad immigration is its entire management on the responsibility, not merely of the colony, but of the government and people of Great Britain. Private speculation has no directing voice in the scheme. It was not started for the aggrandizement of the planter, but to stimulate his prostrate energies, to benefit coolie as much as Creole, and to multiply resources that slavery, during long years of sore trial, was powerless to develop. The immigrants, then, are under the close surveillance of government, and no planter, were he so disposed, can wrong them with impunity. A superintendent, or agent general, of immigrants is appointed, and is invested with special powers. He acts on behalf of the government as the immigrant's protector. He indentures them to their employers; keeps a register, with the names and other particulars of both parties to the contract; provides food for those immigrants who are not employed immediately on their arrival; sees that husbands are not separated from wives, or children from parents; visits and inspects the condition of the immigrants on the estates; and is required to obtain from the planters quarterly returns, in which the increase by birth and decrease by death of the laborers on each estate, with other specified particulars, must be fully stated. The reports are transmitted to the government by the agent general. This officer has also power to cancel any immigrant's indenture if it shall appear to him that the man has been ill used by his employer, or that the accommodation or medical attendance to which he is entitled is bad or insufficient. The system of government supervision is, in fact, perfect and complete, and the consideration paid to the wants and comforts of the immigrant is carried to a point that many consider injurious to the planting interest.

When I speak of coolie immigration to Trinidad I mean immigration exclusively from British India. This is the only immigration conducted here on a large scale, and for it all other plans have been very properly abandoned. It is merely removing British subjects from one portion of the empire to another, where the prospects of the laborer are infinitely better and brighter. He is indentured in order that the parties who have suffered the expense of his importation may be guaranteed from loss. A clerk, sent from England to the Colonial Bank in Trinidad or Barbados, receives his traveling expenses, and is indentured in the same way, though with this disadvantage, that, if found inefficient, he can be turned adrift; the coolie, on the contrary, if inefficient, must be retained or sent back home; and, if disabled by sickness, must be properly cared for. It has been stated that the British coolie immigration is cruelly conducted, but I can affirm that the very reverse is the case. The coolies are imported from Madras and Calcutta at a general expense to the colony—to meet which a duty has been imposed upon rum—and at a special cost to the employer of about $25 per head. The law provides for their free return after they have completed the term of industrial residence for which they were indentured. They are perfectly free men and women, and at their own option leave the squalid filth and misery in which they have been accustomed to live, on a promise, guaranteed by government, of a free passage to the West Indies, certain employment, and fair remuneration for their services. Upon arriving here they have no thought or care about the future. They are immediately provided for. They live on the estates rent free in comfortable cottages; if sick, they receive medical attendance without charge; and their wages are five times more than they could earn at home. The physical appearance of a crowd of coolie immigrants returning to India attests the beneficent results to themselves of an industrial residence in Trinidad. Instead of being a set of naked, half-starved, gibbering savages, ready to eat any dead, putrid animal, fish, flesh, or fowl that lay in their path, they are clothed, sleek and well fed, strong and able-bodied, speaking English with tolerable accuracy, and looking the intelligent people that they really are. I have seen them arrive and I have seen them depart, and speak from actual observation. After they are landed from the ship, not only families, but people from the same district are kept together; their wants are immediately cared for, and, the prospects of work and wages being certain, their condition is far more comfortable and encouraging than that of the mass of Irish immigrants who arrive every week in the city of New York. So jealously does the imperial government watch over the interests of the coolies that no more than 350 or 360 can be carried in a first-class ship. They are not more crowded than steerage passengers in an ocean steamer—not half so crowded as a regiment in a troop-ship going to the East—and the mortality among them, considering their wretched and impoverished condition when placed on board, is inconsiderable. During the voyages from Madras this year the deaths among the coolies have only amounted to three quarters per cent.

The pretension of excessive mortality on board the coolie ships is positively untrue, as far, at least, as Trinidad is concerned. Among the Madras immigrants the mortality on the voyage is not higher than it would be if they remained in their own villages; and if the mortality among the Calcutta immigrants be greater—and I believe it averages five per cent.—it arises from the fact that British agents are permitted to engage these laborers in a weak and sickly condition—men who would die at home quite as readily as on board a vessel. This is strictly prohibited under the French system, and we accordingly find that, though the British only carry one immigrant for every three tons measurement, and the French carry one immigrant for every ton, the average mortality among Africans on the voyage to Martinique while that immigration lasted was only one per cent.

It is impossible to imagine the rights of any people more securely guaranteed than are those of the Indian coolies who emigrate to Trinidad. That they receive adequate compensation for their services is apparent from the fact that all who return home, after completing their term of industrial residence, carry away large quantities of money. I heard of a coolie the other day who returned, after a residence in the island of ten or twelve years, with $9000; yet this man was entitled to, and actually received, a free passage home. A ship-load of coolies, going back, will take with them from $40,000 to $50,000, and, under these circumstances, the heavy tax imposed upon the colony and the planting interest for their return-passage must be considered a hardship, if not a positive injustice. By a colonial ordinance, passed in 1854, the Indian immigrants who have arrived subsequent to that period are only entitled to a free return after a residence of ten years; but the principle of granting a free return at all is absurd. After making heavy sacrifices to obtain a laboring population, the colony, by its own act, deprives itself of that population as soon as it is thoroughly educated and inured to service. That the coolie laborers themselves are fully satisfied with their condition in Trinidad is very evident from the fact that large numbers remain in spite of the bonus, for it is nothing else, offered them to return. After they have fulfilled their terms of service, many voluntarily renew their contracts.

The "indenture" of which I have spoken is the contract of service into which the immigrant enters with his employer, and may be general or specific in its obligations according to option. The immigrant is indentured for three years. As soon as that period has expired, he can release himself from any subsequent indenture by paying $1 20 to the agent general for every month that may be wanting to complete his term. After the immigrants have fulfilled the obligations to which they bound themselves, they receive a certificate of what is called "industrial residence," which empowers them to act as independently as they choose for the future. Under the general contract—where no express agreement has been made to the contrary—the immigrant binds himself to work, except in times of sickness and on Sundays and holidays, for nine hours a day. By refusing or neglecting to work, he forfeits his claim to wages for the time he absents himself, and, being tried for the offense, may, on conviction, be imprisoned for a term not exceeding fourteen days.

There are at present 439 Chinese and about 6000 Indian coolie laborers of both sexes on the sugar estates of Trinidad. The coolies are but the nucleus of the future laboring population of the island, which, if as thickly settled as Barbados, would contain a million and a half of people. Of the sixteen thousand coolies originally imported to Trinidad from Madras and Calcutta, including a few hundred from Cape de Verd, a very large number have been sent home.

A few left the island after the expiration of their terms to seek their fortunes on the Spanish Main. As laborers they are perhaps not all that the planter could desire. They have not the endurance or strength of the Creole, but they are industrious and intelligent. They are gracefully formed, and, upon first arriving, do not look as though they could stand the labor of the fields or the boiling-houses. But the coolie perseveres in his work—the nature of which he learns quickly—and soon becomes an efficient hand. He is mild in disposition almost to effeminacy, docile and obedient, contrasting very favorably, in this respect, with the negro, who has more force and character, and the Chinaman, who has more cunning. The coolie is not addicted to crimes of violence. In the Demarara riots of 1856, said to have been incited by the maniac known as the "Angel Gabriel," but which were a pure outburst of Creole vindictive jealousy against the Portuguese residents, the coolies behaved remarkably well, and the governor, in his report, declared that they rendered important service in protecting life and property. I should say, as far as the Trinidad coolies are concerned, that their extreme docility and gentleness amounted to a fault.

Statistics of the quantity of labor performed and of wages paid on this island show some interesting results. The coolie works, on an average, nineteen and a half days during the month, and receives $5 35; the Creole of Trinidad works sixteen and a half days, and receives $5 91; the Creole from abroad works seventeen and a half days, and receives $6 27; the African works seventeen days, and receives $5 36; and the Chinaman works seventeen days, and receives $4

27. It will be seen by this exhibit that the Creoles from other islands are considered the best laborers, for they are best paid. The statement further shows that no injustice is done to the coolie. He is not brought here under fair promises, and afterward compelled to work, as I have seen alleged, for a sum below the market rate.

The British system of immigration has been most unjustly confounded with that of the French to Martinique, and of the Spanish to Cuba. In the first case the immigrants have all their rights secured by government guaranty and supervision, and no immigration on private account is permitted. The blessing of giving labor and life to the colony is scarcely equal to the blessing that this immigration scheme has conferred upon the coolie himself. He receives, as I have said before, his house-rent and medical attendance free, and he earns from $5 to $6, and as high as $10 a month, which he is at perfect liberty to dispose of as he pleases. A poor pagan, he is brought in contact with civilization, and soon forgets and abandons the gross superstitions in which he was wont to put his faith. Under this system of immigration more might be done toward Christianizing and civilizing the people of India in one year than has been done by all the missionaries that ever migrated to the East under the influence of the most enthusiastic zeal. The coolies who go back after an industrial residence, go back to spread abroad the seeds of civilization and Christianity, and on this ground the free return granted by the government may be advocated with some show of reason. While in the colony, every provision that the law can make is made for the education and industrial training of coolie children; and coolie orphans have an asylum in Trinidad, which one or two leading proprietors have established, and which, in all the details of management, is equal to any similar institution that I have ever been permitted to visit. The children are brought up as Protestants; for though the Roman Catholics are the most numerous in the island, they are not willing to expend the money or the trouble that the support of a rival institution would require.

I have, in these remarks, endeavored to point out how carefully guarded are the rights of the coolie immigrant. The supposition that, by his introduction, an injustice is done to the Creole laboring population may be dismissed with a very few words. I can not believe that any such plea is advanced by intelligent and responsible persons, who have not been misled by falsehood or swayed by mistaken zeal. It is utterly contrary to common sense to dream that the planters of Trinidad would plunge into heavy expenditure to obtain this immigration, or that the people of Trinidad would submit to taxation for the same object, if the labor sought abroad could, by any means, be procured at home. I have shown, in the commencement of this chapter, what tremendous efforts the Trinidad proprietary made in the first years of their distress to obtain Creole labor from other islands, and how unsuccessful those efforts were. None but the very worst class of Creoles will leave their native islands, and this fact the criminal records of Trinidad amply demonstrate. If the reader knows any thing of Trinidad, he will know that never, at any period of her history, either under slavery or under freedom, could she boast of sufficient Creole labor for the proper cultivation of the small proportion of her soil that has been redeemed from wood-land or from wilderness. And when, after emancipation, many of the laborers left the estates for more profitable employment or a more independent status, there was barely a sufficient number left to cultivate the cacao estates, and without immigration the growth of sugar must have been entirely abandoned. The coolies have saved the island from ruin, but so far they have not nearly supplied its wants. The unfinished look of Trinidadian cane-fields, and the inferior quality of Trinidadian sugar, tell to-day of the scanty supply of labor with which the planters have eked out cultivation, and have struggled against crushing misfortunes. But if the negroes abandoned agricultural servitude for pursuits more advantageous to themselves, or more congenial to their tastes, have they any ground for complaint that their loss has been supplied? I have maintained the superiority of the negro as an athletic and industrious laborer when he is properly remunerated for his work; and I have justified him for withdrawing from that work when he could do better in any other pursuit that he chose to follow. I would justify him though he earned no more—though he earned less—upon his own plot than he did on an estate. He has selected, of his own free will, a life of independence to one of servitude, and the choice ought never to be urged to his detriment or represented as his shame. I have passed over with indifference, as I think it deserves to be passed over, the lamentation of the planter that the "negro won't work," because I think that, in the majority of cases, the cry was an ebullition of selfish disappointment at the loss of labor, raised with little consideration for its truth, and without any reference to the subsequent occupation in which the Creole found himself engaged. But it is most unreasonable to say that because the Creole population of Trinidad are unwilling to work in the field, be the reason what it may, the deficiency of labor—out of consideration to them forsooth!—must not be supplied from any other legitimate source. There are a million of acres in Trinidad waiting for the plow; and supposing that every Creole was ready to undertake field labor, the entire number would be insufficient to cultivate one tenth of the island. I can not, therefore, comprehend the assertion that foreign labor for Trinidad is not required, nor the argument that its introduction is an injury to the Creole population. I can not believe that any one would hold these views if he were really interested in the development of the wonderful resources of this island.

It has been, again, stated that the introduction of East Indian coolies into West Indian islands has excited a dangerous jealousy in the minds of the Creole population. On what pretense does such an allegation weigh one scruple in the scale? Such an argument strikes at the root of all colonization, especially American colonization, in which it has been sought to amalgamate races, and not to settle any special district by a distinct and separate people. Such an argument would justify the exclusion of Irish laborers from the United States, for their immigration, beyond all others, has excited "the jealousy of natives," and has reduced the current rate of wages far below its original standard. This is, indeed, a new and obnoxious form of "protection" and "monopoly." This would sustain the monstrous pretension that the West Indies are the sole property of the negro, whose equanimity must be disturbed by the presence of no other people, and that colonies capable of sustaining twenty millions of inhabitants must be reserved as an exclusive inheritance for less than a million descendants of the African race. It is reducing the argument to a positive absurdity. How, in law or in equity, can such a policy be consistently advocated? But I deny altogether that there has been any exhibition of jealousy between the Creoles and coolies of Trinidad. I have looked in vain over the police records of the island to discover even an indication of such a feeling. I have made it the subject of special inquiry and observation, and I believe that neither the Creole nor the coolie have even dreamed of a national hostility toward each other. The fact is that every day the supply of Creole estate labor is diminishing. With increased intelligence, the Creole discovers that he can better his position, if not his fortune, by a more independent mode of life. The coolie quietly takes his place; and the common expectation that, within a few years, the East Indian coolies will have altogether supplanted the West Indian Creoles in the field, and have become the legitimate laboring population of Trinidad, is a wish most likely to be gratified, as it is a consummation most earnestly to be desired.

But the objections raised against coolie immigration are not yet ended; for it is not only stated to be an injustice to the Creole and the coolie, but also an injury to the public, and even to the planter himself.

The public, it is contended, are unjustly taxed to support a system from which they derive no benefit. This is a point, it strikes me, for the colony alone to determine; and if the people are willing to bear a very small proportion of the taxation necessary to maintain an immigration, which, though it be to the direct advantage of the planter, must ultimately increase colonial prosperity and develop colonial resources, the interference of a stranger in a question so obviously local is uncalled for and impertinent. As to the imagined injury inflicted on the planter—the expense to which he is subjected, and the debt with which the introduction of foreign labor is supposed to overwhelm him—these are issues of which he himself is the best judge. The large amount of landed property released from hypothecation in Trinidad during the last five years, or since the introduction of coolie labor has been a declared success, is a stubborn fact very hard to set aside.

I wish it to be distinctly understood that I have been speaking only of Trinidad; not because I believe these remarks inapplicable to many of the sparsely populated islands, but because I started on the principle that each colony should be separately examined, its condition determined, and its wants ascertained, without reference to other colonies within or without the tropics. I can not imagine any one honestly contending that the *principle* of immigration and colonization is contrary to good morals or opposed to sound political economy. Its *practice*, as far as Trinidad is concerned, is honorably conducted; nor can it be otherwise, while the same watchful supervision is preserved, while the cupidity of private speculation is rebuked, and the promise of the imperial government stands solemnly pledged to every individual immigrant. I can not believe that any serious objection would be raised to the transportation of coolies from Eastern to Western India, if it were clearly understood that the liberties of the immigrants were rigidly guarded; and if I am correct in this belief—if English philanthropists are only excited by their own fears of privileges abused or rights violated—let them not blindly seek to abolish what is giving life to a desolated empire, but rather let them do all in their power, and the planters themselves will lend a willing aid, to defend the coolie from every possible aggression and to shield him from every possible wrong. There are minor defects in the system which require to be removed, and improvements which time and experience will suggest. But I am satisfied that that system, as it obtains in Trinidad, is wisely, humanely, and lawfully conducted, and has been attended so far with not a single political or social evil. It seems to have been decreed in the providence of God that these fair and fertile islands should ultimately become an asylum for millions of wanderers from heathenesse; and the scheme of immigration, instead of being condemned, should be upheld, defended, and perfected by philanthropists above all others, as a plan most happily devised for the elevation of a degraded people and for the restoration to prosperity of a splendid inheritance.

CHAPTER XIV.

CULTIVATION AND COMMERCE OF TRINIDAD.

Port-of-Spain, Trinidad, 1859.

I GAVE in the last chapter some leading features of the Trinidad immigration laws; sufficient, I hope, to convey a correct idea of the system under which the colony is being supplied with labor, and of the manner in which that system has been reduced to practice. I do not hesitate to say, and no one in this island will express a contrary opinion, that immigration has been the salvation of Trinidad. It is a blessing both to the employer and the employed. This is no vague assertion; it can be demonstrated; first, by an exhibition of the improved and improving condition of the laborer; secondly, by the increased demand for his services; thirdly, by the extension of sugar cultivation on the island; and fourthly, by the augmentation of its trade.

I have already spoken of the improved condition of the immigrant laborer after an industrial residence in Trinidad of three or five years. He is, indeed, vastly improved, morally, materially, physically, socially. The civilizing influences which surround him make him a new man. The climate agrees with him, and doing much less work than an Irish laborer performs in America, he nevertheless does enough to develop his form and figure. He learns to labor, and labors cheerfully, industriously. I have seen him on the estates where, in the midst of friends and relatives from the remote east, he lives in comfort and contentment, with every want supplied and every right jealously guarded. Statistics fully prove this to be the case. Taking one example from the register of immigrants, I find that, out of 1799 coolies distributed in 1853, there remained in 1858, under indenture, 1184, of whom 623 had never quitted the estates to which they had been originally assigned, while 90 had purchased their remaining periods of industrial residence. Speaking of the condition of the coolies, the agent general of immigrants in his report of the 1st of March, 1859, says: "The year 1853, which witnessed the arrival in Trinidad of 2040 coolies, witnessed also the embarkation for Calcutta of return coolies with their wives and children, and the somewhat agreeable additional impedimenta of $45,000 of declared money in silver, besides concealed amounts. These return immigrants were superior in physical development to the newly arrived, and were, with the exception of a few taken from hospital, in vigorous health. Not only was their appearance above par, but competent evidence had established the fact that they had here acquired habits of continuous industry foreign to their previous character; results which may be attributed to their earning more money than when in India, and perhaps living somewhat better. Nor was improvement confined to physical endowment; external comfort has reacted on their feelings, and the common laborer is evidently less prone to falsehood in his social relations at the close of his industrial residence than he was at the commencement. It is not unusual to see men of this class trusting fully to their employers, and by them as fully trusted in return."

2. To prove the increased demand for coolie laborers in Trinidad I quote from the same authority. The agent says: "In 1852 the applications made to this office were eighty in number for an aggregate of 2000 coolies, averaging about twenty-five for each estate applying; while in 1857 the corresponding demand rose to 7000, from 179 properties, averaging forty to each applicant, accompanied by a voluntary offer on the part of the employers to double the fees payable to government on the contract for each immigrant when the question of labor was at stake." This year 2500 coolies have already arrived out of 3000, whose importation will cost the colony £33,000 sterling, besides an expenditure of £3300 for the return of 300. The total estimate of immigration expenses for the current year exceeds $270,000.

3. The extension of sugar cultivation in Trinidad is a matter with which I have made myself personally acquainted, by visiting the estates and learning the fact from the planters themselves. Within the last twenty years the crop has more than doubled, and the land in cane cultivation has increased from 15,000 to 29,000 acres. Cacao cultivation has also increased, though in a less proportion, because, as an article of export, the cacao is not so profitable as sugar. The immense increase of small proprietors, who grow their own provisions but nothing for export, must also be taken into account as an important item in the general wealth and prosperity of the island. But the extension and improvement in the cultivation of the cane can not fail to attract attention. The substitu-

tion of steam for cattle and water-power is now almost universal. Several miles of a tramway to run through the great sugar district of Naparima are already completed and in operation.

On the subject of extended cultivation the report from which I have already quoted says: "It would be no difficult task to enumerate estates which have more than doubled their produce since 1846; others long abandoned, or nearly so, have risen from their ruins, and a few of late years have been established on newly-cleared forest land. It may not be that, in most of these instances, the planters have heavy balances in their favor at the local bank; but mortgages of ancient date and almost hopeless amount have been settled; the laborers earn a higher aggregate of wages, their houses are comfortable, the manufacturing machinery, whether fixed or movable, is more powerful, and the planter himself has fairly contributed, or rather created that increased commerce which has enabled the colony to provide ample means for the introduction of labor from the most distant shores." But, perhaps, the best illustration of the extension of sugar cultivation in Trinidad is to be found in

4. The increase of its trade. Statistics show conclusively that that increase is principally, if not wholly, due to the importation of foreign labor, for it is only since the importation was commenced in earnest that the improvement is to be noticed. In 1854 Trinidad exported 27,987 hogsheads of sugar; in 1855, 31,693 hogsheads; in 1856, 34,411 hogsheads; in 1857, 35,523 hogsheads; and in 1858, 37,000 hogsheads; showing a gradual increase during the past five years, and an average exportation of 33,000 hogs-

heads. Before the introduction of foreign labor the exports of sugar were as follows: in 1842, 20,506 hogsheads; in 1843, 24,088 hogsheads; in 1844, 21,800 hogsheads; and in 1845, 25,399, or an average of 22,000 hogsheads. The highest average exportation before emancipation during the same number of years was 25,000 hogsheads of very inferior weight, not equal to 20,000 hogsheads of the present day. Thus it appears that the export of sugar in 1844, with a very scanty supply of labor, was equal to the export under slavery; while this year, with coolie labor, the export will reach nearly 40,000 hogsheads, and will continue to increase every year hereafter, if immigration be kept up, until Trinidad has reached the point of cultivation that Barbados long ago attained. In the export of molasses the same proportionate increase is to be observed. It is generally assumed that the sugar-crop this year will reach 40,000 hogsheads of an average of 17 cwt. each. The whole number of laborers employed to produce the crop of 1859 is only 17,000; and what, we may ask, can not be done after the resources of the island have been developed—after cultivation has extended inland, and Trinidad shall have obtained all the labor that she requires?

The increase in the exportation of cacao has been also very great. Though these plantations are not worked by coolies, yet the introduction of foreign labor has so far relieved the pressure in the market that the cacao planter now gets all the assistance he requires. Last year 5,200,000 lbs. of cacao were exported, against 3,200,000 lbs., the highest figure ever attained previous to emancipation.

I think that, judged by any of its legitimate results,

the introduction of coolie labor in Trinidad will be found a mutual benefit to employer and employed. These results have followed the transportation of coolies to the Mauritius and to British Guiana, and must follow their transportation to Jamaica, if it be conducted under a well-regulated system, and on a sufficiently extended scale.

THE LEEWARD ISLANDS.

CHAPTER XV.

PROSPERITY OF ANTIGUA.

St. John, Antigua, 1860.

ANTIGUA has been, and still is, in some respects, one of the favored islands of the British West India group. Though small in size, she has often taken a lead in questions of political and social reform that larger, more populous, and more wealthy islands have found it advantageous to follow. Antigua hastened, in advance of all other colonies, to emancipate her slaves. She refused to believe in the virtues of an apprenticeship, or in the doctrine that her bondsmen needed a purgatory to prepare them for freedom. If they were to be liberated, why not at once, and escape the vexation, the heart-burnings, and the suspense of a wretched ordeal? This was her argument, and in 1834 Antigua became a perfectly free colony. Her rulers were wise in their generation. They foresaw that, with the substitution of free labor for slave labor, much had to be learnt and much to be unlearnt; that the success of the new system could only be determined by time and experience; and that an early start in the race was a point to be gained—not to be neglected. And so it undoubtedly was. Antigua has never had any cause to regret the independent course that she then thought proper to pursue. In spite of an insignificant area, a soil by no means superlatively rich, and a climate too liable to drought to make the cultivation of sugar a business of extravagant profit, Antigua has managed to retain a prominent position among West Indian colonies. She suffered severely from an earthquake in 1843, but that calamity, terrible as it was, neither checked her industry nor affected her permanent prosperity.

There is no island in the West Indies more bountifully supplied with safe harbors than Antigua. Those most generally in use are Falmouth, English Harbor (where the mail steamers stop, and men-of-war find shelter during the hurricane months), Parham, on the north coast, and the principal seaport of St. John. The capital, called also St. John, is the best-looking and best-regulated city of its size in the British West Indies. Its board of health is always actively at work. The streets are clean and macadimized; the houses are neat, well built, and of a more modern style than the generality of West Indian domiciles; and it is only in suburban outskirts—the "St. Giles" of the minute metropolis—that a ragged architecture offends the eye. From the midst of the city, its cathedral, built since the earthquake at a cost of $200,000, rises quite grandly. The Moravian and Wesleyan chapels, the city hall, the poor-house, the hospital, and the jail, all commodious and even elegant structures, testify in favor of Antiguan prosperity. And it is a well-earned prosperity. The whole island is only 55 miles in circumference, and its revenue, about £35,000 sterling, is derived from a population that scarcely exceeds that figure. Of this revenue some £10,000 are directly appropriated to religious, educational, and charitable purposes. Among them the schools receive, for the current year, £1000; the established church, £860; the poor-house, £2340; the lunatic asylum, £2000; the board of health, £1700; the hospital, £1350; and the public library, £120. The island government has kept up a strong militia force ever since the regular troops were withdrawn, eight years ago. It also supports a fire brigade, the only institution of the kind, I believe, in the British West Indies. In so small a community it would, of course, be unreasonable to look for any extensive trade; but St. John is sufficiently busy to satisfy any stranger that Antigua has no place among those ruined West India colonies which exist in people's imaginations.

The island of Antigua embraces some 70,000 superficial acres, of which about 58,000 are owned by large proprietors. Sugar, excepting a small quantity of arrow-root grown by settlers, is the only article of export, and the estates average in size 320 acres. Very few exceed a thousand acres. In a geological or agricultural point of view, the northern and southern divisions of Antigua offer a striking contrast. The former, comprising the parishes of St. John, St. George, and St. Peter, is a low, level country, admirably adapted to the cultivation of the cane; and, excepting the towns, villages, and government lands, the entire section is in the hands of large proprietors. The southern division, comprising the parishes of St. Mary, St. Paul, and St. Philip, is mountainous. Sugar plantations cover three fourths of this section, and the remaining fourth, about 9000 acres, is checkered with negro settlements. The hills which trend along the southern coast have seduced many laborers from the estates, and are in other respects a barrier to the extension of cane cultivation that in Barbados does not exist; but even the level lands of Antigua have not that garden-like appearance which makes Barbados a very Eden among West India islands. Not that so many acres of cane in the one yield less than an equal number of acres in the other; I have seen cane-pieces in Antigua yielding three hogsheads to the acre; but the cultivation of the chief staple is less general, and lacks that superb finish which is characteristic of Barbados, and is an undoubted evidence of the superabundance of Creole labor that she alone, of all the British Antilles, has been able to command.

Judged by a commercial or a moral standard, Antigua as a free colony is considerably in advance of Antigua as a slave colony. This island, since abolition, has yielded a single crop of 20,000 hogsheads, the largest on record, and one which, under the most favorable circumstances, it would be difficult to surpass. Antigua, however, suffers so greatly and so frequently from want of rain that her crop varies more than that of any other island. It has fallen, from this cause alone, to 8000, 7000, and even 5000 hogsheads; and it is, therefore, necessary to take an average, in order to estimate correctly the value of Antiguan industry and productiveness. For ten years preceding emancipation, the period of the island's greatest prosperity under slavery, its average annual exportation was 12,500 hogsheads, with a field force of 18,320 laborers, one third of whom must be held to have been non-effective. From 1840 to 1850 the annual average was 13,000 hhds., and from 1850 to 1860 it rises to 13,500 hhds. of a decidedly superior weight, with a field force of 6000 laborers. While it thus appears that the exportation of the principal staple is considerably larger now than it was under a system of forced labor—an increase that establishes the more telling industry of the people—there is other evidence pointing directly to the same conclusion. In this, as in more important colonies, many of the peasantry have left the estates, and have become independent proprietors of small allotments. They grow arrowroot for exportation, and such provisions as the limited capacity of the soil will allow for domestic use. This, then, must be taken into account when a comparison is instituted between the productiveness of the slave and the free population of Antigua. The improved condition of the peasantry is never doubted or questioned in the island itself, and it is well shown by the nature and extent of the imports during late years, as compared with their nature and extent before the period of emancipation.

From 1822 to 1832 the average annual value of goods imported by Antigua was £130,000 sterling, of which about £50,000 value came from the United Kingdom and £40,000 from the United States. In 1858 the island imported to the value of £266,364 sterling, of which £114,631 value came from the United Kingdom and £106,586 from the United States. The American imports were principally articles of food suited to the wants of a thriving peasant population. It must be borne in mind that this great increase of imports has not been called for by an increased population, for, from causes which I shall hereafter explain, the population of Antigua is not so numerous now as it was twenty years ago; but the increase is simply to be attributed to the improved condition and ampler means of the peasantry developed by the dawn of freedom. Thus, too, in confirmation of the largely-extended trade of Antigua, it appears that, during ten years preceding emancipation, the average number of vessels that entered annually the different island-ports was 340, and the tonnage 30,000; while in 1858 the number of vessels was 668, and the tonnage 42,534. Of these vessels, 78, of 12,988 tons, were American; though only twenty, five with cargoes and fifteen in ballast, cleared for ports in the United States. I have already in chapters on Barbados explained the cause of this difference. The proprietors of estates under mortgage to parties in Great Britain are not free to sell their crops to whomsoever they please. They are obliged to dispose of them to their English creditors, and hence the principal staple seldom finds its way to the American market.

The cost of agricultural labor in Antigua is less than it is in Barbados or Trinidad. In Antigua, a field laborer scarcely earns, on an average, 20 cents per diem; in Barbados he earns from 22 cents to 25 cents; and in Trinidad he earns 30 cents. But the production of sugar in Antigua, in proportion to its field force, does not compare unfavorably with the production in Barbados or Trinidad, keeping the same proportion in view, and making due allowance for such drawbacks as unfavorable seasons, from which Antigua more frequently suffers. The following return from a very well managed estate was given me by a prominent planter, and is an interesting illustration of the low rate at which canes can be reaped and sugar manufactured in the island under consideration:

Cost of Mr. ——'s Sugar for the Week ending Feb. 25th, 1860.

	£	s.	d.
Cutting 315 loads of canes	£2	12	6
Carting 315 do.	0	17	6
Loading 315 do.	0	8	9
Grinding 315 do., viz., feeder, two cane-carriers, one megass do., one fuller	2	8	11
Mill-bed cleaner, at 6*d*. per day		3	0
Boiling-house, viz., one at 1*s*., four at 10*d*.	1	6	0
Copper-hole, viz., one at 1*s*., three at 10*d*.	1	1	0
Potting 11¾ hhds. sugar	0	5	9
Premium on 11¾ hhds., at 1*d*.	0	8	9
Total	£9	12	2

Cost per hogshead, £0 16*s*. 4*d*.

Quantity per hogshead, 1350 gallons; 27 loads of canes.

I have estimated the number of field laborers in Antigua at 6000—something above the actual return made several years ago in answer to a call of the Legislature. On a given day, in the middle of the crop season, a census was taken of laborers at work, and the number was found to be as stated above. They earn on an average twenty cents a day during a year of 250 working-days. Estimating the crop at twenty-five million pounds, each laborer, costing fifty dollars per annum, will be found to produce 4166 pounds, which fixes the cost of agricultural labor in Antigua at $1\frac{1}{5}$ cents for each pound of sugar manufactured—a figure, it is needless to add, greatly below the cost of labor in slave countries.

There is more general intelligence, in my judgment, among the people of Antigua than among the Creoles of any West India colony that I have visited. The efforts to educate the masses have been more persevering and better directed in this than in other islands. The Board of Education is composed of both laymen and clergymen, and a dignitary of the Established Church acts in concord and in concert with a Moravian bishop. At the time of emancipation the number of scholars attending Sunday and other schools was 1886. In 1857 there were 36 day-schools in operation, and 3520 scholars receiving instruction. In 1858 there were 52 day-schools and 4467 scholars. There were also 37 Sunday-schools and 6418 scholars. The population of Antigua, between the ages of 5 and 15, is estimated at 8000, and it therefore appears, from the figures just given, that a large proportion of the rising generation attend the various schools of the island. As to the present generation, though far less instructed and less intelligent than their children will be, much can be said in their favor besides the fact, important in an industrial point of view, that they are producing more now than they produced when they were slaves. In 1846 there were in the island 67 villages, containing 3187 houses and 9033 inhabitants. All these villages were founded and all these houses built since emancipation. In 1858, after another lapse of twelve years, 2000 additional houses had been built, and the number of village residents had risen to 15,644. At the same period there were only 299 paupers in the island with no ostensible means of earning a livelihood. It farther appears that education has raised the standard of morality in Antigua. Marriages are much more frequent than they used to be, and concubinage is discountenanced. The number of illegitimate births averages 53 per cent. In some other islands it exceeds 100 per cent.

The prison statistics of 1858 are unusually large,

owing to the numerous arrests of persons implicated in the March riots. Those riots were quite unpremeditated, and neither directly nor indirectly were they connected with any political movement or design. I am careful in making the assertion, for I have heard them differently construed. A report gained currency at the time that the disturbance was the result of a deliberate conspiracy among the blacks to murder the white inhabitants of the island; but the foolish *canard*, if ever believed in Antigua at all, was fully exposed during the searching investigation that ensued. People, it is true, were powerfully excited while the commotion lasted, and the government, with a somewhat undignified timidity, applied to a neighboring French colony for military aid. For these reasons it was prudent, perhaps, to keep up the impression that the lives of her majesty's lieges had been greatly endangered, and her authority in Antigua seriously threatened. But as to the nature of the riot no doubt whatever is now entertained.

It originated in a private quarrel between two rival stevedores—a Creole of Antigua, and a Creole of the island of Barbuda. The latter being victorious, became an object of popular vengeance, and fled for protection to the police station. Thither the mob followed, and, attempting to storm the building, they were met by a discharge of musketry. Five persons were killed and sixteen wounded. This rendered the mob more infuriated than ever; and, considering that the island was without a garrison and wholly defenseless, law-abiding citizens were naturally alarmed. The rioters marched about the streets destroying the houses of the policemen who had fired on them.

They did not attempt to injure the property of private citizens; but having completed their work of special demolition they turned again to the station, and made another attempt to capture it. The governor was now on the ground. He had ridden among the mob exhorting and remonstrating, but their passions were thoroughly roused, and they refused to listen to his counsel. It was not until they had renewed their assault on the station, and had almost gained the arsenal, that the order was given to fire. Three rounds effectually dispersed the mob and quelled the riot, though it was thought advisable to place the island for a time under martial law. Since then a permanent militia force has been kept up. Throughout these disturbances, which lasted several days, the hostility of the rioters was never directed against the whites. They sought vengeance only on the police, themselves black and colored, and the outbreak, wholly unpremeditated, never extended beyond the town in which it originated.

The progress made by the people of Antigua since emancipation would certainly justify an extension of their very limited franchise. Members of Assembly must have an income of at least £66 13*s.* 4*d.* from real property, or of £200 from any occupation or business. To vote, a resident of Antigua must be a proprietor of ten acres in fee simple; of five acres, with buildings equal in value to £111; or of one acre, with buildings of the value of £222. The occupant of a tenancy renting for £88 17*s.* 10*d.* is also qualified. A town voter must own property of the value of £13 6*s.* 8*d.*, or pay rent to the amount of £26 13*s.* 4*d.* It is proper to add, in explanation of their fractional character, that the figures are here converted into sterling money from the local currency specified in the law. These high qualifications exclude the middle classes from the polls. The Legislature is composed entirely of planters, or of those whom the planters choose to put there. In some districts of Antigua the influence of one large proprietor is sufficient to elect two members of Assembly. The application of the vast machinery of the British Constitution, and its inseparable Church Establishment, to each of the lesser West India colonies, is susceptible of the *reductio ad absurdum.* The machinery is so imposing, and occupies so much space, that popular liberty in a small community is squeezed into the narrowest possible compass.

CHAPTER XVI.

WANT OF LABOR IN ANTIGUA.

St. John, Antigua, 1860.

SMALL as Antigua is, there are parts of the island where labor is abundant and other parts where labor is scarce. The planters are seeking to introduce coolies. They are in need, they say, of 2000 laborers; and it is to be presumed that they understand their own wants. At the same time it is very certain that Antigua, with a population of 318 to the square mile, and with six sevenths of her superficial area preoccupied by large proprietors, is not in the condition of Jamaica or Trinidad, with their immense tracts of fertile soil thirsting for settlement and cultivation. The planters of Antigua have never complained of emancipation. They avow, what is unquestionably the truth, that by the introduction of a cheaper system of labor the island was saved in 1834 from impending ruin. They were the first to get rid of slavery, and they have no reason to regret that they did so. In their present demand for labor they use fair and liberal language, and place one prominent cause of the deficiency of Creole labor in this and all other British islands in its true light. "We regard," say the legislative assembly in their reply to the last address of the governor, "we regard the withdrawal of a large number of the laboring population from the estates, either to engage in the cultivation of land purchased by themselves, or to embark successfully in other avocations of life, as the natural consequence of an improved material condition, of the free and equal administration of the law, and of the facilities largely enjoyed for civil and religious instruction; but while we acknowledge and sympathize with this abstraction, it is clear that a deficiency has been thus created in the supply of manual labor to an extent which is not to be compensated either by increased skill, by implemental husbandry, or by the application of extended capital."

While the statement here made is one undoubted cause of the deficiency complained of, it is not the less true that the abstraction of labor from estates was abetted by planters themselves in times—not yet passed away—when want of capital was more pressing than want of labor. If capital was abundant, it surely lay in the power of the proprietary body or of individual planters to retain their land, if they believed that the sale or lease of allotments to the laborers would inflict a serious injury on the planting interest. Yet they did sell, and still continue to sell; and the negroes continue to buy, though land is scarce, and averages in value fifty dollars per acre. In the last government report bearing on this subject I find it stated that there is "no squatting in Antigua of any importance in its effect on the supply of labor. The facility," continues the report, "which the laboring population possess for the purchase or rent of small plots of ground near the villages built since emancipation in various parts of the island, removes the temptation that might otherwise exist to appropriate portions of the unclaimed crown lands."

While agricultural labor in all the British West Indies is the great *desideratum*, and the cry for immigration is echoed and re-echoed, it is amazing to see how the labor which the planter has within his reach is wasted and frittered away; how the particular population upon which the prosperity of the colonies so utterly depends is neglected; how, by mismanagement and unpardonable blunders of policy, the life of a field laborer has been made so distasteful to the peasant that the possession of half an acre, or the most meagre subsistence and independence, seem to him, in comparison with estate service, the very acme of luxurious enjoyment. Can it be credited that solely through want of proper medical care the agricultural population of Antigua has been allowed, for twenty years past, to decrease at the rate of a half per cent. per annum? But evidence of this criminal neglect is on record. The island is remarkably healthy; it escaped the general visitation of cholera in 1854; and yet the mortality is greater now than it was in the days of slavery, before the population was thoroughly Creolized. In 1800 the taxed negroes of Antigua were numbered at 38,000; in 1815 there were 36,000 slaves; in 1821, when the last census before emancipation was taken, there were 1980 whites, 4066 free colored, and 31,064 slaves on the island; in 1851 the total population was 37,163, and in 1856 it was only 35,408, of whom 26,522 were black, 6714 colored, and 2172 white. It is thus shown that the blacks, which are the agricultural portion of the population, are the sufferers—the whites and colored having actually increased. It appears from the latest return of the registrar that during 1858 thirty-two per cent. of the persons who died were children under the age of one year—a mortality that can only be explained by the want of proper medical care. The acting governor of Antigua, Mr. Eyre, a gentleman of ability and well-deserved popularity, recently brought this subject to the notice of the Legislature. He says:

"The returns of births and deaths disclose the melancholy fact that, in Antigua, the deaths are nearly equal to the births, and that therefore, although no epidemic or other unusual grounds for mortality exist, the population is not increasing as it ought to do, especially in a country where the climate and other conditions propitious to life are so favorable, and where wholesome food is so readily procurable; for there is, perhaps, hardly any country in the world where the laborer can obtain all that is necessary to make his home comfortable at a less cost of exertion than he can in most of the West India islands. A large proportion of the deaths appears to occur in infancy or early childhood, and there can be little doubt but that they are for the most part the result of neglect and want of medical attendance. In the days of slavery, hospitals and medical attendance for all were provided by the estates; but now that the majority of laborers have ceased to be residents on properties, and this obligation but partially exists, the greater number of them, distributed about the country in populous villages, are either unwilling or unable to obtain the necessary medical attendance and proper nursing in illness for themselves, their children, or their relatives. It is worthy the best attention of an enlightened Legislature to provide a remedy for this state of things, and to consider whether arrangements can not be made under which medical supervision shall again be extended to the entire population. The value of such supervision is evidenced by the fact that the rate of mortality is less among the resident population on estates than it is in the villages where the laborers reside on their own lands. The great saving of human life, and the large accession of labor which would thereby accrue to the colony, would both justify and compensate for any expenditure of public money which it may be necessary to incur in securing objects so desirable and so important."

The governor, it will be observed, appears to doubt whether the mortality among the laboring population arises from their unwillingness or their inability to procure medical assistance. In answer to this, it need only be pointed out that the eight or ten practitioners of Antigua reside in town, and that it is quite beyond the power of the peasant who lives five or ten miles off to pay for medical attendance and advice out of the four or five shillings that he may earn during the week. It would seem to be but wise and prudent for the governing classes in Antigua to provide for the safety of their present agricultural population, and arrest its decline before they make any large additions to its numbers.

If 2000 laborers are wanted for Antigua, and I do not doubt that the planter's demand is made in perfectly good faith, no one will question the wisdom of a policy that seeks to obtain them from the ranks of the Creole population in preference to all other sources. I do not say that this is possible, even in Antigua, but I do say that the trial has never been fairly made. The last census gives the number of persons engaged in agriculture at 15,310, and those engaged in trade and miscellaneous occupations at 19,758. It is important to know what superior inducements have been held out to this population (sufficiently numerous, in all conscience, for the cultivation of an island containing only one hundred and eight square miles) to work on the estates instead of on their own emplacements, or at the trade or occupation they have selected. These inducements are, 1. The return to a condition of quasi serfdom; and, 2. Wages that do not reach the average of a shilling a day, considerably below the market rate of wages in any other avocation. The West India planter refuses to believe that his position is precisely that of other employers. In Antigua he offers from 8*d.* to 1*s.* per day to a laborer; and because the man refuses the offer, being able to do better, the planter considers himself aggrieved, and asks the government to procure him labor from abroad. No one interferes with the liberty of the individual planter to get labor wherever he can; but when the whole proprietary interest united demands aid from government to import large numbers of laborers into a thickly-settled colony, the question assumes a very different aspect. The Creole laborers, if they have any rights at all, have a right to be heard upon the subject. The question, furthermore, is one of economy for a Legislature to adjudicate upon and statesmen to consider, whether it is not cheaper and better to accept the terms of the Creole, supposing him to offer any terms within the bounds of reason, than to suffer the heavy outlay which a forced system of immigration imperatively requires. In islands like Jamaica and

Trinidad, where there is an absolute deficiency of population, the planter has no choice; but, in Antigua, much more might have been done than has been done to induce the peasantry to work for the estates.

The tenure under which estate laborers hold their cottages and lands is alone sufficient to drive from cane cultivation any people who have the faintest aspirations after independence. In Antigua there is a contract law which exacts a month's notice on either side, before the planter can discharge his laborer or the laborer can quit the service of the planter. The peasant is not now, as he was formerly, at the mercy of an irresponsible overseer, nor lives any longer in dread of being summarily ejected from his tenement and left to starve upon the highway. The history of plantation management in the West Indies teems with such ejectments. The contract law of Antigua, as many will testify, has been attended with beneficial results; but mixing up, as it does, the rights and obligations of a tenant with the rights and obligations of a laborer hired to service, it is at best but a half measure, and of necessity gives rise to complaint, ill-will, and misunderstanding. If I were asked to point out the chief obstruction to a satisfactory solution of the West India labor question, I should answer without hesitation, want of confidence between employer and employed. The planters cling unwittingly to the shreds of the system of coercion in which they were once taught to believe. They do not yet recognize the overwhelming advantages of perfectly free labor, for they have checked its development by imposing upon it some of the heaviest burdens of feudalism and of serfdom. It is only necessary to compare the condition of estate laborers with that of their more independent brethren, to be perfectly convinced that between the prosperity, the morality, and the industry of the one and those of the other, there is a broad gulf of separation. I can not help believing that it is in the power and in the interest of the planters to change all this. There are many, undoubtedly, who strive to ameliorate the condition of the laboring classes; but it is as legislators, and not merely as private landed proprietors, that they are called upon to act. What English or American laborer would accept the lease of a cottage with the understanding that he and his family, his wife and his children, should work only for a certain estate, and be at all times obedient servants at the call of their landlord? Surely the most desperate poverty alone would drive a free-born citizen to accept such a bondage. And here in the West Indies where poverty is unknown, and a man can live comfortably with the smallest effort, it is lunacy to expect that a tenure which would not last a week in the densely-populated districts of England or Ireland, can by any possibility succeed. The planters have counted largely upon the peculiar attachment of the negro to the spot upon which he was born. He is not naturally self-reliant. The realities of his position must be harsh, and the prospects of a change bright indeed, to induce him to leave the familiar scenes of his youth and the friends among whom he has always lived. But even the negro world moves on. As the West Indian Creole becomes enlightened, his home prejudices become weak, and it is utterly unreasonable to expect that he will remain an estate laborer while the penalty is a forfeiture of independence, and the reward a rate of wages that might be doubled in any other employment.

No unprejudiced West Indian need be told that the abstraction of labor from the estates, the burden of such bitter complaint, is a progressive, not a retrograde movement, to the incalculable advantage of the laborer—to his credit, not to his shame. Writers on the West Indies in books and newspapers, who describe what they never saw and draw conclusions from imagined data, have sometimes expressed a contrary opinion. We can not complain of the planters on the one hand, for advocating *à l'outrance* their special interest, nor of a British anti-slavery society on the other, for straining out gnats in their defense of a class that have no voice of their own in the counsels of the empire. They are entitled to the privileges of advocates at the bar of public opinion. But when we find ignorance and error flowing from our most reliable sources of information, when partisan argument is used by the judge instead of dispassionate reasoning, and fiction instead of fact is given by the witness, these we regard as high crimes and misdemeanors, especially when they are converted into weapons of attack, and leveled against the independence of a helpless people—against their liberty purchased at an enormous cost, and guaranteed to them forever under the solemn pledge of a constitution.

CHAPTER XVII.

THE MINOR COLONIES.

St. John, Antigua, 1860.

BESIDES Antigua, there are under the dominion of the Leeward government, the colonies of Dominica, Nevis, Montserrat, St. Kitts, and the British Virgin Islands. They are not largely productive, and are seldom taken into account when the argument of free labor in the West Indies is under discussion. Their trade and exports are, however, considerable in the aggregate, and I propose to give, as briefly as possible, such statistical information upon these points as I have been able to procure.

DOMINICA is a mountainous island, nearly three times as large as Antigua, and embraces an area of 186,436 acres. Its population, prior to emancipation, was 18,650, and in 1844, at the last census, was 22,220. The whites, in proportion to the black and colored inhabitants, are as one to twenty-six. Of the entire population 11,589 are employed in agriculture. There are 2825 direct taxpayers in the island. About 2600 children, on an average, receive instruction in the different schools. In the year 1858 Dominica exported 6,262,841 lbs. of sugar, against an annual average export of 6,000,000 lbs. before emancipation. Her total imports in 1858 were valued at £84,906, against an average of £62,000 for five years preceding emancipation, the period of her greatest prosperity under slavery. In 1830, 224 vessels, of 11,191 tons, the largest number on record, entered the port of Roseau. In 1858, 320 vessels entered, of 8938 tons. A great majority of the Dominican coffee properties were ruined by blight; and, owing to this misfortune, the exports of coffee have fallen from 2,000,000 lbs. to a merely nominal figure. The cultivation of cocoa has, to some extent, taken the place of coffee, and 125,000 lbs. are now annually exported, instead of 9000 lbs., the maximum before emancipation. Lime-juice is an important article of Dominican commerce, and large quantities of fruit, vegetables, and wood for fuel, are exported to neighboring islands.

NEVIS is a single mountain, with an area of some 30,000 acres. The population in 1830 was 9250, and is now 9571. Of this number 2500 persons live in villages built since emancipation, and 1200 pay direct taxes. More than two thirds of the population between the ages of five and fifteen are receiving instruction. In 1858 Nevis exported 4,400,000 lbs. of sugar, against an annual average of 5,000,000 lbs. before emancipation. She exports also arrow-root, tamarinds, vegetables, and fruits. Her imports in 1858 were valued at £36,721, against an annual average value of £28,500 between the years 1820 and 1830.

MONTSERRAT, about equal in superficial area to Nevis, has a population of 7033, a decrease of some 300 on the population of 1828. Of this number, 1184 heads of families were, at the last return, engaged in agriculture. In 1858 Montserrat exported 1,308,720 lbs. of sugar, against an annual average of 1,840,000 lbs. prior to emancipation. She also exported 846 cords of firewood and 119 barrels of tamarinds, besides miscellaneous minor articles. The value of imports in 1858 was £17,844, and between this figure and the average value of imports before emancipation there appears to be no marked variance.

St. Kitts, or St. Christopher, as it is sometimes called, occupies an area of about 45,000 acres. The population, according to the census of 1855, was 20,741, and seems to have decreased nearly 3000 since 1830. There are in St. Kitts 6656 persons engaged in agriculture, 1074 artisans, 472 engaged in trade, 210 freeholders, 220 persons paying direct taxes, 2704 scholars receiving instruction, and 1587 people living in villages built since emancipation. About 9000 acres in St. Kitts are in cultivation. In 1858 the island exported 9,883,309 lbs. of sugar, against an average of 12,000,000 lbs. before emancipation. Salt has become an important article of commerce of late years, and about 25,000 barrels have been annually exported. Potatoes and arrow-root are extensively cultivated in St. Kitts. The total value of exports in 1858 was £137,531, and of imports, £109,005; largely exceeding, supposing the same prices to rule, the value of exports and imports prior to emancipation. This is fully shown by shipping statistics. For the ten years preceding abolition, the annual average number of vessels entering St. Kitts was 376, of 19,000 tons; while in 1858 over 550 vessels entered, weighing 21,886 tons.

The British Virgin Islands and their capital, Tortola, are also in the Leeward government. Most of them are rocky islets unsuited to cultivation. Their population is estimated at 5053 persons, of whom 2087 are engaged in agriculture, and the very large number of 1361 pay direct taxes. The vessels that visit the British Virgin Islands are of inferior tonnage, and their principal trade is with the Danish colony of St. Thomas. The islands annually export stock, sheep and goats, lime, charcoal, salt, vegetables, some five or six thousand pounds of cotton, and about two hundred thousand pounds of sugar. No reliable statistics of the trade of these islands before emancipation can be procured, and I am therefore unable to institute a comparison between the production of the inhabitants under slavery and their production under freedom.

The few figures that I have here given prove that the Leeward Islands, commercially and industrially considered, have progressed under a regime of freedom. In all these colonies the condition of the free peasant rises infinitely above the condition of the slave. In all the people are more happy and contented; in all they are more civilized; in all there are more provisions grown for home consumption than were ever raised in the most flourishing days of slavery; in all the imports have largely increased; in all a very important trade has sprung up with the United States; for emancipation unshackled Commerce when it broke the chain that bound down Labor to a single interest. From all there is an exportation of minor articles which were not cultivated twenty years ago, and which, in estimating the industry of the people under a free system, are often most unjustly overlooked. These are considerations from which the planter turns with contemptuous indifference. Sugar, and sugar alone, is his dream, his argument, his faith. Yet, even in sugar, the exports of the Leeward colonies compare favorably with their exports in the most prosperous days of old, as the following table amply demonstrates:

COMPARATIVE TABLE OF SUGAR EXPORTATION, IN POUNDS, FROM THE LEEWARD ISLANDS.

Islands.	Annual average from 1820 to 1832.	Exports in 1858.
Antigua	20,580,000	26,174,000
Dominica	6,000,000	6,263,000
Nevis	5,000,000	4,400,000
Montserrat	1,840,000	1,308,000
St. Kitts	12,000,000	10,000,000
Total	45,420,000	48,145,000

The imports of the same islands present a still more striking contrast:

COMPARATIVE TABLE OF IMPORTS TO THE LEEWARD ISLANDS IN POUNDS STERLING.

Islands.	Annual average value from 1820 to 1832.	Value of Imports in 1858.
Antigua	£130,000	£266,364
Dominica	62,000	84,906
Nevis	28,000	36,721
Montserrat	18,000	17,844
St. Kitts	60,000	109,000
Total	£298,000	£514,835

Excess cf sugar exportation with free labor....2,725,000 pounds.
Excess of imports with free labor................. £216,835 sterling.

I have given the returns of 1858 throughout, as they are the latest and most complete that I have been able to obtain; and if it be objected that the sugar exportation of one colony was, in that year, higher than the average, it will be found that others are lower than the average. The table at any rate is a fair exhibition, in round numbers, of the sugar production of the islands at the present time, and this is the point I seek to establish. Sugar is the only staple in which it is even pretended that any important decline has taken place under freedom; yet the fact appears that the Leeward Islands, with an aggregate population of 94,000, export annually 48,000,000 lbs. of sugar—nearly 3,000,000 lbs. more than they exported before emancipation, when all the energies of the colonies were concentrated upon this single cultivation. It appears also from this exhibit that about 510 lbs. of sugar per capita are produced in the Leeward islands. Now Barbados, whose trade has doubled under freedom, and whose prosperity and industry are universally admitted, produces an annual average of 70,000,000 lbs. of sugar with a population of 150,000, giving only 466 lbs. to each inhabitant; and the inference is inevitable that if, according to the planting argument, Barbados flourishes, the Leeward colonies flourish still more. But the argument of the planter is not the whole argument. His undivided attention is turned to cane cultivation; it is his special business, his sole occupation; and it is his right and privilege to further it by all legitimate means in his power. But it is the duty of the legislator and the statesman to consider other interests as well as the planting interest; to lay the foundations of a permanent and not of a fictitious prosperity; to consult the happiness of the people, and to rise above the prejudices that have warped the judgment and misdirected the energies of the proprietary body. When the industry of the inhabitants of any of these islands is doubted on the ground that they produce less sugar now than they did formerly, it must not be forgotten that their production of other articles, whether for export or home consumption, the improvement in their material condition, their very independence of daily labor for hire, enter largely into the merits of the question. But I have shown that even the sugar exports of the Leeward Islands exceed, at the present time, their exports during the most prosperous epoch of slavery. In the Windward Islands, Trinidad and Guiana, a similar increase is apparent. Jamaica alone, of all the larger colonies, exhibits a marked decline. Instead of being regarded as the exception to prevailing West Indian prosperity, she, as the most important British dependency in these latitudes, is very erroneously supposed to represent a general ruin. While sugar cultivation in Jamaica has retrograded under a free system, in other colonies it has advanced; and this fact of itself raises the presumption, if it does not actually demonstrate, that causes other than emancipation have combined to blight her industry and destroy her commerce.

JAMAICA.

CHAPTER XVIII.

TIMES PAST AND TIMES PRESENT.

Kingston, Jamaica, 1860.

As briefly as possible, for the theme is threadbare, I must endeavor to give an approximate idea of the decline of Jamaica ere I attempt to explain the causes of that decline, or point out the political and social abuses and anomalies for which, it seems to me, a remedy must be found before the island can be restored to its ancient prosperity. I do not think it can be disputed, if history and statistics are to be believed, that, since the abolition of the slave-trade fifty-two years ago, Jamaica has never for a moment paused in her downward career. I do not think it can be disputed, if actual observation is to be relied upon, that she has not even yet reached the lowest point of possible depression. Lower still she can sink—lower still she must sink, if her people are not imbued with a more pregnant patriotism, if the governing classes are not stimulated to more energetic action, and are not guided by more unselfish counsels.

I know of no country in the world where prosperity, wealth, and a commanding position have been so strangely subverted and destroyed, as they have been in Jamaica, within the brief space of sixty years. I know of no country in the world where so little trouble has been taken to investigate the causes of this decline, or to remedy the evils that have depressed the colony. The partisans of slavery, it is true—the sufferers who have commanded the ear of the world, and have enlisted its sympathies in their behalf—have represented, and with some coloring of reason, that all this widespread ruin is to be attributed to emancipation only. But thinking and intelligent men are no longer convinced by these stale complaints. They can not now be brought to believe that the liberation of 350,000 slaves, whatever may have been its first effect, is the origin, and only origin, of the poverty and distress that prevail in the island at the present day. British emancipation may have been unwise; regarded as a great social revolution, the manner in which the scheme was executed must be utterly condemned; private rights were violated; their sacredness was dimmed by the splendor of an act which gave freedom to a people who did not know what freedom meant; but the ruin attributed to it is, in Jamaica, too broad and too deep to be set down any longer as the effect of that one solitary cause. No other English island has the natural advantages that Jamaica possesses; no other English island exhibits the same, or any thing like the same, destitution; yet all have passed through the same experience—all have undergone the same trial.

Tempora mutantur should be the Jamaican motto. *Tempora mutantur* with a vengeance! Only sixty years ago, and the dream of emancipation had not been dreamt even by a Wilberforce, and the then greatest slave-trading country in the world was but opening its national eyes to the iniquity of the accursed traffic. How vehemently the planters stood up for their right (who dare dispute it?) to steal Mandingoes and Eboes from the African coast! How forcibly in those days did they represent the unfriendliness of slavery to population, and groan over an annual diminution of slave property which only the African trade could keep up to the scanty figure of bare sufficiency! Their representations had, at least, the merit of being true; for though 600,000 slaves, at the lowest estimate, were brought to Jamaica during the eighteenth century, it is well known that at the end of that period the slave population of the whole island was not much more than one half of that amount. It was computed by the political economists of the day that Jamaica required an annual supply of 10,000 slaves to provide against the wear and tear of life; and the statement will appear by no means incredible to those who have examined the statistics of Cuban slavery at the present time. In spite of this immense traffic, ruthlessly and recklessly carried on, Jamaica was never adequately supplied with labor. The slaves were overworked to satisfy their master's lust for gain, and to this the great mortality has been mainly attributed. That great mortality ceased with the extinction of the slave-trade, for the planters found it incumbent upon them to take more care of their property; nevertheless, in spite of all their precautions, the decrease of slaves each year by death, without reference to the decrease by manumission, was considerably larger than the increase by birth; and the deficit, now, could not be supplied.

There are many who believe that great crimes

against society, in the case of nations as in that of individuals, are followed by certain punishment; and, to such, the impoverished condition of the Jamaica planters of the present day will seem but a natural consequence of a long reign of avarice and cruelty, of extravagance and oppression. I do not seek to take up this parable against them. But it is not to be denied that they are the chief, if not the only sufferers. The large landed proprietors and merchant potentates of the island, these are the men who have fallen from their high estate. The slaves of other days, the poor, the peasantry, these are the men who have progressed, if not in morality, at least in material prosperity, as I shall have ample opportunity to show. If the change could be traced solely to emancipation, I should be loth to justify emancipation, believing as I do that it would be wholly inconsistent with morality or the dictates of a sound policy to degrade that portion of the population which controlled the elements of civilization, in order to enrich an ignorant and undisciplined people. But the decline of Jamaica has been so stupendous as of itself to create a doubt whether it can be laid, in whole or even in part, to the emancipation of the slaves. A witness can prove too much; and the advocates for a slave system for Jamaica have appealed to testimony which places their case in this very category.

It will be found upon examination that the most prosperous epoch of Jamaican commerce was that embraced in the seven years immediately preceding the abolition of the slave-trade. Yet it is a notorious fact, to be proved by parliamentary blue-books, that even then over one hundred estates on the island had been abandoned for debt. During the seven years indicated, that is, from 1801 to 1807, the sugar exports of Jamaica amounted annually to an average of 133,000 hhds. During the seven years *succeeding* the year in which the slave-trade was abolished, from 1807 to 1814, the annual exports fell off to an average of 118,000 hhds. During the next seven years, from 1814 to 1821, the annual average was about 110,000 hhds.; from 1821 to 1828 it was 96,000 hhds.; and from 1828 to 1835 it was 90,000 hhds.; thus showing a steady decline, not so alarming, it is true, as the decline of subsequent years (for the whole sugar exportation of Jamaica is now only 30,000 hhds.), but sufficiently serious to demonstrate that Jamaica had reached its maximum prosperity under slavery, and had commenced to deteriorate nearly thirty years before the emancipation act was passed, and many years before the design of such a measure was elaborated, or Mr. Canning's note of warning was sounded in West Indian ears. A comparison of Jamaican exports in 1805, her year of greatest prosperity, with her exports in 1859, must appear odious to her inhabitants. In the former year the island exported over 150,000 hhds. of sugar, and in the latter year she exported 28,000 hhds. The exports of rum and coffee exhibit the same proportionate decrease.

If the city of Kingston be taken as an illustration of the prosperity of Jamaica, the visitor will arrive at more deplorable conclusions than those pointed out by commercial statistics. It seems like a romance to read to-day, in the capital of Jamaica, the account of that capital's former splendor. Its "magnificent churches," now time-worn and decayed, are scarcely superior to the stables of some Fifth-Avenue magnate There is not a house in the city in decent repair; not one that looks as though it could withstand a respectable breeze; not a wharf in good order; not a street that can exhibit a square yard of pavement; no sidewalks; no drainage; scanty water; no light. The same picture of neglect and apathy greets one every where. In the business part of the town you are oppressed with its inactivity. Clerks yawn over the counters, or hail with greedy looks the solitary stranger who comes in to purchase. If a non-resident, he is made to suffer for the dullness of the market. Prices that in New York would be deemed exorbitant must be paid by strangers for the common necessities of life. The Kingstonians remind me much of the Bahama wreckers. Having little or nothing themselves, they look upon a steamer-load of California passengers, cast away in their harbor for a night or a day, as very Egyptians, whom it is not only their privilege but their duty to despoil.

There is nothing like work done in Kingston, except, perhaps, in the establishments of a few European or American merchants, or on the piers, now and then, at the loading or unloading of vessels. The city was originally well laid out, but it is not ornamented with a single tree, and the square, in a central location, is a barren desert of sand, white-hot with exposure to the blazing sun. The streets are filthy, the beach-lots more so, and the commonest laws of health are totally disregarded. Wreck and ruin, destitution and neglect! There is nothing new in Kingston. The people, like their horses, their houses, and all that belongs to them, look old and worn. There are no improvements to be noted, not a device, ornament, or conceit of any kind to indicate the presence of taste or refinement. The inhabitants, taken *en masse*, are steeped to the eyelids in immorality; promiscuous intercourse of the sexes is the rule; the population shows an unnatural decrease; illegitimacy exceeds legitimacy; abortion and infanticide are not unknown. Kingston looks what it is, a place where money has been made, but can be made no more. It is used up and cast aside as useless. Nothing is replaced that time destroys. If a brick tumbles from a house to the street, it remains there; if a spout is loosened by the wind, it hangs by a thread till it falls; if furniture is accidentally broken, the idea of having it mended is not entertained. The marks of a helpless poverty are upon the faces of the people whom you meet, in their dress, in their very gait.

Have I described a God-forsaken place, in which no one seems to take an interest, without life and without energy, old and dilapidated, sickly and filthy, cast away from the anchorage of sound morality, of reason, and of common sense? Then, verily, have I described Kingston in 1860. Yet this wretched hulk is the capital of an island the most fertile in the world; it is blessed with a climate most glorious; it lies rotting in the shadow of mountains that can be cultivated from summit to base, with every product of temperate and tropical regions; it is mistress of a harbor where a thousand line-of-battle ships can safely ride at anchor.

The once brimming cup of Kingston's prosperity has been indeed emptied to the dregs. It offers no encouragement that this splendid island-inheritance, wasted through riotous living in times past, will ever be redeemed. You must look beyond Kingston for the grounds of such a hope. You must escape from its sickly atmosphere and the listless indifference of its people. You must learn, as you can learn from the most casual observation, that the island, unlike others that can be mentioned, is in no exhausted condition, but is fresh and fair, and abundantly fertile as ever, with every variety of climate, and capable of yielding every variety of product. Up in these tremendous hills you may enjoy the luxury of a frosty night; down upon the plains you may bask in the warmth of a fiery sun. There you can raise potatoes, here you can raise sugar-cane. There you will find interminable forests of wild pimento, here interminable acres of abandoned properties—a mass of jungle and luxuriant vegetation choking up the deserted mansions of Jamaica's ancient aristocracy. Scenes most wonderfully fair, most picturesque, but most melancholy to look upon; scenes that a limner might love to paint, but from which an American planter would turn in disgust and contempt.

This magnificent country, wanting nothing but capital and labor for its complete restoration to a prosperity far greater than it ever yet attained, is now sparsely settled by small negro cultivators, who have been able to purchase their plots of land for £2 and £3 an acre. With a month's work on their own properties they can earn as much as a year's labor on a sugar-estate would yield them. They are superior, pecuniarily speaking, to servitude; and by a law of nature that can not be gainsaid, they prefer independence to labor for hire. Why should they be blamed?

But the fact remains that the island is nearly destitute of labor; that partly through want of labor sugar cultivation has been abandoned; and by an adequate supply of labor can it only be revived. Covering an area of four millions of acres, Jamaica has a population of 378,000, white, black, and mulatto. This makes about eleven acres to each person. In the flourishing island of Barbados the proportion is nearly one and a half persons to each acre. If Jamaica were as thickly populated as Barbados, it would contain over five millions of souls, and would export a million hogsheads. Till its present population has been doubled and trebled no material improvement can be looked for. But where is the money—where are the vigor and the energy necessary to obtain this population? Whose fault is it that these are wanting, and that Jamaica, with far greater advantages than Trinidad or Guiana, has failed to follow the footsteps of their success? Is this also the result of emancipation?

The Jamaica question is prolific of controversy, and I can not hope that my allegations and inferences will pass unchallenged. I shall, for this reason, confine myself as much as possible to statements of fact. Perhaps I may be excused for alluding to myself so far as to say that I came to the West Indies imbued with the American idea that African freedom had been a curse to every branch of agricultural and commercial industry. I shall leave these islands overwhelmed with a very opposite conviction; and if I can convey to others any thing like a truthful picture of Jamaica life, and of the civil and social condition of the people who are so erroneously supposed, by their indolence and improvidence, to have plunged themselves and their country in hopeless ruin, my task, however imperfectly performed, can not be a profitless one. If I can stimulate inquiry on a subject so important and so widely misunderstood as the West India labor question, I shall have achieved all the success at which I ever thought of aiming. I hope to be able to show to others as plainly as the conviction has come home to myself, that disaster and misfortune have followed —not emancipation—but the failure to observe those great principles of liberty and justice upon which the foundations of emancipation were solidly laid. The very highest influence has ever been exerted, and is still exerted, to support the old plantocratic dynasty and its feudalisms—things that were meant to die, and ought to have died, as soon as the props of slavery, protection, and other monopolies were removed. Every one admits that the sugar interest is a most important interest, whose expansion should be facilitated by all legitimate means; but only evil has grown out of the attempt to foster it by a system of quasi-slavery, and at the expense of other interests upon which the prosperity of a country must largely depend. The people of Jamaica are not cared for; they perish miserably in country districts for want of medical aid; they are not instructed; they have no opportunities to improve themselves in agriculture or mechanics; every effort is made to check a spirit of independence, which in the African is counted a heinous crime, but in all other people is regarded as a lofty virtue, and the germ of national courage, enterprise, and progress. Emancipation has not been wholly successful because the experiment has not been wholly tried. But the success is none the less emphatic and decided. The crop appears in patches, even as it was sown, forcing itself here and there through the ruins of the old fabric which disfigures still the political complexion of the island and sorely cramps the energies of its people.

CHAPTER XIX.

A TOUR THROUGH THE INTERIOR OF JAMAICA.

Kingston, Jamaica, 1860.

I DO not think I can do better, in the treatment of this West India labor question, than describe a somewhat extended tour that I have made through the interior of Jamaica. The impressions that this trip have left upon my mind are certainly not unfavorable to the industry and capacity of the black population. I do not for a moment pretend that Jamaica is free from idleness and vice. I do not pretend that her peasantry are as laborious as you will find men in a New York, a New England, or an Old England agricultural district. It is not natural that they should be so. But actual observation has convinced me that industry among the free population of Jamaica is the rule and not the exception; and if idleness be an exception broader than we could wish—larger than any part of North America presents—we must look for the cause, not to the intractable disposition of the negro, but to faults of discipline or absence of education for which the governing classes are responsible; and, in no small degree, to the overwhelming temptations that a West Indian climate offers to all, white and black, to enjoy their *otium cum aut sine dignitate.*

There is a railway between Kingston and Spanish Town—the former being the principal sea-port, and the latter the seat of the Jamaican government. The distance, about twelve miles, is performed in three quarters of an hour. There are first, second, and third classes. The prices are reasonable, being two shillings, one shilling, and sixpence sterling respectively. The cars are comfortable, and the road is good. It is, indeed, a blessing, this little line of railway, by means of which you can be hurried in a brief space of time from the stupor of Kingston. As soon as I heard the familiar whistle and felt the air rushing by me, I began to breathe again. This minute effort of enterprise is, nevertheless, a perpetual reminder to Jamaicans of the depreciated credit of their island, and of the low estimate at which its most solemn engagements are rated in the mother land. Last year a bill passed the Legislature for the extension of the railroad from Spanish Town to the sea-port of Old Harbor, a distance of some ten miles. The colonial government guaranteed an interest of six per cent. on the money to be expended in the work; yet neither in the island nor in England would capitalists advance that money, and up to the present time not a single dollar has been raised to further this important undertaking.

The country between Kingston and Spanish Town is low, marshy, and covered with forest and underwood. If it were not for the difference in foliage you might fancy yourself, on some ferocious summer's day, passing through the New York wilderness. You get a glimpse here and there of a rough settlement, or an acre or so of poor pasturage, deeply shaded, but there are few attempts at higher cultivation. I saw upon the route three plots of Guinea corn in a tolerably flourishing condition.

I need not make a long pause to describe Spanish Town, or St. Jago de la Vega, as it was formerly called. Yonkers is a metropolis to it. A *coup d'œil*, if such could be obtained, would reveal a collection of grotesque houses that might be mistaken for some disemboweled Caribbean village of antediluvian foundation. I do not know exactly where the historian of fifty years ago stood when he looked upon St. Jago de la Vega, and described it as "a city of imposing appearance, built in the magnificent style of Spanish architecture." Inspected in detail, Spanish Town will be found to possess two big buildings facing each other on the central square of the "city;" one the residence of the governor, called the King's House, and the other the House of Assembly and public offices. Both are creditable buildings. Upon further scrutiny some neat, quiet little private residences may be discovered, and one inn, such as the adventurous traveler might expect to meet with on the outskirts of a Canadian forest. The floor of that inn is highly polished, every thing is neat and clean, and the table is furnished for the benefit of guests with several volumes printed in the last century. The population of Spanish Town is about 5000, nine tenths of whom, I presume, gain their living by supplying the wants and necessities of government hangers-on, who constitute the other tenth. It is not, on the whole, an uninteresting place. The atmosphere is cooler than it is on the Southern coast, and the streets, though very narrow, are cleaner and far better regulated than the streets of Kingston. Both Houses were in session when I passed through Spanish Town; but, as I shall hereafter have occasion to explain the franchise and the effect of recent legislation in the island, I lay up these matters for further experience. Nor will I do unto others as I was done by, and victimize the reader with the debates of the Jamaican Assembly. The ability of members, with one or two exceptions, did not seem to me to reach even a provincial standard of mediocrity, and the subjects discussed were, of course, most uninteresting to a stranger. I pass from this topic the more readily, as I think it unfair to criticise with severity the representatives of an impoverished and isolated colony like Jamaica, and especially as these representatives are on the eve of abandoning their seats under a new election law. With education in its infancy over the whole island, in some districts almost struggling for existence, the people are largely represented. I think a majority of the small proprietors and settlers are intelligent enough to exercise the right of voting to their own advantage and to the advantage of this great dependency of the English crown, but it is an experiment not yet fully and fairly tried. It is an experiment which, if carried out, will entirely remove the government of the island from the control of the planters—a control that, for some time, they have seemed utterly indifferent about possessing. The plantocracy of Jamaica is a thing of the past, and in its stead democracy is lifting up its head. I am not so enthusiastic a democrat as to believe that the principles of our political faith, much less its practice, will flourish in any soil or in any climate. The untutored negro, of all people in the world, is most easily influenced by a bribe, and demagogues and office-hunters are plentiful in Jamaica. If the experiment of popular representation and responsible government should prove a failure, there will be no resource left but to establish here such a government as exists in the crown colonies of Trinidad and British Guiana. The one is ruled by a council, the other by a court of policy—synonymous terms for a go-ahead despotism, which Canada or Australia would not tolerate for an instant, but which appears to answer very well for an embryo civilization and a mixed people.

These are reflections that belong to the air of Spanish Town. Having emerged from that quaint collection of ancient domiciles as the rising sun illuminated the hill-tops, on a first-rate road, in a comfortable buggy, and behind a pair of excellent travelers, one forswears politics, and begins to feel that exhilaration of spirits which the atmosphere of Jamaica is truly said to produce. The road lies through a wooded and rather swampy district, and, if it be a Saturday morning, the traveler will encounter, for several miles, a continuous stream of sturdy, good-looking wenches, carrying on their heads to the Spanish Town market most marvelous loads of fruit and vegetables. A few of them, more fortunate than their fellows, have donkeys with well-filled panniers, but they do not, on this account, neglect the inevitable head-load. Considering the distance they come, the heat of the weather, the size of their burdens, and the paltry remuneration they get at market, the performance is highly creditable to the enterprise, energy, and activity of Jamaica negro women. I doubt whether our laboring *men* could execute the same task; they certainly would not undertake it for the same consideration.

The descent from St. Catherine's Parish, to which

Spanish Town belongs, into the Parish of St. Thomas-in-the-Vale, through the "Bog Walk" so called, is picturesque and grand. The road winds along a stream from whose banks the hills rise precipitously and form a narrow gorge. Every furlong furnishes some new variety to the scenery. You look back and trace a silvery thread of water through the graceful plumage of a bamboo cluster; now it is a grove of plantains, or some huge gaunt cotton-tree, rising above its compeers, and stretching its arms from hill to hill, that forms the foreground of the picture. Mountains on every side; and the passages among them are at times so narrow and the precipices so steep, that the traveler involuntarily hurries on, fearful lest some sudden catastrophe in this land of untoward convulsions should bring the hills together and fill up the chasm forever.

The valley soon widens. Linstead, the principal village in St. Thomas-in-the-Vale, lies in the centre of an almost circular hollow shut in by mountains. The road-side is studded with the cottages of small settlers. I entered one or two of the most ragged and dilapidated, and invariably found them clean. Some were mere frame-works of bamboo, with thatched roofs of cocoanut leaves. Still they looked comfortable. They kept out the rain and let in the breeze, and this is all that is needed in a West India climate. I found them more tasteful and far cleaner than the dwellings of North American Indians. Supposing the advantages of education equal, I should not hesitate to declare in favor of the superior intelligence, honesty, industry, and sobriety of the West India negro, when compared with any specimen of the American Indian that could be produced, though it has been the fashion to regard the latter as belonging to the superior race.

I did not reach Linstead, of course, without passing abandoned sugar-properties. I do not think that five miles can be traveled, on any road in Jamaica, without seeing one deserted estate at the very least. They are any where and every where a melancholy sight to look upon, and need no particular description to be readily identified. Some two, four, or eight hundred acres, as the case may be, of splendidly fertile land overgrown with brushwood and rank weeds; the plantation-house looking like one of the ruins in the Swiss Valley of the Rhine; patches of corn and vegetables, or groups of plantains, dotting the space once filled by an uncheckered field of sugar-cane. Negro settlers are always to be found clinging round these deserted plantations. They were probably born on them, and are loth to leave. They buy or hire their little plots of ground from the owners of the estate or their agents. I have conversed with many of these people, and I have been amused at their utter ignorance of the fact that the world at large holds them responsible for the ruin of Jamaica. While proprietors say that the negroes are too independent to work, the negroes say that proprietors are too poor to pay, or that they will not pay regularly, which is a great grievance to a people who live from hand to mouth. There is, doubtless, truth in both assertions. But when I see an abandoned estate still surrounded by industrious settlers and laborers, I think it something like *primâ facie* evidence that the proprietor in England has abandoned them, not they the proprietor.

Linstead is a pleasant little village—lively enough on Saturday mornings, when its only street, which is also its only market-place, is thronged with peasants who have come in to buy or to sell. Commend me to a West Indian market as a fit illustration of Babel after the confusion of tongues. These people are quite as anxious to sell as the progeny of Noe were to build. The sum of their ambition is to get rid of the little lot of yams and oranges that they have brought many a weary mile. They get a shilling or two for their produce, and return as happy as though they were millionaires. I never lived among a more cheerful or a more civil people. Each man, woman, or child that you meet along the road—I speak exclusively of the peasantry—gives a hearty "Good mornin', massa," and a respectful salutation. Their spirits are buoyant, and they are ever ready for a joke or a laugh, if you are disposed to bandy words with them. The crowd collected in the Linstead market-place may be heard a mile off, but there is no quarreling of any kind. It is their fashion to make a noise and talk incessantly, as why should they not? Their exuberance of spirit needs an outlet, and their only amusements are to laugh and gossip. There is a police force stationed in every village of the island, and the white uniform and black visage of an officer can be distinguished here and there among the Linstead crowd. They fraternize with the people, but, more ornamental than useful, their official services are seldom required.

Leaving Linstead, we travel through the parish of St. Thomas-in-the-Vale, in a northerly direction. We pass the huts of many more settlers, several abandoned properties, and one or two estates still in sugar-cane, but cultivated negligently, it seemed to me, without any finish, as though poverty was cramping the proprietors, and preventing them from making the barest outlay necessary for moderate returns. One estate, lying at the base of Mount Diabolo, had been abandoned, I was informed, because the owner, who lived in England, could not afford to pay for labor. I am not able to say, of my own knowledge, whether labor could be procured in the neighborhood, but my informant said it could. There was at least an abundance of settlers.

At this point the ascent of Mount Diabolo is commenced. The hill is well named. You enter now a region of primeval forest, and for four miles the journey is extremely toilsome. The huts of settlers are thick as heretofore, and are buried in the trees, often not to be distinguished at all except by the peculiar foliage of the plantain and the cocoanut-trees which invariably surround them. These mountain settlers also grow pimento, coffee, and corn. Most of them have their horses, and are really as independent and well off as one would wish to see any people in the world. Half way up Mount Diabolo a splendid view can be obtained of nearly the whole parish of St. Thomas-in-the-Vale. It gives a stranger some insight of the true state of Jamaica cultivation. This parish—with the exception of three the most densely peopled in the island—presents, when seen from an elevation, merely a wild wood-land, interspersed here and there with small specks of cultivation. Its general character is that of unredeemed forest; yet its fertility is so great that it is fully capable of sustaining 200,000 instead of the 16,000 people who now inhabit it. St.

Thomas-in-the-Vale gives, as I have stated, more people to the square mile than any other parish in the island, except Kingston, Port Royal, and St. Andrew, in which, be it remembered, large towns are located. It is a fact, therefore, worthy of notice, that in this comparatively populous district there are far fewer sugar estates in present cultivation than in parishes less favorably situated with regard to labor. St. Thomas-in-the-Vale has a population of 125 to the square mile, against a population of 79 to the square mile in Westmoreland, one of the principal sugar-exporting parishes in the island, of 102 in Trelawny, the largest sugar-growing parish, and one that includes the populous town of Falmouth, and of 28 in Vere, another flourishing sugar district. These are facts which seem to require an explanation from those who insist that want of labor is the sole cause of the abandonment of sugar cultivation in Jamaica. I admit, and shall prove, that want of labor has been one cause of the island's depreciation; but if it were the sole cause, or even the preponderating cause, it would be only reasonable to expect that those parishes most sparsely populated would be the first to abandon the cultivation of the cane. The reverse, however, happens to be the case.

A projecting cliff shuts out the parish of St. Thomas-in-the-Vale from our view as we continue to ascend the steep sides of Mount Diabolo. The clouds now rest on the summits of mountains at our feet; the wind that rushes to meet us feels cold and bleak; we have entered a region of eternal mist and rain. The transition to this atmosphere from the hot valley below is too sudden to be comfortable. I was, therefore, glad to find myself descending the opposite side of the mountain—once more in the sunshine, and at a sufficient elevation to make the air deliciously cool. The scene, too, has changed. The forest has disappeared, and coffee and pimento plantations have taken its place; the houses of proprietors look no longer dilapidated; the pens and pasturage lands might be mistaken for New York farms. At the Moneague, a village lying on the northern slope of the mountains just crossed, the traveler will pause to sleep, if it be late, but to feed under any circumstances; for the hotel, built only ten years ago (wonderful fact for Jamaica!) is the best in the island.

The Moneague is in St. Anne's, a very charming parish that grows very little sugar. I protest against the West Indian valuation of a place by the quantity of sugar that it actually produces. There is not a sugar estate near the Moneague, but settlers, of whom there are many, have to pay $6 to $10 a year for an acre of land—sums that would purchase land out and out in other districts quite as fertile as this. But the climate here is healthy; the grass can almost be *seen* growing; the horses are strong and the oxen fat; vegetables are plentiful; fruit is luxuriant; and every thing seems to thrive. I do not wonder when the inhabitants of the Moneague declare that no money would induce them to live any where else.

I passed a Sunday in the Moneague, and it was a model of quiet and respectability. The churches were filled with well-dressed and attentive congregations. There was no drunkenness or debauchery, or assemblage of idlers in the village during the entire day. But church attendance and Sabbath observance, it is argued, are no proofs, among a negro population at least, of moral rectitude. The assertion is not destitute of truth. I never knew a people more faithful than these are to the formalities of religion, although chastity, among the lower classes especially, is dreadfully ignored. I do not think, however, that licentiousness in the emancipated islands will discourage or astonish those who have any conception of the immorality that slavery not only engendered but enforced. Comparisons between past and present times will show that marriages are much more frequent in Jamaica now than they were then, and patient investigation will prove that the prevalence of social vice is but an evidence of the island's very recent deliverance from a state of actual barbarism, and of the very little that has been done to civilize and educate a willing people. I really believe that the eagerness of the African populations to attend places of public worship should be construed as an earnest desire, on their part, to learn. At the same time I am unable to agree with those well-meaning enthusiasts who find arguments to support their views of political economy in a crowded church or in popular zeal for devotional exercises. It is upon other grounds altogether that I combat the ridiculous assertion that these people can not be elevated to the level of the Caucasian race, or that any moral or physical defect prevents them from becoming, under a free system, industrious and useful citizens.

CHAPTER XX.

A TOUR CONTINUED.

Kingston, Jamaica, 1860,

I RESUME the description of my tour through the interior of Jamaica at the point abandoned in the last chapter.

From the Moneague village to a place called "The Finger Post," on the route to the north side of the island, the road winds, for several miles, round the summits of hills, now up, now down, bad enough in this dry season, but axle-deep during rainy weather, in a red, slimy mud. The macadamizers are at work here. Within the memory of living man, and men among these mountains live a century, it was never essayed to repair the road until now. But two or three years ago and the same remark might be made of all the roads in Jamaica, showing very conclusively that the plantocracy of other days were not too deeply interested in the permanent prosperity of the island, or too willing to expend a portion of their revenues in an investment that promised no immediate return. It was a grave error, as any sound political economist of ancient or modern times would have told them; as they themselves now admit when they find themselves compelled to abandon the cultivation of sugar, or carry it on at an extravagant cost and loss of stock, in consequence of bad roads. A simple evil, it may be said, and requiring a simple remedy; nevertheless, the fact is not without significance, that the first attempt to make decent roads is under a democratic *régime*.

I had a good opportunity to see the laborers of both sexes on these and other roads in different parts of the country. Most of the male laborers were strapping young fellows of twenty or thereabouts, who seemed to do good service—who must have done good service, to judge by the amount of work performed. They belong to the new race of freemen born; how superior to the old race, born in slavery, and fast dying out, I need not say. The overseers on these roads make no complaints against the men under their charge that they are idle and unwilling to work; and, what is of more importance, they make no complaint of an insufficiency of hands. They have succeeded in getting a larger supply of labor than most people deemed possible, and their success has excited some surprise in districts where the planters have long and bitterly complained that they could get no labor at all.

"Expound to me the riddle," I say to the planter.

"Oh," he answers, "the people are too independent, too well off here—too fickle, arbitrary, and uncertain as to when they will work and when they will not work. They just do as they please. They work on the roads for a month and then give it up. Then they take to something else and give *that* up. This is the way they have treated us. They ride upon our backs, sir. They work for us only four days in the week, and hang about their own properties or go to market on the other two. We can not improve our estates without a full week's labor. Our properties deteriorate every year for want of contract or continued labor. Now, to illustrate the character of the negro, I should like to show you in what style a body of men would clear fifty acres. They would work as well and as cleverly as American backwoodsmen. 'These men lazy?' you would say. 'Pshaw! They are heroes.' But if I wanted their services for six months I could not get them; they would insist on going back to peddle on their own properties; I would be unable, for want of labor, to plant the land I had cleared; the capital I had expended would be wasted, and my plans utterly frustrated." *Sic loquitur.*

There is a great deal of truth in all this.

"Expound to me the riddle," I say to the overseer on the road, to the merchant, the small proprietor, or to any one whom I suppose to be partial to the negro in the controversy between the laboring and the proprietary interests. "Surely it is work less severe to hoe in a cane-field than to hammer stones on the road-side?"

"Well, you see that laborers on the road are paid regularly once a week, while laborers on the estates often have to go two and three months without their wages; and the men do not like that. Sometimes, too, they lose their pay altogether."

Here was something to think about; and I did think about it, making a note thereof, and many notes thereafter to the same effect. I found that there was much truth in what I was told—that many proprietors of sugar-estates are really unable to pay for labor; that, although want of labor, that is, want of such a competition as would prevent labor being tyrannical, is one cause of the island's scanty cultivation, yet another and more serious cause is want of capital. Money is the one essential thing needed by the Jamaica proprietary. They have no money; they have no credit. The post-obits, drawn in the days of a flourishing plantocracy, have been long over-due, and they exceed in amount by a thousand per cent. the actual value of the property pawned. Money can not be raised in Jamaica, and without money, or its equivalent, a country in these days is without labor, life, learning, religion. Every thing must be paid for. Potatoes and principles have their market value. When the millennium comes we may hope to get things for love.

The path that I laid down for myself in this chapter was one of description, and I have wandered somewhat. I return to the "Finger Post" in the parish of St. Anne. The district through which I have been traveling is composed entirely of pasture-land. All the settlers own a horse and stock of some kind. Their cottages are very neat and tidy, and are shrouded with cocoas and plantains. Most of the inferior ones have but a single room. The pitch-pine floor is carefully polished; a bed stands in one corner, or it may be that the inhabitants make up their couches at night on the floor; a table, bearing all the crockery of the establishment, occupies another corner, for the mysteries of a closet are unknown; there are no glass windows, but blinds placed cunningly for purposes of ventilation; there may be, perhaps, a chair and another table in the apartment, and the table, in the better class of huts, is sometimes a piece of fine old mahogany. The negroes seldom enter their huts except when they retire for the night. They congregate at evening outside the door, and do all their cooking in the open air. Their habits of life are singular and very irregular. They eat when they are hungry, and seldom sit down to a family meal. Hence the frightful mortality among them during cholera visitations. In the better class of cottages I have invariably found books—always the Bible, and not unfrequently the ponderous works of one William Wilberforce, the West Indian's demigod.

Within an hour's drive from the "Finger Post" the northern limit of the St. Anne plateau is reached. A large weather-worn cotton-tree, seen from afar, is the spot whence the first glimpse of the ocean can be caught. It is a wonderful picture. The road can be traced winding cautiously round the hill-sides, and descending in slow graduations till it is lost among the specks of houses on the beach. But the precipice upon which we stand, and along whose very brink the road runs, breaks away with appalling abruptness, and exposes to view a valley swept out between a fork of mountains to the sea. The valley is an unchequered wood-land, except where lingering traces of former cultivation can be detected, and where splendid cane-fields cluster round the distant sea-port of St. Anne's. The road descends through forests of pimento, through groves of plantains or of cocoas, or under archways of gigantic bamboo; and while on the right we get occasional views of the valley I have described, on the left the hills grow steep and steeper, and the trees upon their sides, entangled and knitted together by wild vegetation, draperied with vines and ornamented with the most splendid parasites, look like a torrent of foliage rushing down from the mountain-top. The cottages seen on this long descent are superior to those on the southern slope of the hills. They seem to improve with the commencement of the rich pasture-land at the Moneague, and St. Anne's Bay, on the north coast, has every appearance of being a flourishing village. Flourishing, that is, for Jamaica. I can not compare it with any village of equal size in the United States and call St. Anne's flourishing. Perhaps I ought not to call it flourishing at all, in sight of dismantled wharves and other indications of a large trade in days gone by, contrasted now by the presence of two solitary schooners, from whose peaks the American ensign droops in the utter stillness of every thing around. I can say, however, with perfect truth, that in the immediate vicinity of St. Anne's Bay there are cane-lands in high cultivation; that the houses in the village are neat and well built; that the road, or street, as it should be called, is in proper repair; that shops are plentiful, and buying and selling going on at a fair rate for a village of a thousand inhabitants. Under any circumstances St. Anne's is a proper halting-place for a tourist. It has a couple of inns, and the sugar-estates in the neighborhood are at least worth visiting.

We have now reached the north side of Jamaica, and purpose traveling west as far as we can. From St. Anne's Bay to Dry Harbor, a distance of seventeen miles, the hills trend along the coast, leaving between them and the beach a spacious and well-cultivated slope. For seven miles west of St. Anne's Bay, a continued succession of luxuriant cane-pieces will be passed. They are on both sides of the road, and have every appearance of being highly cultivated. The fences are of stone or logwood, and are well kept up. The hills, which, for the most part, are covered with their native forest, are here and there marked with pasture, and with the peculiar foliage of the plantain and the cocoanut-tree; a certain sign, even where a hut is invisible, of the presence of settlers. Passing the sugar-estates, we come to more pens and pasturage, then to wood-land and to denser settlements. The cottages are rudely built, but clean. I entered possibly a dozen that were grouped together. They were in charge of one old woman. The girls and boys were away at work; some in the cane-fields, some on the roads, and some on their own *emplacements*. Quite close to this group of cottages stood a neat little Baptist chapel, built by the laborers at their own expense. A large majority of the Jamaica Creoles dissent from the Church of England, which is the established church in the West India colonies, and the dissenters, even in sparsely settled districts, are not slow to erect their own places of worship. These people, who live comfortably and independently, own houses and stock, pay taxes, poll votes, and build churches, are the same people whom we have heard represented as idle, worthless fellows, obstinately opposed to work, and ready to live on an orange or banana rather than earn their daily bread. This may have been the case with those originally set free, before they comprehended their responsibilities as freemen, and before their extravagant ideas of liberty had been moderated by a necessary experience. But now that intelligence and experience have come to them, the West Indian negroes can not be indiscriminately thrown aside as a people who will not work. Since emancipation they have passed in a body to a higher civil and social *status;* and the majority of them are too much their own masters ever to submit again to the mastership of others. They can not be blamed for this; and any unprejudiced resident of Jamaica will indorse the statement here made, that the peasantry are as peaceable and industrious a people as may be found in the same latitude throughout the world. The present generation of Jamaican Creoles are no more to be likened to their slave ancestors than the intelligent English laborer of the nineteenth century can be likened to the serfs of Athelstane or Atheling.

The village of Dry Harbor, seventeen miles from St. Anne's Bay, is chiefly inhabited by fishermen and small proprietors. The road thence, continuing west, lies over a mountain densely covered with orange and pimento trees. As we are leaving St. Anne's parish, I may as well say here that pimento is its great staple. Jamaica possibly supplies two thirds of the pimento used in the world; and St. Anne supplies two thirds of the Jamaica pimento. It is easily cultivated, and is said to be best sown by birds. It is, however, a precarious crop. In 1858 the island produced nine and a half millions of pounds, and in 1859 it only produced four and a half millions. The decline was owing to no lack of industry or enterprise, but simply to the fact that the season was a bad one. It is, perhaps, worthy of remark that the pimento crop of 1858 was the largest ever reaped in the island.

St. Anne's is considerably the largest parish in Jamaica. It occupies a superficial area of 433 square miles. The population, which is 25,823, gives only 59.63 persons to the square mile. They are almost exclusively pen proprietors and small settlers. I was charmed with every part of the parish that I visited, with its fresh look, fertile soil, and happy, contented, and independent inhabitants; and I certainly thought that if all Jamaica was like St. Anne's there would be no ground for the commiseration that her condition has excited in Europe and America.

The Pimento Mountain, of which I have spoken, separates Dry Harbor from Rio Bueno. On descending the western slope, the stream from which the latter village takes its name (and which is the boundary between the parishes of St. Anne and Trelawny) can be seen winding through the valley below. It rises from a spring in the mountain side, falls in cascade, and empties itself into the ocean, as a Jamaican river of considerable size, a few miles away. The village itself, like most villages in the island, is situated in a snug little bay. A vacant hotel, large enough to accommodate fifty guests, well-built stone piers, and dilapidated, tenantless stores, tell the old story of past prosperity and present decay. The harbor, in which a dozen ships once rode at anchor, is now without a solitary sail, and but two or three inferior vessels come drifting in during a whole year's space. There are the remains here of an old fort, in a position to sweep a fleet from the bay. It requires some ingenuity to discover the spot, for rank vegetation entirely conceals it. The ruin possesses historical interest, for its walls were built to protect the flag of Spain; and the cannon that stretch their rusty throats through the crumbling embrasures were planted there many years before the

United States were a nation born. Hence the Spanish name, yet retained, of Rio Bueno. I like the village—a quaint, quiet spot, with the sea-breeze blowing freshly in. Many fishermen live here, but they find, I fancy, a bad mart even for the best of mullets and snappers. A fish of 10 lbs. weight must be sold to ten different persons, for there is no one, except perhaps the doctor or the parson, rich enough to buy such a monster entire. In the hotel where I lodged the landlord migrated in search of a candle to light up, for once probably in six months, his huge reception-room, which still looked quite grand with its polished floor and pieces of old mahogany. Up in the crazy room where I slept I lay upon an antique bed in the company of lizards, and gazed through holes in the roof upon the twinkling stars. Providentially it did not rain.

Between Rio Bueno and the village of Duncan I passed through a magnificent sugar-estate, with its buildings, steam-mill, and private wharf in good repair—altogether as fine a property as ever I saw in the favored island of Barbados. The cane-fields extended over hill and valley, and were carefully cultivated and finished in all their appurtenances. There is another fine estate between Duncan and the town of Falmouth, and many pasture-lands, large and small. I continued to find the settlers, without exception, at their work. I met them in troops at early morning traveling along the road, every man and woman ready with their polite greetings. I never met a peasantry more civil or more ready to oblige. Nine out of ten of the settlers rely principally upon their own properties for the support of themselves and their families, but are willing, nevertheless, to work for the estates or on the roads when it does not interfere with necessary labor on their own lands. When the choice lies between the roads and the estates, it is not surprising that they should select the employer that pays best and most regularly. I do not mean to say for a moment that the estates have any thing like a sufficiency of labor; they are entirely without that continuous labor required, not merely for bare cultivation, but for extension and improvement. In the remarks I have here made, I merely wish to give point-blank denial to a very general impression prevailing abroad that the Jamaica negro will not work at all. I wish to show that he gives as much labor, even to the sugar-estate, as he consistently can, and that it is no fault of his if he can not give enough. I wish to exhibit the people of Jamaica as a peaceable, law-abiding peasantry, with whom the remembrance of past wrongs has had so little weight that, from the day of emancipation until now, they have never dreamt of a hostile combination either against their old masters or the government under which they live, though insurrections in the time of slavery were numerous and terrible, and were only suppressed after much bloodshed and lavish expenditure. I wish to bear witness to their courtesy. When I had occasion to ask for coconuts or oranges on the way-side, the settler generally refused payment for the fruit; and if he finally took the money pressed upon him, it was with the understanding, distinctly expressed, that he wanted no payment for rendering so simple a service. I speak exclusively of the peasantry, not of the dissolute idlers, loafers, and vagabonds that congregate in Kingston and other towns. They are as different from their country brethren as the New York rowdy is different from the honest farmer in his home in Niagara or St. Lawrence. That the Jamaica peasantry have grave faults of character and grave defects, which it will take long years of training to remove, I do not doubt. It will be a part of my task to expose their vices; but this is no reason why they should be denied the possession of any virtues.

CHAPTER XXI.

A TOUR CONTINUED.

Kingston, Jamaica, 1860.

HAVING entered the parish of Trelawny, it is proper that I should take the reader to Falmouth, its chief town, which contains a population of seven or eight thousand. The town looks more modern than Kingston; the houses are well built, and, being the principal sea-port of the largest sugar-parish in the island, the harbor, during crop-season, is sometimes thronged with vessels. Falmouth is surrounded by a morass, and would undoubtedly be a most unhealthy spot if it were not favored by unremitting sea-breezes that bear away the malaria. I have been told that during the terrible visitation of cholera, from which and small-pox combined thirty thousand persons are supposed to have died, Falmouth suffered less than any town of its size on the island. It is on the faith of this, I suppose, that the authorities neglect the most ordinary rules of health, give the people bad water to drink, and allow the drainage to stagnate in the streets—sufficient to breed a pestilence in a much more favored locality. Next to Kingston, which carries off the palm, Falmouth is the filthiest town in Jamaica. Report says that when the penitentiary convicts worked on the streets they were kept in much better order, but now that the labor must be paid for, it is neglected. Want of money is certainly epidemic in Jamaica. No Creole seems to possess the commodity, and strangers who are believed to possess it are made to pay for the general deficiency. If a traveler appears in the streets of Falmouth, an inn-keeper will run after him, bag him, and make the most of him, for such game only branches here once in a season.

Besides want of money in Jamaica, there is a deplorable want of economy and want of ingenuity to turn things to the best account. Prison discipline is a farce, and a sentence to hard labor perfect moonshine. I have seen these "hard-labor convicts" moving along the roads in gangs at a funeral pace, and looking for all the world as though they were hunting up cockroaches. They are allowed to stop and talk to girls, and amuse themselves in any manner they like. There is no fear of their escaping. Many of the dissipated scamps about town actually steal in order to get into the penitentiary, they are so well treated there. They have good food, their bath, and easy exercise every day. No disgrace is attached to a residence in the penitentiary. The convict, when released, laughs over his imprisonment and boasts of his good fare. He does not consider that imprisonment a bar to future employment, or any reason why he should not be trusted again. I can say, from my own personal knowledge, that a man who had served his time in the penitentiary attempted to breakfast at the public table of a hotel in which I lodged. Luckily there was a judge present who knew the fellow, and the guests were spared the risk of having their pockets picked and the landlady the certainty of having her spoons abstracted. That I may not be thought exaggerating, I refer to an article in the *Colonial Standard* of the 13th of December last, where the writer calls the island penitentiary a "house of sumptuous living, amusement, and sport." "No bread, no beef," say the convicts, "are equal to that which may be had there." A man, after twelve months' residence in the penitentiary, grows fat and sleek, and often expresses regret when his term of imprisonment expires. The writer of the article in question furnishes an illustration of the "hard labor" of two prisoners under sentence for felony; one had to knead bread, and the other to polish the keeper's boots! This is penal labor in Jamaica. The wretched management here displayed does not need pointing out. The people are taxed for repairing the roads some six hundred dollars a mile—a sum that might be altogether saved by making the convicts do the work. They are also taxed to support criminals who do little or nothing for their own maintenance. Here is "payment at both ends" with a vengeance. And worse than that, a premium of good lodgings and an easy life is offered to the idle and dissolute to commit crime. The evil effect of such a system upon the community is incalculable. Public morality as well as the public purse inevitably suffers.

I dislike excessively the sea-port towns of Jamaica, and can make no exception in favor of Falmouth. All the worst fellows in the island collect in them, and give to foreigners a most mistaken idea of the country people. Those who are not bad soon become so by the force of an example that English and American sailors in port are not slow to set. Though I think that, morally considered, the negroes who congregate about the wharves are the very worst class to be encountered, yet I have seen them in Kingston, Falmouth, and other ports, work like very horses in the loading and unloading of vessels. They are usually paid by the job. I do not doubt that many proprieters really suffer from the partiality of young men to towns; but at the same time I do not doubt that many of these young men prefer, and very naturally prefer, the greater certainty of regular payment that town business offers. I know of waiters in hotels who get only a dollar a week and have to find themselves; and it is not rational to suppose that they would flock to Kingston or Falmouth if they had to work there at a pecuniary disadvantage.

While on the subject of town labor, I have something to say about the conduct of American ship-captains who trade at West Indian ports; and what I have to say is not much to their credit. The American captain seems to think it his special privilege to treat the Jamaica negroes in his employ far worse than he dare treat slaves in southern ports of his own country. It is too common to hear one of these bullies accost a man with "You d—d nigger, if I had you in New Orleans I'd sell you," and so forth. The negro, who is exceedingly sensitive about his freedom, passes off the remark very often as a joke, for he is at work on the vessel, and does not like to lose his job. But the feeling here, and in all the British West Indies, against America and the Americans, owing to just such bad taste and brutality, is bitter in the extreme. I have met intelligent mulattoes—men well educated too—who have expressed a wish to go to New York, and have given utterance to genuine fears that if they did so they might be sold into slavery. If a town loafer has a dispute with his neighbor, his bitterest abuse is to tell him what his market value would be in Charleston, New Orleans, or Jacksonville—with which last place they all seem wonderfully familiar.

Falmouth, from which respectable town I have somewhat digressed, is, as I have said, the capital of the largest sugar-exporting parish in the island. I have seen many of the estates, and should judge them all to be in a condition of paying cultivation. They extend for fifteen or sixteen miles round the town. Some properties, formerly cultivated in sugar, but now converted into breeding-pens and pasturage-grounds, lie farther back. I know of no estates in the parish that have been wholly abandoned, though there may be a very few. Trelawny offers some curious facts in connection with the growth of sugar. The land here is notoriously poorer for growing provisions than it is in districts where the cultivation of the cane has been altogether abandoned. The parishes of St. Mary, Metcalf, and St. George, round Annotto Bay, on the north coast, are examples of splendid soil, formerly cultivated in sugar, but now almost wholly abandoned, or yielded to small settlers. Trelawny, on the contrary, continues to export largely. The success of Trelawny may be partly owing to the fact that the negroes can not grow provisions to advantage. But this is not a complete explanation of its success. It certainly can not be explained by population statistics, for the agricultural force of Trelawny is considerably weaker than that of two of the other parishes named. Leaving out the town of Falmouth, it will be found that the population in the country districts furnishes only 75 persons to the square mile, while some parishes, in which sugar cultivation has been given up, have 80, 90, 100, and even 120 persons to the square mile. If, then, Trelawny, with a comparatively poor soil and a population of 75 to the square mile, retains the cultivation of the cane, why has not Metcalf done the same (I take the parish at random), with its rich soil and population of 110 to the square mile? It can not be said that the planters of Trelawny had more capital, were more prudent, or were better managers than others; but it can be said that the roads have been kept in much better condition than those of St. Mary, Metcalf, and St. George. Bad roads, in some places impassable roads, have helped not a little to diminish cane cultivation. The conveyance to port of hogsheads weighing 18 and 20 cwt. has always been one of the planter's most serious items of expenditure; and he has not now the means necessary to supply the constant drain upon his stock caused by bad roads, nor the capital or the credit to build tramways that would pay their own expenses in twenty years' time. The estates around Falmouth have a comparatively easy access to the port of embarkation; but on distant estates, where access is both difficult and expensive, the cultivation of the cane has been generally abandoned, and this is the case over the whole island. Moreover, where the land is rich, the negro is always more independent and more ready and eager to buy than where it is poor. Thus, again, we have another cause, besides the bare want of labor, for the depression of Jamaican commerce in consequence of the abandonment of sugar cultivation.

It is a long drive from Falmouth to Montego Bay, the principal town in the adjoining parish of St. James. The road lies over a sandy beach, and is exposed to the burning heat of the sun. Comparatively few settlers are to be met with.

At "Little River," half way between Falmouth and Montego Bay, there is a road-side inn. I thanked the gods for the same, and for the opportunity of escaping for an hour the blazing midday sun. The breeze here came up freshly from the sea. After leaving this halting-place, we passed through some splendid specimens of Trelawny sugar cultivation, but the estates end with the boundary-line of the parish. Wood-land then; after which, having veered round the butt of a hill, we obtain a full view of Montego Bay and its shipping—to wit, three vessels. We enter the town between a race-course on the one hand and a burial-ground on the other—both overgrown with weeds; we pass in the shadow of a crumbling fort and along a crooked street, ornamented with perfect models of West India houses in the last stage of dilapidation. Leaning like so many Pisa towers, they, nevertheless, do not fall, and we reach the square and the lodging-house in safety.

They had a wonderful eye, those old Spaniards, for a good site, as all the towns they ever planted, both in the Indies and on the Main, fully testify. The town of Montego Bay, in point of population and size the second in Jamaica, is no exception to the rule. It sleeps at the extremity of an elliptical bay, sheltered from storms by an amphitheatre of mountains, and waiting apparently for the last trump to awaken it. The dreaminess of the place is contagious. You can not look upon its quaint old houses, or upon its people moving at a snail's pace, and feel any thing approaching to activity. A sight of the blue waters of the bay, rippled by the gentlest of breezes, or of a panorama of mountains on the left, that stretch away to the misty point upon which the town of Lucea stands, aggravates indolence, and converts it into an uncompromising laziness. The town has still a Spanish look about it, in spite of the lapse of two centuries since Spaniards were its masters. It wears a smile of contempt for the frowns of fortune and the cessation of a once flourishing commerce. It is the chosen retreat of a remnant of the old plantocracy, and their residences, if antique, are always picturesque, and somewhat symbolic of Jamaica's actual condition. Lo! an ancient tenement half buried in luxuriant shrub: decay, which is of man, and the most vigorous kind of life, which is not of man, progressing side by side. I admit that Montego Bay quite charmed me with its clean streets, neat little patches of garden and utter quietude, with its air of by-gone respectability, and the cool complacency of its people, who did not know or care how they lived from day to day. "Well, massa, we do de best we can in dese times," was all the answer I got to repeated inquiries for a solution of the mystery of life in Montego Bay. I have not yet discovered how 10,000 people manage to exist on the trade of the five or six vessels which annually enter the bay from European or American ports. They certainly make little out of travelers, for a stranger in Montego Bay is so rare a sight that he will create as violent an agitation among its inhabitants as a wild elephant, careering among omnibuses, might be expected to excite in the minds of Broadway pedestrians. The people here, that is, those of the laboring class with whom I conversed, say that the planters of the parish will not pay or can not pay for labor. They complain that a great many of the old estates have been sold to Jews, who are too close to do justice to their workmen. I do not give this as a fact within my own knowledge, but simply as a report credited by the laboring people of the parish of St. James. Many people in the town complain of not being able to get work. St. James has not half the number of sugar-properties in cultivation that Trelawny has, and possessing as large a population to the square mile, it ought not to be worse off for labor than the neigboring parish.

The road from Montego Bay to Lucea, in Hanover parish, follows the line of beach, and is winding, hilly, and irregular. There is little to see but forest, and some few sugar-estates. I speak of the northern slope of the hills which trend along the coast. On their southern side, a district which I did not penetrate, I was told that sugar cultivation was rare, but that small settlements and provision-grounds were plentiful. The pleasantest mode of traveling from Montego Bay to Lucea is by water. I left with a steersman and two oars, and we accomplished the distance (about 20 miles) in less than four hours. When it is remembered that this labor was performed at high noon, that the men engaged in it never flagged for an instant, and that it was no extraordinary job for which they had been offered an extraordinary inducement, but a part of their ordinary every-day work, I deem it no light testimony in favor of the negro's power to work, and will to work, when he is properly paid. These men who row their boat to Lucea and back to Montego Bay within the twenty-four hours—an effort that white men could not undertake in such a climate —receive about a dollar each for the trip; but they do not get passengers every day. They are generally professional pilots, and their receipts from the six or eight vessels that enter port during the year must be very small.

Lucea is an unclean, ragged-looking village, without two houses conjoined, and without one house in decent repair. Its population must be about 1500 or 2000. The road thence to Green Island, and round the western extremity of Jamaica as far as Savanna-la-Mar, on the south side, is execrable, and passes through the wildest country that I saw. It took me twelve hours to accomplish fifty miles. I seldom got the horses out of a walk. Sometimes wading in mud, sometimes steering among huge rocks, sometimes swimming over rivers. If it is thus in the dry season, what must it be in the wet? The people on the route look as wild as the aspect of their country. They run away from a stranger, or glare at him half in terror, half in curiosity, from behind a bush.

Immediately after leaving Lucea some fine sugar-estates are passed, but they soon give way to dense woods, and low, swampy lands, where few settlers, even, have cast their lot. The country breaks into cultivation round the village of Green Island—the western *ultima thule* of Jamaica—where there are a few sugar-properties. I was told here that the estates still being worked in the parish of Hanover were doing well, and that those abandoned had been given up for want of means to carry them on. An intelligent resident of Green Island, himself a proprietor, informed me that he knew of no estate in Hanover whose owner, possessed of capital, or even out of debt, had been compelled from mere want of labor to abandon sugar cultivation. When I have put the same question to any respectable landholder in any part of the island, I have, in nine cases out of ten, received the same answer. The want of continued or contract labor is generally deplored as a great evil; but it is wrong to suppose that that want alone has ever compelled resident proprietors to abandon their estates to ruin. I have no doubt that there are districts where the price of labor is too high to make sugar cultivation as profitable as the cultivation of other produce—where the negroes, in fact, are too well off and too independent to work for the wages they are compelled to take in Barbados; but this is no justification for the assertion, so widely made and so generally believed, that they will not work at all. From all that I learned in the parish of Hanover, I came to the conclusion that the settlers would work very readily if work was proffered them at a fair remuneration.

We have now traveled as far west as it is possible to travel on the north side of Jamaica. I propose to bring the reader back to Kingston, in my next chapter, by the south side.

CHAPTER XXII.

A TOUR CONTINUED.

Kingston, Jamaica, 1860.

To the south side of Jamaica, its original Indian name of Xaymaca, a land of wood and water, is more strictly applicable. For while on the north side wood is plentiful enough, the south side, equally luxuriant in forest, is watered by a hundred streams.

Westmoreland is the most southwesterly, as Hanover is the most northwesterly parish in the island. In the former sugar is largely cultivated, and from its chief town, Savanna-la-Mar, the export of the great staple is still very considerable. On the route from Green Island I passed some very fine sugar-estates, and not a few properties of small settlers cultivated in cane. But the roads are abominable, and the expense of transporting heavy hogsheads from this district to the place of export must swallow up a large portion of the planter's revenue. Still, Westmoreland keeps up its reputation as a leading sugar-parish in spite of a scanty population that numbers only seventy-nine persons to the square mile. The soil is excellent for the growth of the cane; and some of the largest and most successful planters, since emancipation, have their estates in the vicinity of Savanna-la-Mar.

The town of Savanna-la-Mar, as its name indicates,

is built on a large morass that stretches seaward. The Creoles call it a healthy place, and I do not know that it is otherwise; but it ought to be unhealthy. A breeze is ever blowing from the shore, and this perhaps keeps the savanna free from fevers. I liked the look of the town, with its broad central street, and piers kept tolerably clean, and houses peeping from among forests of cocoanut-trees. Crop-time was at hand, and a couple of vessels in the bay, forerunners of the fleet that annually visit Savanna-la-Mar, were waiting for their cargoes of sugar.

It was Christmas-eve—a season at which the West Indian negro goes wild with excitement. Old drums, trumpets, kettles, bells, and any thing that can make a noise, are brought out; dancers dance violently, and fiddlers fiddle violently, without any regard to time or tune; and masquerading and psalm-singing are alternately kept up until New-year's day is fairly past. No negro will work for love or money during this carnival time. He is literally demented, and can hardly give a sane answer to the most ordinary question. All night long, and for eight successive nights, an infernal din—a concert of cracked drums, shrill voices, and fire-crackers—is maintained. Those poor devils who can not enjoy this species of amusement suffer the most exquisite torture. I passed the whole season in the country, and saw exhibitions of excitement that made me think the actors fit subjects for a lunatic asylum; but, though I mixed freely among the people, I was always most civilly treated, and never on any of these occasions did I see a negro in a state of intoxication. I do not remember having ever seen a West Indian negro drunk; and the temperate habits of the Jamaica Creoles are the more remarkable, as the spirit manufactured in the island can be obtained for a very trifling cost.

I allude to these Christmas festivities because they afforded me an opportunity to see the people in their holiday time, when, if ever, they would be disposed to be as saucy and insolent as I have heard them characterized. I found them nothing of the kind. The accusation may be true as regards Kingston loafers, who hang about the wharves for chance jobs, and follow strangers with annoying persistency; but it is not true when applied to the peasantry. The people are no longer servile, though they retain, from habit, the servile epithet of "Massa," when addressing the whites; but I have ever seen them most respectful to their superiors, and most anxious to oblige, when they are treated as men, and not as slaves or brute beasts. Individual testimony on this point might be discredited or deemed insufficient, but there is no discrediting the fact that, since their freedom, no people in the world have been more peaceful than the Creoles of Jamaica. They seem to have forgotten all ancient grievances, and never to have entertained a thought of retribution. The contrast in this respect between the reign of freedom and the reign of slavery carries its own lesson and its own warning. Twenty-five years of freedom, and not a murmur of popular discontent! Twenty-five years of slavery—I take any period—and what fears and anxieties and actual outbreaks! It cost the government $800,000 to suppress the single insurrection of 1832, during which private property to the value of $6,000,000 was destroyed. But the outbreak from which the planters then suffered would have been light compared with the one that was ready to burst over the island when liberty appeared in the gap and brought them salvation.

I have also heard the Jamaica people denounced for making Christmas, instead of the anniversary of emancipation, their great gala season of festivity. It is argued that they can care little for the boon of freedom if they do not keep it in remembrance, or regard it as a fit opportunity for national rejoicings. But I do not think that the absence of any general enthusiasm in the West India islands on the first of August demonstrates at all that the people fail to appreciate the blessings of freedom. Any one acquainted with these colonies knows that the reverse is the case. Negroes, very like other people, are creatures of habit, and in their Christmas festivities they keep up the customs that they were taught to observe. They have a week's holiday, and they make the most of it, according to their noisy fashion. Probably they do not reflect on the great event that the season is designed to commemorate, any more than civilized people do who drink Champagne and eat roast turkeys.

It is a hot drive, along a beach road, from Savanna-la-Mar to Black River. The country is covered partly with forest, and partly with pens and pasture-land. There is an abundance of pimento and orange trees. American schooners very often come to the bays along this coast, and load with oranges and other fruit. I did not notice a single sugar-estate on the way. The houses of small settlers are also, comparatively speaking, scarce, until a more open country in the adjoining parish of St. Elizabeth is reached. The hills in the distance are covered with dense forest, but are nevertheless inhabited by small proprietors, who grow their own coffee and pimento for the Black River market.

The town of Black River is situated in a deep bay, looking out upon the setting sun, and back upon lofty ranges of hills. For a place that can not number more than 2000 inhabitants, it is doing a thriving business, though the parish, of which it is the only outlet, is by no means a first-class sugar-growing district. There are few estates in St. Elizabeth, and, I think, only two that transport their sugar by the roads. The remainder send their produce down the river, which, at a little expense, might be made navigable for boats for a distance of forty miles. A more fertile district, or more splendid soil for the cultivation of every article of tropical growth, can scarcely be imagined than this portion of the parish of St. Elizabeth, and a conveyance by water is not the least of its many advantages for the cultivation of the cane. It has been aptly called the Demerara of Jamaica, and vegetation here is indeed quite as luxuriant as it is in that wonderful colony. But Jamaica's curse—want of capital—is upon the rich alluvial soil and easy communication of the Black River country. The forests remain uncleared, and sand and mud are allowed to choke up the river channel. Yet, in spite of great natural advantages neglected and thrown away, the richness of this district is not altogether hidden from view, nor are its resources entirely wasted. The trade of Black River is principally in coffee, pimento, and different kinds of wood. Some forty or fifty vessels arrive in port during the year, and many American schooners come here for return cargoes. I was told that about a hundred tons of logwood, fustic, and ebony are daily moved in the Black River market. The coffee is excellent, and is raised, without an exception, by small proprietors.

The decline in the exportation of coffee is a great argument in the mouths of those who urge the necessity of large accessions to the laboring population of the island. But I can not see the force of the argument, for the cultivation of coffee does not demand any thing like the labor required in the cultivation of the cane. It is an undoubted fact, that the exportation of coffee has declined from twenty-five and thirty millions of pounds to five and six millions; but the exhaustion of Jamaica coffee-land will almost account for the deterioration. It must also be remembered that where one pound was used in the island prior to emancipation ten pounds are used now. What master would ever have dreamed of giving coffee to his slaves? What settler nowadays would dream of depriving himself of his *tasse de consolation?* I never yet passed a settler's *emplacement* in the mountainous districts of Jamaica that I did not see coffee in cultivation; and it is my firm conviction that there is no such great discrepancy between the amount grown now and that grown at the time of emancipation. The same statement will apply, with much greater force, to provisions of every description. It is undoubtedly true that most of the large coffee properties in cultivation prior to emancipation have been abandoned, or turned to other uses. But want of capital prevails quite as much among coffee-planters as among sugar-planters. Coffee, too, like cacao, requires new land, and the clearance of fifty acres of wood is a sort of Herculean enterprise that, in these days, a Jamaica planter would not willingly face. But, whatever large coffee-planters may say about their profits and losses, it is a notorious fact that thousands and thousands of settlers grow the delicious berry to advantage, as any merchant engaged in the trade will be able to testify. They come to the towns and villages with one, two, six, or a dozen bags, and in this way many a cargo is made up for foreign ports. The population of St. Elizabeth parish numbers 119 persons to the square mile—a larger proportion than can be found in most of the sugar-growing parishes. But I know of no locality in Jamaica where labor for sugar-cultivation is more needed than here. The settlers have their own properties to look after, and it would be surprising indeed if they neglected them to hire themselves out as field laborers at a shilling a day.

We leave Black River village and St. Elizabeth parish, and soon after begin to ascend the Manchester mountains. Fresh horses are needed, for the long miles of this day's traveling would make twenty Sabbath-day's journeys. Possibly we reach the summit of the May-day mountains about sunset, and then one of the finest spectacles in all Jamaica can be witnessed. That last hill, over a mile above the level of the sea, was killing work, and so steep that no animals but stout Jamaica ponies, accustomed to such travel, could ever have dragged us up. We pause for breath, and can look back at the country through which we have lately passed. We are upon a ridge of hills running north and south; a parallel ridge rises up in the distance, standing out black against the sun now slowly setting beyond it. The valley below, full twenty miles broad, resembles, from this height, a vast plain; but, having so lately traversed it, we know it is no plain, but an uneven country, covered with formidable hills, that have shrunk away to seemingly a level surface. The vast meadow-lands that we crossed, and which were filled with stock, have dwindled down to specks of light—oases of cultivation in a wilderness of wood—and the huge cotton-trees that flung their shelter over a hundred oxen can scarcely be distinguished even at our feet. Hills piled on hills, and thunder-clouds upon hills, are massed together on the right. On the left, over a mountain-top, there lies a line of sea in which the sun is about to make a golden set. The valley now is dark, its light has gone out, but the crests of the hills are all ablaze. Night comes on apace, and there are yet ten miles of bad road to travel before a village can be reached. The air, at this height, feels bleak after sunset, and a cloak is not to be despised.

The sun never rose upon a more picturesque village than that of Mandeville, the capital of the parish of Manchester. It reminded me a little of a newly located town in an American territory, for the houses did not look very old, nor were the streets out of repair—two exceptions to very general rules in Jamaica. Though a mile above the level of the sea, Mandeville lies in a hollow surrounded by hills. The air is fresh and the climate wholesome. This parish is the only one that entirely escaped the cholera.

There are no large sugar-estates in Manchester. Coffee, pimento, and provisions are raised in great abundance by the settlers; but pens and pasture-lands form the principal feature of cultivation. Immense herds of cattle may be seen grazing together, though stock-raising is not as profitable as a stranger might be led to suppose. Like most other pursuits in Jamaica, this one depends very much on the sugar-crop. If sugar-planting is abandoned, or if the planters are in reduced circumstances, there is a diminished demand for stock, and the breeders suffer in proportion. The fact is thus: though it is singularly illustrative of prevailing apathy that, possessed of a soil that can not be outrivaled for richness, and of a climate that favors the growth of temperate as well as tropical products, the Jamaica proprietary should submit to destitution because they have not the money, or the means, or the protection, or the labor, or whatever else it may be that is wanted to cultivate the cane. I have no patience to listen to their complaints, when I look at the unbounded wealth and wonderful resources of the country. They cry out at the high price of labor, and pretend they can not grow corn, when corn is grown at five times the cost in the United States and exported to Jamaica at a handsome profit. They import beef, and tongues, and butter, though this very parish of Manchester offers advantages for raising stock that no portion of America possesses. They import mackerel, and salmon, and herrings, and codfish, though Jamaica waters abound in the most splendid kind of fish. They import woods, though Jamaica forests are unrivaled for the variety and beauty and usefulness of their timber. They import tobacco, though their soil in many districts is most excellent for its growth. The negroes, who have never been taught these things, are learning them slowly by experience, and a gradual decline in certain articles of import demonstrates that they now raise on their own properties a very large proportion of their own provisions.

In a parish like Manchester, where there are no estates, the settlers grow provisions not merely for themselves, but for the supply of neighboring sugar-parishes, where the inhabitants are principally engaged in field labor. Thus Portland supplies St. Thomas-in-the-East; St. Anne supplies Trelawny, and Manchester supplies Clarendon and Vere. In Manchester, at the time I write, so far from there being any want of labor, there are a number of people in quest of labor and can not get it. This is, doubtless, to be accounted for by the fact that there are no sugar-estates in the parish; for it is the cultivation of the cane alone that demands that extraordinary force which the planters say they are unable to obtain. A Clarendon planter recently offered employment to five hundred Manchester negroes if they would change their residence; they refused to do so, and the refusal was published to the world as a complete justification of the planters' arguments and pretensions. Now I was in Manchester at the time, and I felt certain that the offer would be rejected, and for reasons that any one acquainted with the negro character would readily understand. The laborer has been so often the victim of promises, carelessly made and as carelessly broken, that he may be pardoned for declining to travel fifty or a hundred miles upon the vague assurance of a distressed proprietor that he will give regular work and remunerative wages. Were work and wages both guaranteed, I doubt whether the negro could thus be induced to leave his home. He has an invincible dislike to move his household gods. It seems an unaccountable prejudice; but, throughout the whole island, the people may be found clinging to the plots of ground upon which they were born and their fathers before them.

The road from Mandeville, in Manchester, descends into the parish of Clarendon. Neither this parish nor the one contiguous to it, St. Dorothy, need any special notice. Sugar-cultivation in both is scanty, for the soil is not very favorable for the growth of the cane. The sugar-lands in the former parish lie to the north of the Mocho mountains. In the latter, the smallest parish after Kingston and Port Royal, there are only one or two estates in cultivation. The population of Clarendon is 54, and of St. Dorothy 91 persons to the square mile, and the settlers grow provisions and minor articles for export. At the small village of Lime-Savannah, some distance from the sugar properties of Clarendon, the people are about building an independent church.

The parish of Vere, forming the most southern promontory of Jamaica, when seen from the hills of Clarendon, which it adjoins, presents a rich alluvial country—something like Barbados, which it nearly equals in size, but without the garden-like appearance of that exquisite island. Some of the best estates in Jamaica are situated here, and they occasionally suffer from severe drouth. If money, enterprise, and labor were forthcoming, it would not be an impossible, nor yet a very expensive undertaking, to turn some of the mountain streams into the parish, and save the vast sums that planters not unfrequently lose from dry weather. But there must be a great change in Jamaica before money, enterprise, and labor are readily found there. It is worthy of remark, as proved by this and other parishes, that only first-class estates, or, in other words, estates that have had means at command, are now in cultivation. Here, again, we find, as an explanation of prevalent distress, want of capital; for if it were solely want of labor, the large estates that required most labor would be the first to suffer. In a precarious business like sugar-cultivation, where the loss of an entire crop must now and then be expected, there is no salvation for the Jamaica planter who can command neither capital nor credit when an unfavorable season overtakes him. He was accustomed, in times past, as some are accustomed even to-day, to hope against hope, that a sudden rise in sugar, or some other lucky stroke of fortune, would free him from trouble, and his estate from an incumbrance three times its actual value. One in a hundred, perhaps, realized his dreams, and, warned by experience, either prudently withdrew, or curtailed his extravagance and altered his plans so as to meet the new order of things introduced with emancipation. The other ninety-nine met the fate that must inevitably overwhelm the desperate gambler, who, with a few shillings in his pocket, plays against the certain chances of a bank.

This want of capital—quite irrespective of a want of labor, which I admit to exist—has been a fruitful cause of the abandonment of sugar-cultivation. The most hasty tour through the island will convince any one that contract or permanent labor—wholly independent of the valuable but transient work of the negroes, who have their own properties to look after—is absolutely needed before the cultivation of the cane in Jamaica can be largely extended or real estate command its positive value. I do not believe that the absence of this contract labor explains the present great depression of Jamaican commerce. My belief is that the contract or permanent labor of coolies is needed, as a supplementary labor to that of the Creole, alike on the richest and the poorest estates. There is sufficient labor in Jamaica now for the bare wants of its reduced cultivation, if the planter had means enough to pay his laborers, fairly and punctually, the wages they earn. Those wages are not too high, for they are scarcely one fourth of what a day-laborer can command in America. This I state unhesitatingly. But, at the same time, I state with equal confidence that, in Jamaica, permanent labor, that is, daily labor throughout the year—that kind of labor which will enable the planter to improve his property and extend his cultivation—is wholly wanting, and it seems to me that, without it, neither capital nor confidence will ever fully return to the island. The point I make is this: Jamaica wants labor, but that want is not the preponderating cause of her decline. In this parish of Vere, large estates are now in flourishing cultivation; yet its entire population is only twenty-eight to the square mile, considerably less than that of any other parish in the island.

Returning from Vere, the road joins a turnpike highway near the village of Old Harbor, in the parish of St. Dorothy. From thence to Spanish-Town, through St. Catharines, it is luxurious traveling, after recent experience of Jamaica roads. A few sugar-estates are passed, but the main features of the cultivation are pasture and provision grounds.

My account of a tour through the interior of Jamaica is already sufficiently long, without adding a detailed description of the eastern parishes that I visited. There is, moreover, nothing essentially new to be told about them. With the exception of St. Thomas-in-the-East—one of the finest sugar-districts in the island—none of these parishes can boast of any thing like a general cultivation. Yet the eastern section of Jamaica (the county of Surrey) has probably more natural advantages than either of the other two counties, Middlesex and Cornwall. In the parishes of St. Mary, Metcalf, St. George, and Portland, on the north coast, a great many estates have been abandoned; some five or six have been lately resuscitated, and the settlers are in an independent and thriving condition. The physical aspect of these parishes is wild, and the roads in many places are impassable for vehicles. A fine road is now in course of construction from Kingston to Annotto Bay. In the vicinity of the latter place, and also in the vicinity of Port Maria and Port Antonio, some few estates are in cultivation, but the interior country is occupied exclusively by negro settlers. St. Thomas-in-the-East is such another parish as Westmoreland. St. David, on the south coast, is almost an unbroken wood-land, and Port Royal, the smallest parish in the island, is still celebrated for its extensive coffee properties. Such information concerning Jamaica as I have been able to obtain and to give, I have picked up, as it were, by the way-side. For my inferences and conclusions I have had to depend altogether upon my own observations. No reliable statistical returns can be procured in official quarters. The colony has passed through an agricultural crisis of the severest kind; the question most vitally affecting all interests is admitted to be the labor question—and yet no effort has been made to obtain authentic data as the proper basis for legislation. Legislators have legislated abundantly, but in the dark. They do not yet practically believe that the actual condition of Jamaica and the demonstrations of her past experience are the only safe axioms by which the problem that puzzles them can be solved, and the only safe beacons by which the colony can be guided to prosperity and life.

CHAPTER XXIII.

THE OLD PLANTOCRACY.

Kingston, Jamaica, 1860.

THE planters of Jamaica constitute no longer the overruling oligarchy, or "plantocracy," that they once actually were, and are still somewhat insolently designated in the bitterness of party spirit. Poverty may not have humbled their pride or changed their belief in the "divine right" of the white man to enslave the black; for, in their own homes and on their own estates, and in public whenever an opportunity offers, they wage, under different guises, the old war against free labor. But as a political body, with power to control the destinies of the island, they no longer live. One after another the relics of the system of coercion to which they clung are being swept away. Their complaints have been disregarded—their petitions have been rejected—until, in despair or disgust, they have almost altogether retired from the contest, and left the field open to their undisguised and uncompromising opponents.

The planters of Jamaica, it may be thought, have not had a full measure of justice meted out to them. They, especially, and far beyond all other West India planters, have had to bear the brunt of the anti-slavery attack. But this is not a little owing to the persistency of their own hostile attitude, to their misrepresentations, to the selfishness of their aims, and to the mistakes of their policy.

It is a curious and instructive study to track the decline of the old West Indian plantocracy; and though I have attempted such an invidious task in a former chapter on Barbados, I must, to make myself understood, attempt it again with special regard to the Jamaica proprietary. Throughout many changes, social and political, the same selfishness will be found at the root of all their schemes; the same disregard of truth in their public statements; the same opposition to popular freedom, progress, and enlightenment in their acts. It was on the ground of humanity that, in the commencement of the present century, they opposed the abolition of the slave-trade. They urged that there was an annual decrease of two and a half per cent. among the negroes, and that if the same quantity of labor should continue to be exacted as the number of slaves diminished, the loss would be greater every year, and would augment with accelerated rapidity. The unfriendliness of slavery to population was a strong argument in the mouths of slave-traders. If the slave-trade were abolished, the sugar-estates of Jamaica, it was prophesied, would be dismantled within thirty years, and the 130,000 negroes then engaged in the culture of the cane would be utterly extinct! The planters of the day, when they petitioned Parliament, based their grounds for redress on the expense of the slave system which prevented them from competing, without a constant supply of fresh labor, with those colonies and countries in which the African slave-trade had not been abolished.

Twenty-five years later, when Parliament, in obedience to the tremendous pressure of public opinion at home, formally declared its determination to abolish slavery in the West Indies, the planters essayed to demonstrate the cheapness of slave labor as compared with the free labor about to be introduced. Emancipation, they said, would ruin them, and preclude any competition with countries where slavery continued to exist. It is not surprising that the planter thus argued. He was the owner of the slaves who cultivated his property. It was a matter of doubt whether he would be compensated for them at all in the event of abolition. Under the old *régime* he was not compelled to make the weekly disbursements that the new order of things would demand; and he could still go on hoping that a rise in sugar would furnish him with means to liquidate his most pressing debts. He dreaded a change that would certainly expose his bankruptcy.

During all this time the prosperity of Jamaica was on the decline. The exportation of sugar had gradually decreased from 150,000 hhds. in 1805, to 85,000 hhds. in 1833. It was not emancipation or the thought of emancipation that dragged down the island suddenly from the pinnacle of its prosperity. The deterioration progressed slowly. Between the years 1814 and 1832 the coffee-crop was also reduced one half; and during the fifty years that preceded emancipation it is estimated that two hundred sugar-estates were abandoned. The planters say that the fear of impending abolition induced them to withdraw capital from their estates. But abolition was not dreamed of when the decline of Jamaica set in. While the slave-trade was yet in operation over one hundred properties had been deserted—deserted, too, for the same cause that compelled their desertion in later years—debt and want of capital.

Sugar-cultivation, it is hardly necessary to say, to be carried on with profit to the proprietor, and with ordinary chances of ultimate success, requires an enormous capital, not only at the outset, but to provide against the losses that unfavorable seasons very frequently entail. I can not do better than transfer here, from Mr. Edwards's History of the West Indies, a picture of Jamaica sugar-cultivation sixty years ago. Himself a planter, a slaveholder, and opposed to the abolition of the slave-trade, the author represents that the estates at that time were very much understocked with slaves, and speaks of a West India property "as a species of lottery," giving birth to a spirit of adventure, and awakening extravagant hopes, "too frequently terminating in perplexity and disappointment." Mr. Edwards proceeds to say:

"The total amount of the annual contingent charges of all kinds (on an estate yielding 200 hhds. of sugar) is £2150, which is precisely one half the gross returns, leaving the other moiety, or £2150, and no more, clear profit to the planter, being seven per cent. on his capital, without charging, however, a shilling for making good the decrease of the negroes, or for the wear and tear of the buildings, or making any allowance for dead capital, and supposing, too, that the proprietor resides on the spot; for, if he is absent, he is subject in Jamaica to an annual tax of £6 per cent. on the gross value of his sugar and rum for legal commissions to his agent. With these and other drawbacks, to say nothing of the devastations which are sometimes occasioned by fires and hurricanes, destroying in a few hours the labor of years, it is not wonderful that the profits should frequently dwindle to nothing; or, rather, that a sugar-estate, with all its boasted advantages, should sometimes prove a millstone about the neck of its unfortunate proprietor which is dragging him to destruction. * * * It were to be wished that people would inquire how many unhappy persons have been totally and irretrievably ruined by adventuring in the cultivation of these islands without possessing any adequate means to support them in such great undertakings. On the failure of some of these unfortunate men, vast estates have, indeed, been raised by persons who have had money at command; men there are, who, reflecting on the advantages to be derived from this circumstance, behold a sugar-planter struggling in distress with the same emotions as are felt by the Cornish peasants in contemplating a shipwreck on the coast, and hasten with equal rapaciousness to participate in the spoil. Like them, too, they sometimes hold out false lights to lead the unwary adventurer to destruction, more especially if he has any thing considerable of his own to set out with. Money is advanced and encouragement given to a certain point, but a skillful practitioner knows where to stop; he is aware that very large sums must be expended in the purchase of the freehold, and in the first operations of clearing and planting the lands and erecting the buildings, before any return can be made. One third of the money thus expended he has, perhaps, furnished; but the time soon arrives when a farther advance is requisite to give life and activity to the system by the addition of the negroes and the stock. Now then is the moment for oppression, aided by the letter of the law, to reap a golden harvest. If the property answers expectation and the land promise great returns, the sagacious creditor, instead of giving farther aid, or leaving his too confident debtor to make the best of his way by his own exertions, pleads a sudden and unexpected emergency, and insists on the immediate repayment of the sum already lent. The law on this occasion is far from being chargeable with delay—and avarice is inexorable. A sale is hurried on, and no bidders appear but the creditor himself. Ready money is required in payment, and every one sees that a farther sum will be wanted to make the estate productive. Few, therefore, have the means who have even the wish efficaciously to assist the devoted victim. Thus the creditor gets the estate at his own price, commonly for his first advance, while the miserable debtor has reason to thank his stars if, consoling himself with only the loss of his own original capital and his labor for a series of years, he escapes a prison for life. * * * At the same time it can not be denied that there are creditors, especially among the British merchants, of a different character from those that have been described, who, having advanced their money to resident planters on the fair ground of reciprocal benefit, have been compelled, much against their inclination, to become planters themselves; being obliged to receive unprofitable West India estates in payment, or lose their money altogether. I have known plantations transferred in this manner which are a burden instead of a benefit to the holder; and are kept up solely in the hope that favorable crops, and an advance in the prices of West Indian produce, may some time or other invite purchasers. Thus oppression in one class of creditors, and gross injustice toward another, contribute equally to keep up cultivation in a country where, if the risks and losses are great, the gains are commensurate. * * * In this, as in all other enterprises where success depends in any degree on human sagacity and prudence, though perhaps not more than one man in fifty comes away fortunate, every sanguine adventurer takes for granted that he shall be that one. Thus his system of life becomes a course of experiments; and if ruin should be the consequence of his rashness, he imputes his misfortune to any cause rather than to his own want of capacity or foresight."

This is a picture of Jamaica cultivation sixty years ago, when monopoly favored the proprietor, and sugar was sold for treble the price that it will now command. Nor is it so unlike the cultivation of the present day that it can not be recognized, for half a century has brought to the Jamaica planter but little knowledge of the labor-saving arts. The evils, however, which were then only taking root, have since overshadowed the island. Hypothecation, rendered necessary by the expenses of the slave system and the extravagance of the planters, increased so fast that nine out of ten estates at the time of emancipation were mortgaged far beyond their value. The creditors were English merchants, who vainly tried to keep up the cultivation of the property that reverted to them. How could they do so? Estates that yielded an average annual income of seven per cent., with the proprietor resident, could not, with the proprietor absent, pay attorneys and overseer, and still be worked at a profit. Many proprietors tried the impossible experiment and failed, while their agents and overseers made money, or ultimately bought in the estate at a nominal cost. Many proprietors have since tried the experiment, and have failed, and will continue to fail as long as they neglect the common teachings of experience. They will attribute their failure to any but the right cause. They shut their eyes to the fact that, in times past and in times present, the successful estates in Jamaica have always had, and have still, resident proprietors. Absenteeism, it is true, is less prevalent now than it was about the period of emancipation. But the seeds of the evil were sown years and years ago, and the fruit must be reaped. No country, since the world was made, were its resources tenfold greater than those of Jamaica, could continue to prosper with the large body of its landed proprietary permanent absentees. And even those who were nominally residents usually passed half the year in Europe, and spent their money there. England was always their home, and Jamaica merely a place out of which the most was to be made. I feel it almost a plagiarism to enumerate these causes of the decline of Jamaica, they have been so often explained by other writers—they are so perfectly obvious to any unprejudiced inquirer after truth. They were evils sufficiently serious to ruin the island had emancipation never taken place. They exhausted capital and destroyed credit, and without these it would be impossible for any country to flourish. Since emancipation this want of capital has been the chief cause of an unceasing depression. The sum received by the planter for his slaves was insufficient to pay off his mortgages; he had no money to improve his estate or even sustain a naked cultivation; he had no money to keep roads in repair or build tramways; he had no money to pay for labor; he had no money to meet misfortune. What was the inevitable consequence? His mortgages were foreclosed; he reduced his cultivation; he sold small lots to settlers to meet pressing wants; the roads were so bad that the transportation of sugar to the shipping-port became one of his heaviest items of expenditure; the laborers whom he neglected to pay went elsewhere; the day of misfortune came, and overwhelmed him with ruin. He was bankrupt before emancipation; but it was emancipation that tore down the veil which concealed his poverty. I speak generally, for I do not doubt that there were many exceptional cases. Many of the three hundred estates in cultivation at the present day are exceptions. There were planters who continued to cultivate sugar after emancipation—who were successful then, and are successful still—and since 1853, when the general abandonment of estates may be said to have ceased in Jamaica, the number of these successful planters has considerably increased. I need not pause to explain that they were all men of capital, and that their properties were economically managed, for both assertions are proved to demonstration by the fact that only first-class estates are in cultivation to-day.

But the old plantocracy steadily and fatally ignored, in early as in later times, the real causes of the island's decline. They shrunk from the idea of putting their own shoulders to the wheel. In the days of their prosperity they never faced labor; in the days of their adversity they did not face misfortune. If they thought freedom the worst system of labor in the world, their manhood should have taught them to make the most of what was done and could never again be undone. They would not give it a fair trial, but preferred to see their heritage pass away without a living struggle to redeem it. They have complained loudly enough, and have waited in the modest expectation that the government of England would wrong the people of England to relieve *them*. They expected a restoration of protective duties on sugar, and the imposition of a heavy tax on the British nation, in order that they, who gave nothing in return, might live in sumptuous and easy luxury. They have iterated and reiterated the false accusation that the negro will not work, in order to raise up a seeming justification for themselves, and they have done all they could to bring him again under a yoke of coercion. By these means they succeeded in keeping morbidly alive the anti-slavery spirit of the British people, and of fanning into flame a philanthropic zeal that, I do not hesitate to say, has proved injurious to the best interests of Jamaica. If, instead of trying to create sympathy for their class by the false assertion that the negro would neither work for love or money, they had simply urged a want of labor, there can not be a doubt that, like the Mauritius, Guiana, or Trinidad, Jamaica at this day would have an ample population.

I do not deny that the planters of Jamaica have had misfortunes to contend with. It was their misfortune that they inherited a system of labor that demanded extravagant expenditure. It was their misfortune that slavery so deeply degraded labor, that, even under freedom, the effect of such a curse could not speedily be removed. It was their misfortune that, within the century prior to emancipation, there were over thirty servile insurrections in the island, each one of which entailed a heavy expense upon the proprietary, and, in some cases, brought them to the verge of ruin. It was their misfortune that, with the rise and progress of the United States, Jamaica lost the prominent position she once occupied as a dépôt of trade between Europe and the Spanish Main, and that a large amount of commercial capital was in consequence withdrawn from the island. It was their misfortune that their expenses were aggravated by the mistaken policy of the imperial government, which placed restrictions and prohibitions on colonial intercourse with the American republic. It was their misfortune that they were never adequately paid for their slave property. It was their misfortune that they found themselves compelled to mortgage their estates—that their debts continued to increase—and that when an unfavorable season overtook them they lifted up their eyes in hopeless bankruptcy. It was their misfortune that among the island merchants they found too many like those whom, sixty years ago, Bryan Edwards likened to Cornish wreckers. It was their misfortune that, between 1815 and 1825, the price of their great staple fell twenty-five per cent.—that between 1825 and 1835 it fell another twenty-five per cent.—and that between 1835 and 1850 it fell twenty-five per cent. yet again. It was their misfortune that the British nation would no longer consent to be taxed to support them, and that the protective tariff upon West India sugars should have been abolished. It was their misfortune to have been distrusted at home and abroad, and to have been the victims of a jealousy that refused for years to Jamaica, alone of all the British West Indies, the privileges and the advantages of a wholesome immigration.

But it was their fault that, under the most expensive system of labor known, they were ever reckless and improvident. It was their fault that they prosecuted a precarious business in the spirit of reckless gamblers. It was their fault that they wasted their substance in riotous living. It was their fault that they obeyed not the commonest rules of political economy—that they saved no labor and spared no land. It was their fault that they faced not labor themselves, but were absentees from their estates, and followed a road that could lead to no possible end but ruin. It was their fault that they listened to no warning—that they heeded not the signs of the times—that they opposed all schemes for gradual emancipation, and even for ameliorating the condition of the slaves, until the crushing weight of public opinion broke the chain of slavery asunder, and threw suddenly upon their own resources an ignorant and undisciplined people. Theirs were the faults of policy and government that drove the Creoles from plantations, that kept the population in ignorance, that discouraged education, and left morality at the lowest ebb. It is their fault that, under a system of freedom from which there is no relapse, they have made no brave attempt to redeem past errors and retrieve past misfortunes, but have been content to bemoan their fate in passive complaint, and to saddle the negro with a ruin for which they themselves are only responsible.

This was the old plantocracy—the generous, hospitable, improvident, domineering plantocracy of Jamaica. Their power no longer predominates. They command no credit and no respect, and they obtain but little sympathy in their misfortune. Even from domestic legislation they have sullenly retired, and their places are being fast filled by the people whom they have so long and so vainly tried to keep down. I am not going to speak of the change in terms of extravagant admiration. The mass of the inhabitants are still too ignorant to exercise the franchise with discretion, and all are more or less imbued with the prejudices of caste. But imperfect and defective as it is, representative and responsible government in Jamaica is greatly preferable to the oligarchy of a planter's reign. The interests, moral, political, and educational, of the people, are more cared for, and on their progress, much more than on the success of large plantations, the permanent prosperity of the island most assuredly depends.

Nor are the new class of resident planters who have appeared in Jamaica within ten years past by any means to be ignored. They work their estates with prudence and economy, though they lack the advantages that latter-day science has given to American and Cuban proprietors. Capital and labor are both needed, but the art of economizing labor is needed still more. A Cuban planter makes twice the quantity of sugar from an acre of land that a Jamaica planter does. Nevertheless, it is a fact, of which I have had ample proof in all parts of the island, that many Jamaica planters who look after their own business have relieved their estates from incumbrance, and are, even now, making handsome fortunes. Since 1858 as many properties have been resuscitated as abandoned; and I regard it as one of the most favorable signs of improvement that the work of regeneration, however small its commencement, has been at least inaugurated by new men.

CHAPTER XXIV.

THE MIDDLE AND LABORING CLASSES.

Kingston, Jamaica, 1860.

If I were asked to describe, in as few words as possible, the effect of emancipation in Jamaica, I should say—the creation of a middle class. There was no middle class under slavery, and could be none. Master and servant made up the population. They were alike in this respect, that their thoughts were all of the present. Neither had any patriotism; neither had any interest in the moral, social, or political progress of the colony—the one because of his selfishness, the other because of his ignorance. The proprietary never even attempted to lay the foundations of a durable prosperity. On the contrary, they exhausted a substance that was deemed inexhaustible, so that they might accumulate wealth and escape the sooner from confinement in a tropical island, and from the limited resources of an unpolished society.

Emancipation struck at the very root of the existing system, and the revolution brought with it a large admixture of good and evil. But one most beneficial result stands out to-day so prominently, and in such bulky proportions, that the most prejudiced can not close their eyes to its presence. Emancipation has created a middle class—a class who are born in Jamaica, and who will die in Jamaica—a class of proprietors, tax-payers, and voters, whose property, patriotism, happiness, and comfort are bound up in the island's permanent prosperity.

It is but twenty-two years ago that the slaves of Jamaica were fully liberated. The apprenticeship was, in a moment of bitter excitement, cut short by the planters themselves, and 320,000 slaves—an undisciplined, degraded, half-savage crowd—were, without any preparation or training, left to their own devices. The free colored Creoles numbered 60,000, and the total black and colored population of the period consisted, therefore, of 380,000 souls. By the census of 1844, the last taken, the total black and colored population was only 361,657; and if the estimate of mortality by cholera and small-pox within a few years past be correct, I do not believe, after making every allowance for a proper increase by birth, that the black and colored population of Jamaica exceeds at the present day 350,000. It will be remarked, and possibly with surprise, that the population of Jamaica, between 1834 and 1844, must have annually decreased at the rate of nearly a half per cent. This decrease, it is true, is nothing like the decrease that went on prior to emancipation, but it is sufficiently serious to demonstrate the existence of some very aggravating causes of mortality among a people of temperate habits, and in a climate of unquestioned salubrity. In the absence of statistics on the subject, it is impossible to arrive at exact conclusions; indeed, official neglect in all matters statistical is so conspicuous that I am not disposed to place implicit faith in the returns of the census itself. But supposing a decline, undoubted as I believe it to be, fully established, I do not think it difficult to assign more than one reason. Within a quarter of a century some 15,000 whites have withdrawn from the island, and the increase of half-castes has been, in consequence, greatly checked. Another important cause of the decrease of population, particularly among the blacks, is the lack of medical practitioners in remote country districts. The mortality among children from want of proper attention is frightful. Nor, unfortunately, is this the only evil that deprives Jamaica of a legitimate increase in her population, and of the wealth that such an increase would of necessity bring. Many of the vices engendered by slavery remain a heavy burden and curse upon society, and, among them, immorality of the grossest kind pervades all classes, tainting alike the civilization of towns and the unchecked intercourse of laborers in the cane-fields. The natural growth of the population has been thus arrested, and some of the most detestable crimes known to society are, even now, of frequent occurrence.

Perhaps it is not fair to judge the people of Jamaica by a standard of European or American civilization. Their recent deliverance from a rule that frowned down morality and education, and the very few opportunities for improvement that have been since allowed them, would explain, if they did not palliate, deficiencies and shortcomings of a graver character, and much more widespread existence, than those which have so deeply injured the reputation of the West Indian Creole. But Jamaica, with all her faults of omission and commission, offers, I believe, the best examples that can be produced of the emancipated negro; her inhabitants are more independent and better off than the inhabitants of other islands, in which overcrowded labor or a less productive soil have kept the masses in the same position that they occupied as slaves. Here the masses have made a great step forward; and my object in the present chapter is to measure that step—to describe the present civil and social condition of the people, and compare it with their condition at the time of emancipation.

In a material sense we have the spectacle presented of a large body of ignorant, penniless predials, elevated, by their own exertions, to the rank of landed proprietors, tax-payers, and voters. Of the 320,000 slaves that were liberated, only the tradesmen and head people, numbering not more than 45,000, had ever picked up the merest waifs of knowledge. The others—field-laborers and domestics—were almost as savage and untutored as their fathers were when they were dragged from their homes on the African coast. The change they have undergone within twenty-two years is assuredly no sign of incapacity, no proof of indolence, no indication of unconquerable vice. At the lowest estimate that I have heard given, there are now, in the island of Jamaica, fifty thousand small proprietors, owning, on an average, three acres of land. The improvement in *their* condition of life even a champion of plantocracy would not ask me to point out. Yet these are the men whom, under a strange and fatal misunderstanding of their true interests, the planters would force back to field labor. The planters—I speak of them as they exhibited themselves to the world some few years ago—struck out no new path, nor devised, in a patriotic spirit, any comprehensive measure to meet and neutralize the deficiency of labor of which they complained; but they schemed to deprive the independent settlers of their means of livelihood, to destroy their market, and compel them to accept again the shilling a day and the slavery of plantation-work that the master condescendingly offered. It was fortunate for all parties that these schemes proved a total failure.

The latest Blue-book returns give the number of males and females engaged in agriculture at 187,000—more than one half of the population of the island—tending in itself to disprove the assertion that the people are averse to the tillage of the soil; but when the farther fact appears that out of this number 50,000 men, with their families, have elevated themselves to a proprietary rank, it speaks volumes, not merely in their own favor, but in favor of general intelligence and a wholesome progress. These small proprietors can not be said to live comfortably, in our sense of the word. Their huts are usually made of bamboo-sticks, thatched with cocoanut-leaves. Most of them prefer the floor to sleep upon, and few understand the enjoyment of a regular meal. They eat when they are hungry, and will sometimes take enough in the morning to last them the entire day. But I have always found them clean in their personal and domestic arrangements.

I have spoken, in former chapters, of dwellings very superior to these here mentioned. I am now attempting to describe the social condition of an average Jamaica peasant, owning one or two acres, though I think a majority are proprietors of five and six. They grow provisions for themselves and families, and for the village market; they raise for sale coffee, pimento, arrow-root, fruit, vegetables, and sometimes sugar-cane; they have their horses and stock, and are about as independent of labor for daily wages as it is possible for any peasantry to be. Yet there are many of them who give to the estates such labor as they can spare from their own properties. It is a transient labor, with which we can not expect the planter to be satisfied, for it is insufficient for his purposes; but it is a labor which reflects no discredit upon the people, and offers no justification for the complaints that have been maliciously made against them. Statistics of exports have been brought forward to exhibit the decline of Jamaica. Statistics of exports can also be adduced in proof of the rise and progress of a middle class. I note here some of the minor articles grown or collected now exclusively by small settlers, and institute a comparison between the exportation in 1859 and the exportation before emancipation had taken effect:

	Exports—1834.	Exports—1859.
Logwood, tons	8,432	14,006
Fustic, tons	2,126	2,329
Mahogany, feet	1,936	35,000
Succades, cwt	none.	279
Cocoanuts, number	none.	712,913
Ebony, tons	none.	28
Beeswax, cwt	none.	770
Honey, gallons	none.	6,954

Here we have the production of some minor staples by small settlers compared with the production of the same articles by large proprietors prior to emancipation, when attention was almost altogether turned to the cultivation of the cane. The exhibit speaks for itself. It is to be noticed that in 1855 there were 124,000 feet of mahogany exported, and that the Jamaica woods are being fast drained of this valuable timber. In the article of pimento it is also worthy of note that the exportation in 1858 exceeded by two million pounds any yearly exportation prior to emancipation. To show the progress made by the people of Jamaica under freedom, I institute again a comparison as follows:

	Exports—1841.	Exports—1858.
Arrow-root, lbs.	none.	72,023
Logwood, tons	9,550	12,558
Fustic, tons	394	1,638
Santa, or Shrub, gallons	none.	129
Beeswax, lbs.	none.	88,967
Honey, gallons	none.	8,108
Cocoanuts, number	none.	784,422

It is but fair to exhibit here the decreased exportation of principal staples under emancipation, viz.:

	1841.	1845.	1858.
Sugar, hhds.	34,000	47,926	33,031
Rum, puncheons.	11,769	16,997	18,193
Ginger, lbs.	1,834,120	1,888,480	709,620
Pimento, lbs.	3,595,380	7,181,220	9,465,261
Coffee, lbs.	6,433,370	5,021,209	5,237,689

I have selected the year 1841 for a comparison, as the general withdrawal of field laborers from estate-service had not then commenced. The sugar-crop of that season was unusually light; in 1842 it amounted to 50,000 hhds. But the diminution of later years proves nothing against the peasantry when it appears that the energy and industry employed during slavery, and since, to produce large crops of coffee and sugar are, under freedom, exerted, even in a greater degree, to purchase land and erect houses and villages, of which the number established in Jamaica within a quarter of a century is almost incredible. The immense quantity of provisions that the settlers grow for home consumption must also be taken into account; and it is partly demonstrated by the diminished importation of necessary articles of food, as illustrated in the following table:

	Imports—1841.	Imports—1858.
Flour, bbls.	127,820	94,038
Meal, bbls.	25,995	14,081
Bread, bbls.	16,000	none.
Bread, cwt.	2,202	3,024
Corn, bushels	83,718	20,704
Beef, bbls.	3,455	3,024
Pork, bbls.	21,185	12,012

There is, indeed, a vast difference between the living of the free peasantry of Jamaica and the living of her slaves. The people enjoy luxuries now where they had not common necessaries before. The coffee, vegetables, and meat that are now indispensable to them, they never so much as tasted before they were emancipated. A settler with an acre of land in cultivation estimates its value at £30 sterling a year. He grows upon it, at the same time, corn, yams, cocoas, plantains, bananas, tobacco, peas, ochro, coffee, and even sugar-cane. An acre or two like this will support a family of seven in clothes and provisions, and enable the proprietor to save money besides. I know settlers who have accumulated by this, and no other means, £80 and £100, and the sum is generally devoted to the erection of improved dwellings. Of course their work is not as well directed or as valuable now as it was before emancipation. They are poor farmers as yet. All their agricultural learning has come to them by instinct. Digging cane-holes was the early experience of most of them. They have not the remotest idea of economy in labor. Their implements are of the most primitive kind, and it is surprising to find how many of them manage to manufacture sugar. I know of settlers who produce, from four or five acres, some forty barrels of sugar, weighing two hundred and fifty pounds each. They obtain the juice from the cane by hand-work, and I can not describe their rude wooden implement better than by calling it a huge lemon-squeezer. Their preparation of coffee is less primitive. An ingenious mechanic of Kingston has invented a cheap coffee-cleaner, and he informed me that he sold numbers of them. His best customers, he said, were negroes, who always came cash in hand. But in all they grow they may be held to waste five times as much as they reap. They are not an ingenious people, but they are an intelligent people, and will imitate with the greatest alacrity. They see the planter's partiality for the cultivation of sugar, and they at once determine to have their little cane-piece also. Of a thousand things indigenous to Jamaica that might be raised with great profit and no expense, they are as ignorant as children. They never reason out the fact that their soil is probably the richest in the world, and that with five acres, and knowledge to assist them, they could produce as much as they do now with fifty acres and no knowledge. An acre of good Jamaica land can be made to yield thirty tons of grass, or five hogsheads of sugar. I have seen the experiment successfully tried. The soil, for general purposes, needs little attention, and four crops of provisions are gathered in the year. But the people have no opportunities to learn. No friendly settler from abroad has ever appeared among them to stimulate their exertions by showing them what science has accomplished in other lands. They know nothing of what passes beyond the limits of their island. They are utterly without training. A spirit of emulation has never been generated among them. They have no cause for rivalry, and nothing to call out their ambition. They may thank the planters for adopting a system of persecution which literally drove them into their present independent position. Their singular adhesion to the estates upon which they were born rendered it very improbable that any but the most enlightened would have ever voluntarily forsaken them for an uncertain venture. They went into the mountains, built their own huts, and cleared their own lands, and, from that time to this, they have worked steadily up to their light. It is not their fault that that light is weak, for they only conquered their independence and all the knowledge they have acquired in the face of determined opposition, and in defiance of hostile legislation. Let me not be mistaken. I am not setting up the West Indian Creole as an object for hero-worship. I do not place him on an equality with the American or the Englishman. His courage to face labor, his perseverence under difficulty, and his power to overcome obstacles are but hesitating, halting steps when compared with the Anglo-Saxon's rapid and determined strides. I do not say, because I do not know, how far judicious training will remedy the negro's defects of character and judgment. I simply vindicate his actions as those of a reasonable and intelligent being, fully capable of comprehending his own interests, of managing his own business, and of appreciating the blessings of freedom. I think that the position of the Jamaica peasant in 1860 is a standing rebuke to those who, wittingly or unwittingly, encourage the vulgar lie that the African can not possibly be elevated. The American writer who could be found to say that "any attempt to improve his condition was warring against an immutable law of Nature," should visit this island and study more closely the object of his sage conclusion. I think the Creoles of Jamaica have disproved, by their own acts, the calumny of a hostile interest, that they do not work. The most ignorant work whenever they can get work. There are fully twenty thousand, of both sexes, who work for the estates, and who may still be regarded as a laboring class. There are probably ten thousand who work as domestics. There are three thousand at work now upon the roads, where scarcity and idleness of laborers are made no grounds of complaint. The small proprietors work on their own lands and on the estates also whenever they can. Very large numbers work as merchants, mechanics, and tradesmen, and not a few of the ex-slaves of Jamaica, or their children, are members of the Legislature, and fill responsible offices under government. In the Assembly alone there are seventeen black and colored members out of a total of forty-seven. The whole people of Jamaica work; and if their work is often misdirected and wasteful, the blame does not surely rest with the unlettered classes. They work, as I said before, up to the light they possess, and when I look at the feebleness of that light, I am utterly amazed at the progress they have made.

It would be false to deny that the most deplorable ignorance prevails throughout the lower orders of society, and especially among the field laborers. How could it be otherwise when the planter's policy has been to keep the people uninstructed, and the government has never even encouraged education, much less insisted upon it as one of the most important of reciprocal duties between a free state and its citizens. No general system of public instruction has been introduced in Jamaica, and it is surely unreasonable to expect that this people, or any other people, could acquire a knowledge that has never been placed within their reach. It is estimated that there are 65,000 children in Jamaica between the ages of five and fifteen, and for their education the Legislature voted last year the sum of £2950—less than a shilling for the instruction of each child during a space of twelve months. About 7000 scholars were benefited by this grant, the schools in connection with the Church of England getting two thirds, and the Dissenters one third, although five persons go to "chapel" where one goes to "church." The total number of scholars receiving instruction at the present time is barely 20,000; and of these 13,000 are educated by different charities, missions, and private subscriptions. It is deemed discourteous "to look a gift horse in the mouth," and the Creoles of Jamaica, I suppose, must he thankful for the crumbs of learning they are allowed to pick up. The Presbyterian, Wesleyan, Moravian, Baptist, Independent, and, though last, not least, the American

Missions, are all doing good in their way. Within four years past the number of scholars attending their schools has considerably increased, while within one year past the number of scholars attending the schools supported by government has decreased nearly thirty per cent. But all these schools are of a sectarian character. If they do good they also do harm, by encouraging a sectarian prejudice, most injurious, in my judgment, to the best interests of the negro population. At the present moment there are populous districts in the island without any schools at all, and others where the schools already in existence are in debt, unable to pay for teachers, and will be compelled to close unless they receive some timely assistance. If this neglect to instruct the rising generation is so glaring to-day, when civilization every where admits the principle that a free government can only rest on the basis of popular intelligence, how much greater was the neglect ten or twenty years ago, when the education of the masses in Jamaica was deemed unnecessary and impolitic? The natural intelligence of the negro is not disputed, at least in this island; why not, then, improve it? The desire of the people to learn can not be denied, with the fact in view that 200,000 out of a population of 350,000 attend the different places of worship every Sabbath day. It is only at the point where the moral responsibility of the untutored negro ceases and the duty of the government begins, that we find a deplorable lack of common prudence and common sense. The old plantocracy, with wretched foresight, opposed the training and education of a people upon whose training and education their own prosperity depended, and the governing classes of to-day seem inclined to follow their example. If they do, they can only reap the same bitter disappointment. When government fails, as it fails in Jamaica, to care for human life, and to see with unaccountable apathy the country destitute of medical aid, it is not surprising that the population should exhibit an annual decrease. When government fails, as it fails in Jamaica, to give any consideration to popular education, it is not surprising that vice and immorality should alarmingly prevail. Under a rule of such pernicious neglect, it is not surprising that the governor, in proroguing the legislative session of 1858, should say that "in many of the county districts the people are abandoned to the spells and debasing superstitions of the working Obeah and Myalism, and to the scarcely less injurious practices of other ignorant empirics of the lowest grade." I am only surprised that the great middle class of Jamaica —the small landed proprietors, the mechanics and tradesmen of the island—should have been able, in the face of so many obstacles and such mountains of opposition, to compass the difficulties that surrounded them, and emerge from a darkness that still envelops many of their less fortunate and weaker brethren.

If I have presented a faithful picture of the civil and social condition of the Jamaica Creoles, the reader will infer that education in the island is too partial, and general intelligence too limited, for the establishment of a purely democratic government. Universal suffrage must fail where the mass of the people are unenlightened. It seems to me that the very best form of government for Jamaica is the one on the British model that she now enjoys. Every voter has a stake in the country. His intelligence and industry are to a certain extent guaranteed by the required property qualification. The election law now in force, and passed in 1858, is a decided improvement on previous enactments of a similar nature. Under its provisions a voter must possess a freehold of a clear rental of £6 sterling a year, or he must pay £20 rent, or have an annual income derivable from business of £50, or, finally, he must pay taxes to the extent of £2 per annum. There are probably 50,000 freeholders in Jamaica with a clear income of £6 a year, but the number of actual voters does not exceed 3000. A tax of ten shillings *per capita* for registration explains the discrepancy. The negro does not care so much about voting as to be willing to pay government ten shillings for the privilege. The principle of taxing a vote may not be considered orthodox; but it is the only tax to which the country people are liable, and I am satisfied that the plan will work better in Jamaica than one which would throw open the polls, without discrimination, to the entire population.

Of past Legislatures I need scarcely speak, after having exhibited some of the duties they have failed to perform. But it must not be supposed that Jamaica legislation is perfect now, because it is no longer the exclusive prerogative of the plantocracy. It is, in fact, most wretchedly imperfect. Planters, too, of the right sort, are much needed in both houses. The island depends—no one can doubt the fact—upon the extension of sugar-cultivation for a revival of prosperity. The sugar interest must always be a predominating interest. The error, in times past, was believing it to be an exclusive interest. But the men who represent it must utterly forsake the policy of their predecessors, and leave the track in which they fancied they might forever travel. The work of developing the resources of Jamaica has yet to be performed, but it will never be performed by non-resident planters. It must be done by men who can consent to make the island their home; and if it is not done by whites, it will be done by blacks. But the governing classes have to learn, above all things, that the extension of knowledge is the truest political economy, and that one intelligent free man will contribute more toward the prosperity of a country than a dozen ignorant serfs.

The government of Jamaica is possibly better than the pure oligarchy of Barbados; but the latter island has advantages in a dense population that the former does not possess. In Barbados the plantocracy are still able to rule as they please; in Jamaica they have been borne down by an independent middle class, who would not be denied their rights or defrauded of their privileges. In Barbados the prejudices of caste are bitter in the extreme; in Jamaica they exist in a modified form. But they must be swept away entirely if the colony is ever to attain a position of enlightened prosperity, and a "brown party," a "black party," or a "white party" must be discarded from the political index.

CHAPTER XXV.

FREE AND SLAVE LABOR IN JAMAICA.

Kingston, Jamaica, 1860.

THE superior economy of free labor, as compared with slave labor, can be demonstrated even from the imperfections and shortcomings of Jamaica. The planter, who complains the loudest against the parent government for admitting slave-grown sugars on a par with free-grown sugars, does not deny that free labor is the cheaper of the two. He attributes his misfortunes to the abolition of one system without a corresponding introduction of the other. He offers to compete with slave labor provided he can command a sufficient supply of free labor. While I believe, and have already endeavored to show, that an undoubted scarcity of labor was aggravated by the course the planters themselves pursued, and is not to be attributed, as some pretend, to Creole indolence; while the planters of Jamaica, as a class, have been opposed to improvement, and, in their obstinate determination, even at this day, to follow the old routine, find themselves, as manufacturers or agriculturists, behind the age, and from this cause alone unable to compete with the planters of Cuba and Porto Rico; while it is certain that the scanty laboring force of the island is not economized, and the enemies of immigration have found in the fact a powerful argument of opposition, it is at the same time true that free labor in Jamaica was never allowed a fair start. With its present force of 20,000 uncertain laborers engaged in sugar-cultivation, and utterly destitute of capital, Jamaica can not be considered the rival of Cuba, nor ought any conclusion unfavorable to free labor be deduced from the depression of the one and the high prosperity of the other. It is not a competition between slave and free labor, but, practically, between slave labor and no labor at all. And herein we find a state of things for which the imperial government is, in a measure, responsible. It was not that they committed the dazzling mistake of a too sudden emancipation; it was not that they withdrew protection from the infant system, and left it unaided to fight out the battle, but that they cut off the re-enforcements which, in a sparsely-settled country, free labor imperatively and constantly demands; they refused supplies of labor, more needed in Jamaica than in northern colonies, and without which even the most enduring energy would have been compelled to halt in the race for empire. It is folly to dream over the mistakes of British emancipation if we fail to read in them a practical lesson; and such a lesson as will benefit Jamaica at the eleventh hour is yet to be learnt. By the light of experience we are able now to see that if a free immigration had been poured into the island *before* abolition—if free labor had been introduced to fight slave labor on its own ground—slave labor must have been defeated in the contest; and no violent revolution would have marked its extinction. If free immigration had been poured into Jamaica *after* abolition, there can not be a reasonable doubt that the island would have been redeemed from bankruptcy, and from other burdens laid upon it by a slave system and the peculiar aristocracy that it fostered. Other colonies have thus regained their lost position. Other colonies establish beyond a peradventure the superior economy of free labor, and even Jamaica, exceptional Jamaica, with its ruined proprietary and scanty population—desolate, deserted, degraded Jamaica, points feebly to the same result.

Before I produce figures on the labor question of Jamaica, I will admit that they are to be obtained with difficulty, and must be received with caution. Statistics of all kinds are imperfect, and there is not an agricultural return to be found among the proceedings of the Assembly for twenty-five years back. This neglect is the more deplorable, as information from every estate in the island is required for a solid and reliable basis of legislation. Plantation management in Jamaica is a confusion of contradictions. The books of a south-side sugar-estate would give no adequate idea of the cost of manufacture on a north-side estate, and neither would be applicable to an estate in the interior. I myself know of cases where the expense of producing a hogshead of sugar has been £4, and of others where the expense has been double and treble that amount. So, too, I know of cases where the planter has been in distress for labor, and of cases where the laborer has been in distress for work. Most positive assertions of a most opposite character and tendency are violently made by persons who ought to know the truth, if they could divest themselves of prejudice; and it is not, therefore, surprising to hear so many contradictory opinions on the labor question expressed abroad, when so many contradictory opinions are entertained within the island itself. While I am tempted to make an estimate of the cost of sugar-production in Jamaica, I am, at the same time, free to admit that estates in districts where labor is scarce will think my average below, while others, well stocked with labor, will deem it above the mark. I can only say to this that my sole object has been to arrive at the truth—that my information has been obtained from intelligent sources—and that whenever I am proved wrong I shall be most willing to acknowledge the error.

Every planter in Jamaica knows from his own books, if they go back far enough, that free labor is cheaper than slave labor. He knows that the cultivation of an acre of cane does not now cost him $40, when in other times it cost him $80. He knows that, under slavery, the cost of digging an acre of cane-holes was from $35 to $45, while, under freedom, it is from $8 to $15. He knows that under one system 30 per cent. of his laboring force were non-effectives, and had to be fed and clothed like the rest, while under freedom no work is paid for that is not actually performed. He knows that a free laborer is not bought with a sum that can be otherwise laid out at profitable interest—that ten and even fifteen per cent. are allowances no longer to be made for death and depreciation. These are facts readily admitted; any one who takes the trouble to think about them will see their force; but it is not so readily admitted that Jamaica planters, in spite of the great scarcity of labor, have it in their power to produce sugar at a cheaper cost than it is produced in Cuba and Porto Rico, and much cheaper than it was produced by their predecessors before they quietly accepted the destiny of ruin which they considered impossible to avert, and the merest folly to fight against.

The average exportation of sugar from the island of Jamaica during the past few years has been about fifty millions of pounds, and of rum about eighteen thousand puncheons. I estimate the laboring force on the estates at twenty thousand—about equal to the number of acres in cane-cultivation. This would give some sixty or seventy laborers to each estate. I have received this estimate from many reliable sources, and believe it to be as near the truth as it is possible to get in the absence of precise returns. But it must not be imagined that these are steady laborers, working on the same estates from year's end to year's end. Many of them are perpetually on the move, others only work on estates for a month or two out of the twelve; some offer their services when they are least wanted; some have provision-grounds of their own, which require their attention when the estates are most hardly pressed for labor; nearly all, if they chose, might be independent of the planter for their daily bread. Jamaica labor is essentially of this transient and uncertain character. It is not the negro's fault; very few estates can afford to keep up a large and constant agricultural force—*that* was one of the necessary extravagances of slavery—and when the crop-season comes, and a simultaneous rush is made upon the labor market, it is found altogether inadequate to the demand. The negro, who has his own acre to look after, is bitterly denounced by the planter when he is independent enough to decline the high wages which, during the few weeks of crop-time, the latter would doubtless be willing to pay. But, in my judgment, the very fact that large numbers of the agricultural population are able to refuse the work and wages that, at certain seasons, the planters offer, is to their credit rather than to their shame. When, therefore, I estimate the actual laboring force at twenty thousand, I mean that this is the number usually employed on the sugar-estates throughout the year. There are possibly forty thousand laborers in all who give transient work to the estates, but at one and the same time the number actually at work, or the number that can be commanded, does not average more than twenty thousand. These twenty thousand laborers, taking them *en masse*, do not work for estates more than one hundred and seventy days in the year, sometimes three and sometimes four days in the week. They devote the balance of their time to their provision-grounds, and go to market on Saturdays. When, therefore, it appears, from these data, that each laborer annually produces 2500 pounds of sugar, and very nearly a puncheon of rum, it must be borne in mind that he produces besides, from his own grounds, a sufficient quantity of provisions to supply the wants of himself and family, and very often a considerable surplus to sell at market.

I take a high average when I place the price of estate labor at thirty cents a day. A good workman can earn fifty cents by digging cane-holes, and occasionally by job-work he may earn a dollar; but these are exceptional cases. No planter will pretend that an ordinary field laborer can earn fifty or even forty cents on his estate all the year round. I know that the highest price paid for labor on the roads, or in the

M

mines, is thirty-six cents, and a large majority receive only twenty-four cents. In nearly all the cases that fell under my own immediate observation, the price of field labor was twenty-four cents, and I know of cases where labor could only command eighteen cents. At thirty cents, then, per day, the laborer who produces 2500 lbs. would receive $50 for a year of 170 working-days—or, to be more exact, for a year of 167 working-days—which establishes the average cost of agricultural labor in Jamaica sugar-production at *two* cents per pound.

We can arrive at this conclusion by another process of calculation, and from a basis that may be considered more reliable than that of rough estimates. The Vere Agricultural Society in 1845 offered and awarded prizes for the largest quantity of sugar made on any estate in the parish at the least proportionate expense for labor in cultivation and manufacture. Its report is, I believe, the only official exposition of the kind that has appeared since emancipation. I need scarcely add that what could be done in 1845 could be done now, and is undoubtedly done on many first-class properties. The first prize was awarded to "New Yarmouth Estate." From the return of the overseer, it appeared that the total expense of manufacturing 168 hhds. of sugar and 62 puncheons of rum was £1038 18*s.* 7½*d.* Deducting 10*s.* per puncheon as the estimated cost of manufacturing the rum, there remains £1007 18*s.* 7½*d.* ($4838 07) as the cost of 168 hhds. of sugar, equal to $28 80 per hogshead of 16 cwt., or 1⅗ cents as the cost of production per pound, labor and manufacture included. The second prize was awarded by the same agricultural society to the estate of "Caswell Hill," which manufactured 202 hhds. of sugar and 105 puncheons of rum for £1401 4*s.* 7½*d.* Deducting as before £52 10*s.*, the cost of rum manufacture, there remains £1348 14*s.* 7½*d.* ($6473 91) as the total cost, labor and manufacture included, of 202 hhds., equal to $32 05 per hogshead, omitting fractions, or $1\frac{4}{5}$ cents per pound. Only three estates competed for the prize. The expenses of the third—"Amity Hall"—far exceeded those of the other two. It manufactured 131 hhds. and 35 puncheons for £1317 17*s.* 9*d.* The total cost of labor and manufacture on the sugar was £1300 7*s.* 9*d.* ($6241 86), equal to $47 64 per hogshead, or $2\frac{66}{100}$ cents per pound. It must be remembered that these are not estimates, but attested statements of moneys actually expended, not merely for agricultural labor, but for manufacturing purposes also. My estimate of 2 cents per pound for labor *alone* is based on the assertion of planters themselves that they pay their laborers on an average 30 cents a day, that the total labor force of the island is 20,000, and that the men work about 170 days in the year. Taking an average of the three estates named, it will be found that the cost of labor and manufacture *combined* is less by a fraction than my estimate of the cost of labor *alone*, and one of two corrollaries (both equally creditable to the laborer) may be deduced: 1. That the proprietors of these estates paid less than thirty cents a day for work admitted to have been most satisfactorily performed; or, 2. If they paid thirty cents a day, the number of laborers in their employ must have been below the average, and the production of sugar per man, as a necessary consequence, exceedingly above the average. The production of sugar on the estates mentioned proves that the laborer worked very fairly for very low wages, or worked unusually hard for the average hire of thirty cents a day.

Perhaps the illustrations given will be deemed exceptional cases, though I may mention that the committee in their report "regretted exceedingly that there were only three competitors, which obliged them to award a prize to Amity Hall, the expenses of which were considerably higher than those of the other two." But I have before me the estimates of several practical planters, all of whom agree in placing the average cost of purely agricultural labor at £8 for an acre yielding a hogshead and a half of sugar; that is to say, $38 40 for 2688 lbs., or $1\frac{42}{100}$ cents per lb. Taking, for argument's sake, $1\frac{1}{2}$ cents as an average of the cost of labor on the Jamaica sugar-estates, it would give an annual payment for labor of $750,000; or, estimating the force at 20,000 laborers, it would place the average earnings of each man, during a year of 170 working-days, at $37 10, or about 22 cents per diem. The man thus paid would, according to these figures, produce annually 2500 lbs. of sugar, besides a puncheon of rum and provisions for the maintenance of himself and family—a positive exhibition of industry that disproves all vague assertions of general idleness. It does not strengthen the planting argument to say that the proprietor pays more than $37 a year for wages. I am prepared to admit that he does. But when he does—and if his own estimate for labor of £8 per acre be correct—the production of each laborer is proportionately increased, and my assertion of his industry fully borne out. In any case it will be admitted that my estimate of two cents per lb. as the average cost of labor in Jamaica sugar-production is above rather than below the mark.

Let us now go back to sugar-cultivation in the days of slavery and institute a comparison. The total annual production for ten years preceding emancipation averaged 160,000,000 lbs., and the laboring force engaged in the business was, during the same period, variously estimated at 70,000, 80,000, and 90,000. I will take the lowest figure. The slave certainly cost his master $100 a year. The interest on his value, his food and clothing imported from America and Europe, his medical attendance, the depreciation of his value, and his total extinction by death, were, with the exception of the first, all items of heavier expense than are now paid for the Louisiana slave, whose cost is estimated at $125 a year. Old planters, who have lived in this island under both systems, have told me that their slaves cost them £15 sterling a year, exclusive of interest on their value and of a loss by death which averaged $2\frac{1}{2}$ per cent. per annum. It is, therefore, demonstrable from these data that, under the old system, the Jamaica slave produced within a fraction of 2286 lbs. of sugar, and that the cost of labor alone was $4\frac{37}{100}$ cents per pound. The planters of those days, as any authority will show, expected to make a hogshead of 15 cwt. for each slave in their possession. This was looked upon as a very fair remuneration, and the result of good management. Yet under such a return, the proprietor paid within a fraction of six cents per pound for his labor, or twenty per cent. more than my estimate.

It follows, if my figures are correct, that the cost of

labor in sugar-cultivation was in Jamaica, under slavery, $4\frac{37}{100}$ cents per pound, and is now, under freedom, two cents per pound—that the slave, under compulsory work, produced annually 2286 lbs., while the free laborer, working only six or seven hours a day, and only 170 days out of the year, produces 2500 lbs.

Governor Hincks, in a recent publication, has instituted a comparison between slave labor in Cuba and free labor in Barbados; and in support of the general argument that the latter is the cheaper of the two, I introduce here his excellency's conclusions. The governor's Cuban figures are those of 1852, but they are as applicable now as then, though the crop and the labor force, under the influence of the slave-trade, have increased one hundred per cent. within the last eight years. In 1852 there were 120,000 slaves on the Cuban sugar plantations, and the total quantity of sugar produced was 22,690,460 arrobas of $25\frac{7}{16}$ lbs. each, or an average to each slave of 4810 lbs. Estimating the annual cost of each slave at $144 30—an under estimate for a Cuban slave—the cost of production per pound is ascertained to be three cents. This is the general average, though a particular average on choice estates is a fraction lower. Governor Hincks takes seventeen of the most important estates in the island, and shows that the prices paid by them for labor is $2\frac{3}{10}$ cents per pound of sugar produced. I am able, from figures in my possession, to corroborate this estimate. I have before me the expenses of an economically managed sugar-estate, embracing $55\frac{1}{2}$ caballarias of land, producing 1,700,000 lbs. of sugar, and stocked with 350 slaves. The maintenance, clothing, and medical attendance of the slaves are put down at $20,000. The interest on their capital ($800 apiece, or $280,000,) is $28,000, making a total annual cost of $48,000, or $137 14 per head. Each slave produces 4857 pounds, and the cost of labor is, therefore, $2\frac{82}{100}$ cents per pound. But this is an exceptional case; the general average, as I said before, is three cents, and even that is fifteen per cent. lower than the estimate of Cuban planters themselves.

In the island of Barbados, 68,000,000 lbs. of sugar, and sometimes much more, are produced by 22,000 laborers. They work about 200 days in the year, and the daily rate of wages is from 20 to 25 cents. Taking 22 cents as the average, a laborer is paid $44 a year, and produces 3090 lbs. The cost of labor in Barbados is, therefore, $1\frac{2}{5}$ cents on each pound of sugar manufactured.

The island of Trinidad yielded, in 1858, a sugar-crop of 65,000,000 lbs., with an agricultural force of 17,000 laborers. This gave 3823 lbs. to each laborer, who worked 220 days for $66, or at the rate of 30 cents a day. The cost of labor in Trinidad was in that year $1\frac{72}{100}$ cents per lb. It must have been considerably less in 1859, when the sugar-crop exceeded 70,000,000 lbs.

The cost, then, of labor required for the cultivation of the cane in some of the principal West India islands is as follows:

Islands.	Pounds of Sugar produced.	Labor Force.	Av. of lbs. per Laborer.	Cost of each Laborer pr. Annum.	Cost of Labor per lb.
Cuba.............	577,200,000	120,000	4810	$144 30	3 cts.
Jamaica (slave)	160,000,000	70,000	2286	100 00	$4\frac{37}{100}$ cts.
Jamaica (free).	50,000,000	20,000	2500	50 00	2 cts.
Trinidad........	65,000,000	17,000	3823	66 00	$1\frac{72}{100}$ cts.
Barbados........	68,000,000	22,000	3090	44 00	$1\frac{2}{5}$ cts.

From this table the first and most important result appears that the cost of labor in the free countries is much below the cost of labor in the slave countries. The slave in Cuba produces more pounds of sugar than the free laborer, because one works on the plantation four or five hours longer per day, and at least two days longer in the week, than the other. The comparatively small quantity produced by the Jamaica slave may be attributed to the fact that he only worked five days in the week, being allowed to cultivate his own plot on the Saturday, and also to the great waste of labor that marked the reign of slavery and marks still the reign of freedom in the island.

It farther appears, from the same figures, that the cost of labor is lower in Barbados than in the other free colonies, and the reason undoubtedly is that the Barbados labor market is plentifully supplied. Barbados offers the most perfect example of free labor, and of the capacity and willingness of the African to work under a free system. It is not fair to cite Jamaica as an illustration of the failure of free labor while the laboring class is so exceedingly small, and so utterly unable to meet the necessities of an extended cultivation. But its depreciation, in point of fact, is not a sequence of emancipation but of slavery. The doctrine of emancipation, that free labor is cheaper than slave labor, is proved to demonstration; but where the free-labor force is insufficient for the cultivation of the soil, as in Jamaica, there can be no competition with a slave labor, as in Cuba, that is being constantly re-enforced. It is important to know how that insufficiency originated; for if it arose, as the planters pretend, from the positive refusal of the negro to work under a free system, it is mere child's play to show on paper that free labor is cheaper than slave. Now Barbados is a living proof that the negro does work under a free system; and if Barbados were an exceptional case in that bare fact (which it emphatically is not), it would have been the simple duty of the governing classes in other colonies to imitate as closely as possible the successful example of the sister island; and by increasing their population —if want of population were the sole defect—relieve an agricultural distress from which they themselves were exclusive sufferers. I do maintain, without any hesitation, that the Creole of Jamaica works as diligently as the Creole of Barbados; but with this difference—that the former works for himself, while the latter works entirely for a master — that the work of the one is more profitable because it is well directed and economized, while the work of the other is less profitable because it is ill directed and wasted. It was to demonstrate these truths, and not with any desire to rake up old grievances against the planting interest that, in former chapters, I endeavored to explain the causes that have so greatly reduced the laboring force on Jamaica plantations under a *régime* of freedom. That force, at no period in the island's history, was equal to the demand; and when, after emancipation, the planters, under a heavy pressure of debt and misfortune, attempted to coerce their liberated slaves to work for them on illiberal terms, it is not surprising that a large proportion of the laborers abandoned the estates and entered upon the new path of industry and independence that freedom had opened to them. If they had acted differently they might have been justly condemned as men unable to appreciate the blessings of liberty and averse to moral and social improvement; for their progress in this respect—their superiority over the small remnant of laborers who still constitute a permanent force on the estates is so marked, that even the most prejudiced can not fail to recognize it.

The obstinate determination of the planters to pursue the old system of management—to regard their laborers as serfs in whom every spark of ambition should be quenched—has been attended, I am convinced, by the worst consequences. The aid of settlers is still steadily refused for the cultivation of the cane, except it be given in the particular way, and at the particular time that the planters ask for it. If the settler is looking after his yams and plantains during the week or month that the planter requires his services, if he is selling his produce at the time, or enjoying his Christmas holiday, or in any other way making practical use of his purchased independence, he is denounced as an idle, worthless vagabond. Mention the Metairie system to a Jamaica planter, and he will think you a fool, or intimate, perhaps, that you mean to insult him. He refuses to co-operate in any way with a people who will admit no more his patriarchal authority, and will recognize no longer his right to command their services whenever he pleases, and at any disadvantage to themselves. But, more than this, the labor that he can even now obtain, the Jamaica planter neither economizes nor takes any trouble whatever to retain. He himself aggravates and increases the scarcity of which he so bitterly complains. He practically ignores all the mechanical and agricultural improvements of the century. Except in the one particular of steam, introduced at the last hour, his mode of cultivating and manufacturing sugar is the same now as it was in the year 1800. He rides his worn-out hobbies in spite of the demonstration of scientific men that, from the present amount of land in cane-cultivation, with slight additional labor or expense, one hundred thousand instead of thirty thousand hogsheads might be annually produced. No one who understands American character will entertain a doubt that, if this island had been American, emancipation would never, for a day, have checked its progress, and that now, depreciated and dead as it is, there wants but the touch of enterprise to kindle it into burning life. No one who thoroughly understands the present condition of Jamaica can entertain a doubt that if her planters had as signal advantages over those of Cuba and Porto Rico in the supply as they have in the cheapness of their labor, they would still be unable to compete with rivals so far ahead of them in all that pertains to economic science.

If obstructions so serious impede the progress of the resident proprietary of Jamaica, how much more serious are the obstructions in the way of non-residents, who, besides other drawbacks, pay annually for oversight about $20 on each hogshead of sugar produced! This alone is sufficient to swallow up their profits. The ultimate fate of any property in the world cultivated and managed in perpetuity, under such an expensive agency, or under agency at all, is so certain, that it is an insult to the understanding of an intelligent reader to point it out. As soon as Jamaica cane-cultivation was left to stand or fall on its own merits by the equalization of British duties on foreign and colonial sugars, it was most natural that nine tenths of the estates owned by absentee proprietors should have been abandoned. This absenteeism has cursed, more than aught else, the island and its industry. This, the most prominent among a host of evils, led to the abandonment of so many estates, and to the wide-spread ruin that ensued. I do not, however, say that, because the proprietors ruined their own interest, the interest itself should be allowed to die. One of the means prescribed for its recovery is immigration; and though it is not to be expected that immigration, unaided, will accomplish every thing, we know from the experience of other colonies that it can accomplish a very great deal. With the examples of Trinidad, Guiana, and the Mauritius understood and appreciated, the benefits to be derived from a well-regulated scheme of immigration will be conceded by those who take an unprejudiced view of Jamaica's actual condition, and who earnestly desire to see a reign, not of particular, but of general prosperity inaugurated. At the same time it will be admitted that many deficiencies besides a deficiency of labor must be supplied before Jamaica can affect to rival her wealthy neighbor; that among the causes to which her ruin may be traced, the refusal of the African Creole to work for proper remuneration finds no place; and that emancipation, far from being the origin of her many misfortunes, only ushered into life a cheaper, a wiser, and a better system of labor.

CHAPTER XXVI.

WANT OF LABOR IN JAMAICA.

Kingston, Jamaica, 1860.

When I enumerated, in a former chapter, the causes that, in my judgment, have combined to ruin Jamaica, and attributed them, as I think they ought to be attributed, to faults and errors committed by the planters themselves, it was with no feelings of hostility to an interest that I believe to be of paramount importance, and no desire to see its lawful energies cramped or its success obstructed. When the planters were compelled to receive an inadequate compensation for their slaves, they did so with the understanding that their staple should be protected in the British market. The wrong, if wrong it was, lay with the government that held out such a promise, not with the government that abolished, with an odious monopoly, the heavy tax paid by the English people for the support of a West Indian aristocracy. The planters could not be expected to take an abstract view of a measure that consummated their own ruin. They complained bitterly of injustice; and, though their complaints carried with them no argument for the restoration of protection, they should have silenced all factious opposition to wholesome plans devised for the restoration of Jamaica's prosperity. Whether labor was or was not as urgently needed as a large party in the island contended, there can not be a doubt that population was required, and that, if immigration had been encouraged immediately after emancipation, the colony would have been saved from many of the evils that have since befallen it.

That I may not be misunderstood, I state my conviction distinctly, in the commencement of this chapter, that *population is one of Jamaica's most pressing necessities.* The laboring classes must be strengthened if sugar-cultivation is to be extended beyond its present limits; the middle classes must be strengthened, if it be at all advisable to promote agricultural and mechanical knowledge, to ennoble and stimulate labor, to engender a spirit of emulation, and to multiply the exportation of minor staples; and finally, the large proprietary must be strengthened by men of capital, men of energy, and men of enterprise — men who are not averse to improvement, if the great resources of the island are ever to be thoroughly developed. But, for laborers, Jamaica does not want mere beasts of burden, to be the slaves, as in the French and Spanish colonies, of a selfish and unprincipled management; she wants no new settlers, as was once contended, to monopolize the provision market, and drive the legitimate peasantry from the cultivation of their properties to a state of dependence on the planter and a labor for daily hire; she wants no new planters who can not consent to attend to their own business, and who will refuse to consider their interests in any way connected with the durable prosperity of the island. In this kind of population there would be no guaranty for the future. Jamaica, even now, has a larger number of inhabitants to the square mile than any state in the Union except Connecticut, Massachusetts, New York, and Rhode Island. But she stands in need of immigration more than any state in the Union, because a working-man in America does as much as ten men do in Jamaica. She stands in need of labor, because sugar can not be largely cultivated without an exclusively laboring class; and that class in this island, always unequal to the demands upon it, grows weak and weaker every day. The Jamaica laborer of yesterday is a proprietor to-day. He has bought his acre of land, and is independent; and as long as land is cheap and plentiful, the drain upon the laboring force must inevitably continue. The vacancy can only be supplied by constant immigration. In America the process is natural, in Jamaica it must be forced and fostered. I believe that the prosperity of Jamaica depends very much upon the extension of sugar-cultivation, and that the extension of sugar-cultivation materially depends upon a labor that is not adequate to the task. It can not be questioned that the most flourishing plantations in the island might be raised to a much higher point of perfection than they at present exhibit, and be made to give double the quantity of sugar that they now yield to the acre. If such an improvement demands more scientific culture, better machinery, and closer economy, it also demands a continued supply of labor such as few planters in Jamaica can procure. It demands a certain labor, available at any and all times—a labor that is not transient or dependent on the pleasure of the peasantry, who, at critical seasons, will leave an estate almost deserted to plant or look after their own provision-grounds.

The statement that an increase of labor is indispensable to the prosperity of Jamaica, bears, however, some qualification. Want of labor has not ruined the island, and it is mere folly to expect that an indiscriminate importation of labor will, without other aid, regenerate it. I do most unequivocally state that, after diligent inquiry, I have been unable to discover a single property abandoned for want of labor alone. There are, without doubt, successful planters in the island who could command means to extend and improve their estates, if they could also command the necessary field force; there may be some few estates, in districts remote from populous villages, where the want of labor during crop-time is severely felt; I will not even undertake to deny the assertion (though I think it unlikely) that canes, for want of labor alone, have been left uncut to rot upon the ground; but the rule—and I must be guided by the rule, and not by exceptional cases—the rule is, that capital is wanted to employ the labor that may already be found in the island. I agree with the planters when they say that an abundance of labor would bring an abundance of capital; but I differ from them when they say that capital in Jamaica, as a rule, is unable to command labor. Let it be remembered that the destitution of labor in Jamaica is nothing like the destitution that has prevailed in Trinidad or in Guiana. Jamaica, with an area of four millions of acres, had an agricultural laboring population in 1838 of 200,000; the field-laboring force of Trinidad, with an area of two million acres, was at the same period only 12,000; and the laboring force of Guiana, with an unbounded territory of the richest soil adjoining its settlements, was 55,000. Yet Jamaica, with advantages of labor, sank lower than Trinidad or Guiana, because she was weighed down by a heavier debt, and cursed more deeply with absenteeism and mismanagement. Want of labor, therefore, is so far qualified by want of capital, that the one is utterly useless, and, indeed, can not be obtained at all without the other.

Want of labor in Jamaica bears a farther qualification. The labor that the planters now command they do not economize; the labor that they lost years ago, and that year after year they continue to lose, they so lost, and so continue to lose, in a very great measure by their own fault. If want of labor were the sole cause of diminished cultivation, we would expect to find such labor as there was, were it ever so scanty, closely economized instead of recklessly wasted in the manner that it unquestionably is. Economy of present labor should naturally precede the introduction of fresh labor. Now, when we find the planter pursuing a policy that tends to alienate the laboring classes from his interests, how can we put implicit faith in his profession, that on the industry of the people whom he disdains to conciliate, his own success or ruin depends? The righteous instinct of the British nation has demanded a guaranty (which the planters, to do them justice, have readily conceded) that the immigrant laborer shall not be made the slave or tool of oppression—a mere lever with which the proprietary may enrich themselves at the expense of popular liberty and popular enlightenment. The introduction, under a specious disguise, of a new race of slaves would never benefit the colony, and, more than this, the honor of England is pledged that these men shall be free. This foreign immigration, which has so advantaged other colonies, has been only allowed to Jamaica within a year past; and the opposition that colonial legislation encountered from the mother country must be attributed to the distrust with which all measures emanating from the planting interest of Jamaica have been hitherto regarded. The planters of to-day are paying the penalty of old faults and follies. They are inheriting the consequences of a very mistaken policy that some, even now, are not too willing to discard; they are suffering from the defeat that their predecessors sustained in the long and bitter war that they foolishly waged against free labor.

The mouth-pieces of the planting interest continue to-day to misrepresent the character of the negro, under the stupid belief that it will create a reaction of sympathy in favor of their party. They say that the Creole can not be induced to work for love or money. They have a fancy for his picture as he "lounges about his own grounds—caring little for the comforts of life, and unwilling to purchase them at the expense of even a trivial and transient labor." The planters, and all connected with the planting interest, unite in believing, or professing to believe, that want of labor, lost through Creole idleness, is the only cause of Jamaica's ruin at all worthy of consideration. Any one who thinks differently is set down as grossly prejudiced, possibly bought up by the Anti-slavery Society (Jamaica's signal enemy), or, at the very least, ignorant of the subject upon which he has ventured an opinion. How can a stranger understand or appreciate the wants of Jamaica? Surely political economy in Jamaica is unlike political economy any where else!

I plead guilty to the charge of being a stranger.

But the Jamaica resident of a month old must have neither eyes nor ears if he fail to read in the ceaseless wash of partisan newspapers, or to hear from eager communicants the minutiæ of the planter's *argumentum ad crumenam.* The anxious inquirer in Jamaica will be like the man with the ass in the fable, if he depend for information on what people say; for A will flatly contradict to-morrow what B told him to-day. He must rely upon his own powers of observation. If my powers in this respect are deficient, I can not help it; but I stoutly maintain that I have been looking only through my own spectacles. If it be true that the negro declines work, I am ready to admit it; but it is untrue. If it be true that want of labor has ruined the island, I am anxious to see it; but it is not.

A stranger in Jamaica, and especially an American, who knew nothing of its past history or present wants, would never dream that labor was the great desideratum. He finds, on arriving at Kingston, a dozen boatmen eager to convey him ashore—a dozen porters ready to carry his luggage—a dozen messengers quarreling to run his errands. He is pestered with able-bodied men and their offers of assistance for a paltry remuneration. He sees as many attendants in a petty Kingston shop as in a Broadway store, and a government clerk with as many servants as a foreign embassador. Servants must have under-servants, and agents sub-agents. If he travel through the country, he finds half a dozen men watching a herd of cattle, and as many looking after a team of oxen. He *sees* labor every where—on the roads, the streets, the wharves; and it is only upon the plantations that he *hears* any complaint. Yet even there he detects none of the labor-saving machinery that he has been accustomed to see at home, where labor is really scarce and dear; but he witnesses a cultivation conducted on primitive and most wasteful principles. He will infer, of course, that the labor market is overstocked rather than understocked, and his inference will neither be wholly wrong, nor yet wholly right. It will be nearer the truth to say that the actual labor force of the island is misdirected and frittered away. The laboring classes of Jamaica—I mean the men and women who live by labor for daily wages—dislike plantation-work, and prefer to earn their livelihood whenever they can by any other kind of toil. They disliked it at first because it was the badge of a slavery still fresh in their remembrance—not, as the planters say, because they were too idle to work, for they *do* work, and work hard, as I am going to show, at any other occupation. But their dislike was not an invincible dislike. It might have been overcome by elevating instead of degrading labor; by kind treatment, by wise legislation, by the cultivation of friendly relations, and by some little regard for the happiness and comfort of the people. It was, on the contrary, strengthened by systematic harshness, oppression, and injustice.

The Jamaica planter, who wants more labor than he can command at a particular season, hurries to the impatient conclusion that the negro will not work. The laborer indignantly denies the imputation. I found it unnecessary to strike a balance between the contradictory statements, or to rely upon either—for there was other and more unbiased testimony at hand. I sought information from the chief commissioner of roads, who has 3000 men under constant employment, and he assured me that they worked diligently for five days in the week—going to market, after their custom, on the sixth, or devoting it to the cultivation of their own grounds. He had no complaints to make of idleness, and instead of there being a deficiency of hands, he could obtain an additional thousand at any time he chose. The men, he said, preferred breaking stones on the road to estate-labor, though the former was much the severer work of the two.

I inquired farther of the superintendent of the Rio Grande copper mines, in the parish of Portland, an intelligent, practical, energetic Englishman, who, for eight years, has had a large body of men under his command. He told me that, at first, the planters ridiculed his idea of getting labor; nevertheless, in all his experience, he has not known what it was to want labor. If he stood in need of five men, fifteen or twenty would apply. These men worked eight hours a day, and for six days in the week—and though some of them had been in the superintendent's employ five or six years, he never had occasion to complain of their idleness. "They work," he said, "like very slaves, stripping themselves to the task; they work harder and more persistently, I am convinced, than if they were forced to it."

All the impartial testimony that I could obtain in Jamaica summed up a crushing contradiction to the unqualified pretension of the planter that the negro would not work. And when I asked the negro himself why he preferred the toil of the mine to the comparatively easy labor of the plantation, his explanation was very simple—"Buckra don't pay."

On flourishing estates, where planters and overseers can afford to pay punctually, they are seldom in great straits for labor. On other estates, where the case is different — where laborers are kept two and three months without wages, which, in the end, are arbitrarily cut down, and sometimes not paid at all, it is natural there should be complaints of want of labor. I am not making a vague or untenable assertion. Several instances of unpunctuality in payment and questionable honesty fell under my notice. In these particular instances, at least, they proved the existence of a practice that would ruin the credit of a business man in America within a month. The mining superintendent to whom I have referred, informed me that when his operations were suspended, an overseer from a sugar-estate near Annotto Bay came to the Rio Grande to seek labor. About twenty men accepted his offer of *thirty-six* cents a day, and left for the estate, thirty miles distant. They worked for three months without receiving any wages, and at the end of the time were paid off at the rate of *eighteen* cents a day.

It is the practice, among an inferior class of proprietors, to cut down the laborer's wages, if exception can possibly be taken to the work performed; and when the laborer complains of injustice he is summarily dismissed. It is a farce to talk of legal redress or the negro's love of litigation. He is in a country district, has no one to advise with, and must bear the wrong or quit the estate. The planters themselves admit that they can always get men to dig cane-holes—the severest of plantation-work. But this is a definite and specific job. The negro contracts for the payment of so much money for so many cane-holes, and if he does the work he can not be deprived of his due, except by open dishonesty. Here, then, is a distinction between estate-work and other work sufficient to account for the Creole's preferences. Upon the roads, or in the mines, he *knows* that he will be paid, once a week, the shilling, or the shilling and a half per diem that he has earned; while, owing to some pernicious examples, he is taught to believe that on the estate payment is a matter of uncertainty, depending on the arbitrary will of the overseer. I do not assert for a moment, or seek to insinuate, that dishonesty is a common practice on Jamaica sugar-estates, or that irregularity of payment is any thing like a rule. The simple fact that three hundred estates are in successful cultivation proves the contrary. But to account for the notorious preference of the negro for the severest work rather than plantation-work, I give irregularity of payment as one among other causes. It is perfectly obvious that the practice on one estate is enough to excite distrust throughout a whole parish, especially among a people who indulge in exaggeration and gossip, and who never could be induced to work again for a master whom they suspected of dealing with them unfairly. This, then, is one important reason why the planter can not command the labor that already exists in the island, and that other capitalists can readily obtain. To it may be added the low estimate, amounting to positive degradation, at which field labor is rated in the popular mind. No sum of money would tempt a mulatto to work in the field. It is the province of the blacks alone. It ceases to be their province as soon as they buy the acre of land, and the independence after which their souls yearn. It was the badge of slavery; and it is no matter for surprise that there should be a prejudice against the emblem long after the reality has passed forever away.

The planter's plea that, for such labor as the island can give, he can not afford to pay the price demanded, is unworthy of consideration. He says, for instance, that he can not raise corn to advantage. What! with a soil five times as productive as any soil in America, and able to procure first-class laborers at fifty cents a day, he can not compete with American corn in the Kingston market! The statement is absurd on the face of it. A laborer in America earns a dollar a day. Laborers in Jamaica on the roads, or in the mines, get, according to their value, twenty-four cents, thirty cents, and thirty-six cents—no higher. A task-laborer on an estate, if he work hard, may earn fifty cents, and I have known laborers by contract earn their dollar. But these are very exceptional wages. Laborers in the parish of Manchester are willing to work for eighteen cents a day and can not find employment. Taking the whole island, the average price of daily labor throughout the year does not exceed, if it reaches, thirty cents.

There are undoubtedly many Jamaica Creoles who will not work for estates under any inducement. They are small proprietors of a superior class, and different from the laborers, pure and simple, of whom I have just been writing. But because they cultivate their own grounds, and are too independent to hire themselves out at thirty cents a day, they should not be denounced as an idle, worthless, and unproductive people. These men, years ago, were driven from the estates by a series of mistakes and blunders which the planters of to-day can readily recognize. The history of estate abandonment in Jamaica is a history of systematic injustice and oppression on the part of the proprietary body, accompanied by a most fatal blindness to their own interests. They strove, by harsh measures and petty persecutions, to compel the people to remain on the estates, and a system of tenancy-at-will, held over them *in terrorem*, though practically broken up by the negroes themselves, remained in force long enough to destroy here, as it has destroyed in other islands, all confidence between planter and laborer. That confidence has never been restored. The better class of Creoles bought land, cultivated for themselves, and earned, as they still earn, an honorable livelihood by supplying the provision markets and the export markets with minor staples. All attempts to dislodge them from their independence have but widened the breach between them and their old employers. The planter even now, after twenty years' disastrous experience, will not allow that he has aught in common with the small settler, or that he is under any necessity or obligation to conciliate a people who might still be of the utmost service to the large proprietary interest that he represents. I know of an abandoned estate in the parish of Portland which the settlers offered to resuscitate on condition that the proprietor would give them one half of the produce. The offer was refused; and I have heard of other cases where similar proposals met with the like rejection. I have no doubt in my own mind that, under some such arrangement as this, abandoned sugar-estates throughout the whole island might be resuscitated with economy and profit to all parties concerned.

When, therefore, I stated, as I did in the commencement of this chapter, that labor in Jamaica is wanted for sugar-cultivation, I do not mean it to be inferred that the Creole population will not work. So, again, when I state that labor of a certain kind and in certain localities can not readily find employment, I do not mean it to be inferred that the planter can always command it. My object in this chapter has been to explain the coexistence in Jamaica of unemployed supply and serious want of labor—an anomaly produced, in my judgment, by very grave errors of political economy and plantation mismanagement. There seems to have been a fatality in the course pursued with the West India negro, arising from a determination to regard him as a being who reasoned differently and acted differently from other people. I have ever found him doing exactly what a white man would do under the same circumstances. While I believe in immigration, I believe that the planting interest of Jamaica could make, and ought to make, far more of the present laboring force than it does. Immigration, to insure success, can only be carried out on a large scale and at a large expense. Capital, then, becomes an important prerequisite. Jamaica, in this respect, is worse off than Trinidad or Guiana ever were, because her credit is utterly ruined. Men might be found to risk capital once more on her productive soil if it were not for the quicksands of her unsteady legislation. But though a fresh and vigorous population were poured into the colony to-morrow—though, under its influence, the most enthusiastic hopes were realized—though enterprise revived and prosperity regained the sway that ruin now usurps—the governing classes would do well to erect a beacon on the Charybdis that wrecked their island-ship. For they must remember, in all time to come, that the permanent prosperity of Jamaica, or of any other country in the world, depends not upon the accumulation of capital in the hands of a few large landed proprietors, but on a general distribution of wealth and education among an industrious, a free, and intelligent people.

CHAPTER XXVII.

NECESSITY FOR IMMIGRATION.

Kingston, Jamaica, 1860.

IN preceding chapters I endeavored to show that labor can not readily be commanded by the planters of Jamaica, and for reasons which I shall here briefly recapitulate:

1. Because, at the period of emancipation, there was barely labor enough for pressing wants, and every year that has elapsed since the abolition of slavery has witnessed the permanent and perfectly legitimate withdrawal of large numbers from estate-service without any corresponding introduction of labor from abroad.

2. Because Jamaica exports, besides sugar, very large quantities of coffee, pimento, ginger, and woods of various kinds, all of which have helped to weaken the labor force absolutely required for the production of the principal staple.

3. Because, for years after emancipation, the planters pursued a policy of coercion that compelled the negroes, in simple self-defense, to abandon estate-service; and the confidence between the proprietary and laboring interests then destroyed has never been restored.

4. Because land in Jamaica is very cheap and plentiful, and the negro has discovered that cultivating

for himself is more to his advantage pecuniarily, socially, and morally than cultivating for others.

5. Because a very large number of estates were abandoned for want of capital, and the negroes, obliged to seek other means of livelihood, bought land, and have since attained an independence of which, if it were possible, it would be extremely unwise and impolitic to deprive them by compulsory legislation.

6. Because the planter steadily refuses to co-operate with the small settler, and to accept his services in the cultivation of the cane under the Metairie or any other system. In the management of his estate he insists, as a *sine qua non*, that his tenant shall be his laborer, and that his relations with the latter shall be strictly those of master and servant.

7. Because want of means on divers estates led to unpunctual payment. In some cases the laborers were not paid for months; in others their wages were cut down or not liquidated at all; and this, though an exception and not a rule, created a wide-spread and general distrust most injurious to the planting interest.

8. Because a strong prejudice exists in the minds of the Creole population against field labor, which, in other days, was the badge of slavery; and no efforts have been made to remove this prejudice, either by educating the masses, or by elevating the work itself to the dignity of honest, independent industry. Many of the dissenting ministers, whether rightly or wrongly I will not pretend to decide, advise their people not to work on estates when they can find other employment.

9. Because economy of labor is practically ignored

in Jamaica; labor is wasted, and labor-saving arts are unknown.

10. Because the governing classes have shamefully neglected the welfare of the masses. They have not made the annual decline of population a subject of earnest consideration, nor have they essayed to check it by the adoption of the most ordinary precautions.

11. Because the native laboring force of the island has been weakened by large emigration to the adjoining continent—especially to Panama, while the railroad across that isthmus was in course of construction.

12. Because the laboring force of the island has been decimated by cholera and small-pox. It is supposed that, from these visitations, upward of 30,000 people died.

13. Because the character of the labor that the planter can now command is essentially transient; and, if the supply were sufficient in mere numbers, its uncertainty, at particular seasons, deters capitalists from undertaking sugar manufucture in Jamaica, and cramps the energies of those present proprietors who are able to extend their operations and improve their estates.

I confess that if none of these reasons existed—if the planters of Jamaica could command a plentiful supply of labor for all present necessities, I should still advocate immigration in view of the mere fact that three million acres of cheap unplanted land are open for settlement, that the soil of the island is wonderfully productive, and its climate salubrious. These arguments do not encroach upon debatable ground. The advocate of immigration may consistently refuse to believe that the planting interest is paramount, or he may treat with indifference the consideration that, with population, Jamaica could export 500,000 instead of 30,000 hogsheads. There are reasons, other than those given by the planter, in favor of immigration, and (that I know of) not a valid one against it. They are reasons that must weigh with statesmen and patriots, if there are any in Jamaica, and with Englishmen who care for the prosperity of one of the most splendid dependencies of the empire. I do not speak of political reasons which make the colonization of Jamaica a matter of the last importance to British commerce in these seas. They are obvious enough while the United States, on the one hand, are coveting Cuba, and France, on the other, is fostering her West Indian possessions and seeking to enlarge them. The most forcible argument that can be urged in favor of immigration is that Jamaica now supports a population of 350,000, when she could support with ease a population of 4,000,000; that, capable of yielding every article of tropical growth, her resources have remained undeveloped and her wealth almost unknown during two centuries of occupation. There have been costly attempts to raise cotton in Africa and India; but here, in Jamaica, within fifteen days' steaming of London, cotton grows wild, and labor for its cultivation is the only desideratum.

It is deplorable that Jamaica, every where regarded as a representative of the emancipation experiment, should have been the special victim of a mistaken philanthropy — that immigration, upon which free labor and the island's prosperity so largely depended, should have been opposed and discouraged in England, or even left to the management of a bankrupt and broken-down provincial interest. By such a course the people of England, under a mistaken apprehension of the true issue, flung away their opportunity to vindicate, in this island, the rightful superiority of free labor; though, with curious perversity, they seized and turned to profitable account a similar opportunity in the Mauritius, Guiana, and Trinidad.

The advantages to be derived from an immigration based on colonizing principles—and the British government countenances no other—can not be disputed. Carried out on a large and liberal scale, its first palpable effect in Jamaica would be to restore a confidence that has been torn up root and branch. It would bring capital, and capital would bring re-enforcements to the white population now seriously threatened with extinction. It would remove prevailing poverty, and check its demoralizing influences. It would enable the planter to free himself from debt, and extend and improve the cultivation of his cane-fields. His labor would be cheaper than slave labor, and, other things being made equal, he would be able to compete successfully with the Cuban planter. An extension of sugar-cultivation would be immediately followed by an increased demand for the superior kind of labor that the Creole prefers, and that he alone is capable of rendering. It is mere folly to say that he would be supplanted in his own market. Immigration can not be otherwise than beneficial to him. It would open to him a wider field of exertion; his services would be more wanted, would be better remunerated, and would be willingly received on his own terms; his provision-grounds would yield him a larger income; he would altogether emerge from the serfdom of estate labor, and, as a mechanic, a skillful workman, or farmer, would help to build up the middle class of Jamaica. The immigrant laborer is not introduced as the Creole's competitor. He is introduced to displace no one, but to fill a blank in the civil and social condition of the island. Unless field labor in this climate receives constant re-enforcement, cultivation not merely stands still, but retrogrades. The friends of freedom have only to insist that the liberties of the immigrant laborer shall be carefully guarded—that he shall not be made the slave of any particular interest—and he, of all others, becomes most benefited by the change. He is removed from the over-populated districts of the East to these sparsely-settled islands of the West, at no expense to himself and with no misgivings about the future. For the first time in his life he is adequately paid for his work, and for the first time the path of social and moral progress is opened to him. Immigration must further the cause of civilization. By abolishing female labor on estates, it will create among the Creole population a respect for the sex, now terribly wanting, and will arrest one of the principal sources of degrading immorality. These are not fanciful expectations; but results that have flowed directly from immigration in Trinidad, Guiana, and the Mauritius. It can be shown in all these colonies that exports have multiplied—that planters have relieved their properties of debt—that the investment of capital has recommenced—that Creoles and immigrants have both, in their respective spheres, materially improved, and live together in perfect harmony and contentment.

The Indian coolie, after the Creole, is the favorite

laborer in the British colonies. In point of fact, the West Indian planter can only choose between the coolie and the Chinaman. The African can not be procured without encouraging wars on his own continent and giving an indirect support to the slave-trade; and his introduction into any of the British possessions is not contemplated, and will not be tolerated by the English people. The Chinaman is not liked; he is close, cunning, avaricious, unprogressive, quarrelsome, and seldom becomes a permanent colonist. His habits of life are repulsive both to Creole and European. In California and Australia the Chinese have been an unproductive and injurious element of the population. They would never make for Jamaica a thriving peasantry such as it is her object to secure. The Indian coolie, on the other hand, is found to be docile, peaceable, intelligent, industrious, eager to learn, and apt at improvement. He is, moreover, a British subject, and his transportation, at his own free option, from one portion of the empire to another, is conducted with the most jealous protection of his rights and the most careful regard for his interests.

I know that, in the United States, British immigration to the West Indies has been confounded, and most unjustly confounded, with immigration to French and Spanish islands, and I have made, on this account, a special study of its prominent features. Familiar, too, with its practical working, I do not hesitate to say that the immigrant is as free as any other laborer, under contract, in the British dominions. He has, moreover, privileges which laborers who emigrate to other countries do not enjoy. His prospects are not even doubtful, for, from the day he arrives, he is supplied with work, or with lodging and provisions until work can be obtained. He is employed at the current rate of wages, of which a minimum is fixed by law. He is guaranteed proper medical attendance, and government officers are appointed for the express purpose of protecting him and affording him immediate redress in the event of any possible wrong. The planter is powerless to exact from his laborer more than the terms of the contract into which both have entered; and that these terms are perfectly fair and liberal I shall presently undertake to show. I have already explained the system of immigration that obtains in other colonies, and shall only observe here the peculiarities of the Jamaica law which came into force in 1858.

By the provisions of this act the immigrant laborer is entitled, free of all charges, to a certificate of "industrial residence" after he has worked five years under indenture. He can shorten this term of service, and receive his certificate, by paying a commutation fee of $20 at the end of the third year, or of $10 at the end of the fourth year. At the end of the second year, and of each subsequent year, he can, at his own election, change his employer, and give his service to whomsoever he pleases. The contract between the immigrant and his employer explains the obligations of both, and is thus worded:

JAMAICA, SS.—This indenture made the 10th day of February, 1860, between Oh Swanne, immigrant laborer, of the one part, and John Jones, of St. Thomas-in-the-Vale, in the said island, of the other part, *witnesseth:* That in virtue of "the immigration act of

1858," and in consideration of the covenants of the said John Jones, hereinafter contained, he the said Oh Swanne doth bind himself to the said John Jones for the term of five years, to be computed from the date hereof; and doth hereby covenant with the said John Jones, that he, the said Oh Swanne, will, during the said term, or the continuation of these presents, truly and faithfully serve the said John Jones, his heirs and assigns, as laborer on the Silver Spring estate, in the parish of St. Thomas-in-the-Vale, according to the laws and regulations made concerning immigrant laborers in this island; and the said John Jones doth hereby covenant with the said Oh Swanne, that he, the said John Jones, will, during the said term, or the continuance of these presents, provide the said Oh Swanne with suitable and sufficient lodging, medicine, and medical attendance; and such medicine, medical attendance, and lodging shall be in conformity with the laws or regulations made concerning immigrant laborers in this island; and also will pay wages to the said Oh Swanne at the same rate which may be at the time paid to the laborers, not under written agreement, working on the said estate, according to the quantity of work performed, being at the rate of not less than —— per diem, subject to deductions at the following rate (for medical attendance, lodging, and repayment of advances, if such have been made). In witness whereof we have hereunto set our hands.

(Signed) OH SWANNE,
(Witnesses.) JOHN JONES.

Under this contract the immigrant either works out his five years' term or pays the commutation; and in either event he receives the "certificate" which frees him from service and conveys the right of naturalization. While under contract he may be a landed proprietor, and cultivate for himself, provided he does not neglect the service due every day, Sundays and holidays excepted, to his employer. After his contract has expired, and he has obtained his certificate, he may return home at his own expense, or, if he choose to remain in the island another five years, he may then return home at the expense of the colony, or receive, instead of this privilege, ten acres of land exempt from taxation during three years. The wisdom of this provision, or of any other that holds out inducements to permanent settlement can not be questioned. Colonization, and not a temporary supply of labor, is the chief object to be attained. The principle of granting back passages, and allowing immigrants no choice but to accept them, is, in my judgment, an erroneous one. It is not sound political economy, nor is it just to the people who bear the burden of the immigration outlay. It looks like an expiation of some wrong inflicted on the coolie, and is so interpreted abroad. It offers a bonus to the immigrant to go away after he has become an efficient, acclimated laborer. To offer him a bonus to stay would be the wiser policy.

It only remains to add that, under the Jamaica law of 1858, the entire expense of immigration is imposed upon the planting interest. This is the interest, it is true, which the importation of labor is chiefly designed to benefit; but there can not be a doubt, if the experience of other islands be accepted as an indication of the result in Jamaica, that the benefit to the planter will be shared by the merchant, the stock-breeder, the mechanic, and the settler.

Such are the main features of the Jamaican immigration law to which the sanction of the imperial government was so reluctantly given. The law is quite as favorable to the liberties of the immigrant as any similar law in Trinidad, Guiana, or the Mauritius, and yet the most strenuous exertions were made in England to have it vetoed. The Anti-slavery Society exerted their powerful influence against its passage, and memorialized government with objections either untrue in fact or illogical in argument. They "denied the scarcity of available labor," though men of all parties in the island, and of wide experience, thought differently, and so expressed themselves. They objected to "wages being fixed arbitrarily by the proprietor," when the immigrant's contract distinctly stated that he should be paid at the current rate. They found fault with a scheme of immigration that "imposed a tax on the whole colony," when the law clearly provided that the expense should be borne altogether by the planter. They urged that the measure "would reduce the present inadequate rate of wages paid to Creole laborers," when, judging from the experience of other colonies, it would, on the contrary, increase the rate of wages, and procure for the Creole more lucrative and more satisfactory employment. They deprecated "the introduction of pagans and idolaters," when, by this very introduction, these pagans and idolaters are civilized and christianized. They deplored the consequences of "an African immigration," when none was in contemplation. They represented that the immigrant "was not allowed to choose his own master," which was only so far true that for two years, and no longer, the laborer's employer is selected, for very obvious reasons, by an immigrant agent, who is an appointee of the crown, and responsible for all his acts. They made out a mortality on shipboard, and after arrival, not warranted by fact. There has been mortality, undoubtedly, among West Indian immigrants, but nothing like the percentage alleged. It arose in one case from an outbreak of cholera, and in others from an unwise selection of sickly emigrants. Except in these cases the average of deaths among the people has not been greater than it would have been if they remained at home. The Anti-slavery Society farther pretended that the Jamaica law "did not sufficiently provide for the protection of the immigrant," when it appeared that officers were created for this very purpose, in the interest of immigrants exclusively, and armed with special powers of supervision and interference. They finally concluded that the measure "was not wished for by the masses," though it was passed by their representatives, without a single dissenting petition, and with the support of every journal in the island.

Untenable as these objections were, the opposition that pressed them was unyielding and powerful. Such a hostile spirit can only be explained by the existence of a very strong distrust of all measures emanating, or supposed to emanate, from the planting interest. And this distrust is not difficult to account for. While the planters of other days were making representations of a great dearth of labor, they were driving Creole labor from the estates by a mistaken policy and oppressive legislation. While they were bankrupt, ruined, and appealing for aid, they untruthfully pretended that Creole indolence was the cause of their misfortunes. While they proclaimed that immigration was their only hope, their own schemes of immigration were being grossly mismanaged, and ultimately turned out most pitiful failures. It is not generally known outside the island that, at various times since emancipation, over 17,000 immigrants—Africans, Indians, Chinese, American negroes, and Europeans—have been brought to Jamaica. I do not believe that one tenth of this number can be found upon estates to-day. Immigration agents abroad appear to have lacked the sense or the honesty (for they were paid so much per capita) to select their men from an agricultural population; the coolies were picked up in the streets of Calcutta; the Europeans were idlers from large cities; the American negroes were mechanics and tradesmen; and the Africans, with some coolie exceptions, were the only serviceable field laborers. A quarter of a million sterling was expended, and the island is still in debt for a portion of the sum wasted in these fruitless efforts. It is not surprising, therefore, that fresh immigration measures should be opposed by an organization that assumes a protectorate over West Indian interests, and undoubtedly represents a preponderating English sentiment. Under former immigration laws the planters of Jamaica paid only two thirds of the expense; but under the present law, as a penalty for past mismanagement, and a concession to the opposition that they have with such difficulty combated, they have to bear the whole burden of expenditure. The present scheme of immigration is, in fact, a victory of the Anti-slavery party of Jamaica, whose views the planters have been compelled to adopt. A few years ago the proprietors scouted any plan that did not indenture the laborers for ten years. They are now content that the indenture shall not exceed two or three years—sufficient to guarantee the planter a return for his outlay, and to give the laborer a necessary industrial training. The Jamaica law of 1858 was opposed in England, very unwisely as I think, and much more strenuously than it was opposed even by ultraists within the colony. It can not, under any circumstances, be considered a triumph of the planting interest; it is rather a fair expression of the liberal public sentiment of the island on a much debated question of the highest importance. A separate bill authorizes the governor to borrow sums not exceeding £50,000 sterling in one year, to defray the charges of immigration in the first instance, and these sums are to be repaid by employers in ten semi-annual instalments.

Legislation on the subject of immigration can do no more for Jamaica than it has done. The island is now waiting for the capital, the energy, and the practical ability necessary to carry out its laws. The opposition of the Anti-slavery Society has been silenced, and the planters of Jamaica are at liberty to bring in 50,000 coolie laborers within a year; but who believes they will do it? If it was true that they were in such desperate straits for labor—if it was true that labor, and not capital, was their most pressing want—why are not a dozen ships laden with coolies now on their way from Madras to Kingston? There is a law on the Jamaica statute-book authorizing the introduction of labor on private account, provided that the contract between employer and immigrant shall be binding for only three years, and that the latter be paid the current rate of wages. Why are not the planters, who complain that their capital is lying idle, and their estates going to ruin for want of labor, availing themselves of this special enactment in their favor? The burden of all that I have written is an answer to these questions, and if it is not I have been writing to a vain purpose.

Immigration for Jamaica should be advocated wholly irrespective of the deficiency of labor to meet present demands, and upon a broader basis than that of building up the planting interest, or giving it any undue preponderance. That was the wrong of slavery. The planting interest is, I believe, the most important money interest at stake, and should not be cramped or checked in its legitimate expansion; but it should not, on the other hand, be fostered at the expense of other interests. When that happens, it necessarily and naturally becomes oligarchic, selfish in its aims and purposes, opposed to popular enlightenment, education, and moral discipline. Immigration should be advocated on the ground that the island is capable of sustaining forty people where it now sustains four. Every class of its inhabitants—planters, settlers, laborers—all want the new life that immigration only can give them. They all belong to a past age; and even those that float upon the surface of Jamaica's ruin are but wrecks of a demolished system. New men, with new ideas—men of perseverance, energy, capital—men determined to face the responsibilities and difficulties of their position—men willing to work, no matter whence they come—would soon startle Jamaica from her apathy and stupor. There are such men in the island now; their estates flourish; they make fortunes; they find labor; but they are exceptions—their influence is limited. I do not doubt that, before long, they will be representatives of the Jamaica proprietary interest. Their examples must be beneficial. They must eventually open the eyes of the world to the undeveloped resources of this island, and to the wealth that it is yet destined to yield.

Jamaica was ruined by its proprietary, and in its proprietary the hope of redemption lies. They have the experience of their predecessors to profit by. The work that they have to perform they must perform themselves, and not find consolation in the maudlin belief that it will ever be performed by others. They may enrich themselves, as their predecessors did, by the re-introduction of serf labor, but if they neglect, as their predecessors did, to educate the people, and give them sound moral and industrial training, they will establish, at best, a fictitious prosperity that the first storm will sweep away. Their schemes of immigration will fail if the main object of colonization is forgotten. They will fail if the welfare of the people is again made subservient to a mere money interest. They will fail if no discrimination is used in the selection of laborers, who are to become at a future period the mainstay of the island. They will fail if, after the introduction of immigrants, they are turned into beasts of burden, and slavery, under another name, is reinstated. Their schemes of immigration will fail if there is a want of capital to carry them out —not by driblets—but on a scale sufficiently extended to insure success. They will fail if, finally, false representations are made to seduce laborers to the island, and expectations are held out to them that can not be realized. I have seen a circular in Canadian journals offering colored laborers who will emigrate to Jamaica wages "varying from fifty cents to one dollar and fifty cents, and even two dollars a day." Now a field laborer in Jamaica can not earn any of these sums throughout the year. It will take a very good and very industrious laborer to earn fifty cents for one hundred out of the three hundred and sixty-five days. But neither Canada nor the United States, where wages are so high, are places to look for mere laborers. The American negro may make a good farmer or settler for Jamaica, but to perform inferior service in a dependent position he can not be obtained in available numbers.

Upon the colonizing principle Jamaica is ready to receive and sustain a million of free, intelligent, and industrious laborers. And not alone laborers. The island is in want of settlers and farmers from Europe or America, who will stimulate, by the force of example, the sluggish energy of the Creole peasantry—who will teach them to economize the labor that they waste, to cultivate more wisely, and to reap more abundantly—who will introduce among them comforts of which they are now utterly ignorant—who will create an independent public opinion, and who will elevate the middle classes of Jamaica far above the present standard of questionable civilization. If the advantages of this colony had ever been fairly placed before the world, and a cheap line of travel established, there is no reason to doubt that many of the British and German emigrants who wandered to the Rio de la Plata, the Brazils, and the sickly slopes of the Amazon, would have turned their steps hitherward, where the climate is so salubrious, the land so fertile, and political equality so fully recognized. A few settlers of this kind distributed throughout the different parishes could not fail to stimulate Creole enterprise, and, with abundance of labor to satisfy the demands not only of the planting interest, but of all other interests, down to those of the settler himself, there need be no speculation about the future of the island or the ultimate triumph of the free system. Acquainted, as I profess to be, with her wonderful resources and the immense field for industry that she offers, I can not refuse to believe that there is in store for Jamaica a prosperity that she never approached in her days of barbaric grandeur. For, if her present proprietary are unequal to the work of regeneration, others will be found to take it up and carry it out to the uttermost limit of completion.

CHAPTER XXVIII.

RÉSUMÉ.

Bridgetown, Barbados, 1860.

I HAVE endeavored, and I hope successfully, to show that each of the British West India colonies has had its own distinct and separate history, its own elements of prosperity, its own resources to develop, its own political and social evils to eradicate, its own policy to pursue, its own destiny to work out. I have endeavored to combat the error of judging the islands by rules that might apply to a continental dependency, and of tracing their depression, past or present, to the same or to a single origin. The fact that some islands need immigration, while others do not—that some are being colonized with Asiatics, while others are already densely peopled with Africans—points out the mistake of supposing their fortunes identical, or their cases exactly parallel. Emancipation, it is true, was granted to all at the same time and on the same conditions; but it was admitted to each island under different auspices, and breathed in each a different atmosphere. In Jamaica—where slavery was the primary formation upon which the social and political structures rested, and the revolution to be effected was most comprehensive—the change was resolutely and systematically opposed by a powerful plantocracy. Freedom, in Jamaica, was met and encountered at every point, and found, among the governing classes, a very limited number of willing workers. In the small and comparatively unimportant island of Antigua, freedom was received by the monopolists of the day, if not with cordiality, at least as an innovation which they were forced to accept, and which merited, under the circumstances, a fair and impartial trial. Emancipation was an isolated experiment in each of the different colonies. Precedents and rules of action for one were no precedents or rules of action for another. *Here* there were obstacles to overcome and difficulties to surmount which *there* did not exist, or existed only in a mitigated form. Each colony was a field of battle upon which the banners of free labor and slave labor were flung to the winds; and while in some, where resistance was feeble, all trace of the contest has disappeared, and prosperity has revived, in others, where resistance was strong and determined, the exhaustion that follows a long war and a long reign of oppression weighs heavily upon a dispirited people. Let us not be deceived. Let us not misinterpret the true meaning of Jamaica's desolation at the present time. Let no one be so mad as to believe that it is the work of freedom. Let no one fancy that even an aristocracy were ruined by the system from which they so long and so stubbornly withheld their allegiance. Let no one question the victory, though its choicest fruits are yet to be reaped; let no one doubt that freedom, when it overturned a despotism and crushed a monopoly, unshackled, at the same time, the commerce, the industry, and the intelligence of the islands, and laid the foundations of permanent prosperity.

I have addressed myself exclusively to the argument of the planter, for his pretension is, in reality, the only one to be disputed. It could not have been expected that he would act otherwise than he did. It was his part to resist. The new system was meant to effect a radical change in plantation management, and it was only natural for the proprietor to look upon any change that he had not proved with distrust and aversion. His monopolies and his privileges were to be swept away, and he could not encourage the scheme that doomed them to destruction, and opened to wide competition the field of profit he had hitherto exclusively enjoyed. Many of the planters went down with the privileges and the monopolies by which alone they had managed to keep afloat; but are the Act of Emancipation and the abolition of a protective tariff to be condemned because they tore down the veil of fictitious prosperity and exposed a helpless bankruptcy? Are these West India colonies ruined in their sugar interest, or any other interest, because some five hundred third-rate sugar-planters had not the stamina, pluck, capital, strength, wit, or what you please, to stand alone when the props of favoritism and partial legislation were removed? If free labor be tested by any other gauge than that of sugar-production, its success in the West Indies is established beyond all cavil and beyond all peradventure. If the people merit any consideration whatever—if their independence, their comfort, their industry, their education, form any part of a country's prosperity—then the West Indies are a hundred-fold more prosperous now than they were in the most flourishing times of slavery. If peace be an element of prosperity—if it be important to enjoy uninterrupted tranquillity and be secure from servile war and insurrection—then the West Indies have now an advantage that they never possessed before it was given them by emancipation. If a largely-extended commerce be an indication of prosperity, then all the West Indies, Jamaica alone excepted, have progressed under a system of free labor, although that system hitherto has been but imperfectly developed.

I have endeavored to convey a correct idea of the depreciation of commerce and the decline of sugar-cultivation in Jamaica; and I have also endeavored to show that this depreciation is an exception to the present general prosperity of the British West Indies—that it commenced before emancipation was projected, and can be traced directly to other causes than the introduction of freedom. Long before Mr. Canning, in his place in Parliament, became the unwilling organ of the national will, and explained, in terms not to be mistaken, that the demand of the British people for the liberation of the slaves could no longer be resisted, West India commerce was in the most alarming state of depression, owing to the heavy outlay and expenditure that a system of slave labor imperatively required. Testimony pointing directly and overwhelmingly to this conclusion has been given by planters themselves—by men put forward as the special champions of the planting interest—and fills a score of Parliamentary Blue-books. Upon their statements the report of the select committee on the condition of the West India colonies, printed in 1832, declared that "there was abundant evidence of an existing distress for ten or twelve years previous." That report described an impending, if not an actual ruin that we look for in vain at the present day. Jamaica, in 1860, and she only in the one particular of sugar-cultivation, is the single British island whose industry and enterprise remain, as we are told they formerly were, exhausted and paralyzed.

Let us appeal once more to figures. The colony of British Guiana, for four years prior to emancipation, exported an annual average of 98,000,000 lbs. of sugar, while, from 1856 to 1860, its annual average export rose to 100,600,000 lbs. The colony of Trinidad, for four years prior to emancipation, annually exported an average of 37,000,000 lbs. of sugar, while, from 1856 to 1860, its annual average export rose to 62,000,000 lbs. The colony of Barbados, for four years prior to emancipation, annually exported an average of 32,800,000 lbs. of sugar, while, from 1856 to 1860, its annual average export rose to 78,000,000 lbs. The colony of Antigua, for four years prior to emancipation, exported an annual average of 19,500,000 lbs. of sugar, while, from 1856 to 1860, its annual average export rose to 24,400,000 lbs. This is a total exhibit of 265,000,000 lbs. annually exported now, instead of 187,300,000 lbs. before emancipation, or *an excess of exports, with free labor, of seventy-seven million, seven hundred thousand pounds of sugar.*

In the matter of imports, we find that the colony of British Guiana, between the years 1820 and 1834, imported annually to the value of $3,700,000; that the annual imports of Trinidad, during the same period, averaged in value $1,690,000; that the imports of Barbados averaged in value $2,850,000; and those of Antigua $600,000. In the year 1859 the imports of

Guiana were valued at $5,660,000; those of Trinidad at $3,000,000; those of Barbados at $4,660,000; and those of Antigua at $1,280,000. The total exhibit represents an annual import trade, at the present time, of the value of $14,600,000, against $8,840,000 before emancipation, or *an excess of imports, under a free system, of the value of five million, seven hundred and sixty thousand dollars.*

In the exports I have made mention of sugar only; but if all other articles of commerce be included, and a comparison be instituted between the import and export trade of the colonies of Guiana, Trinidad, Barbados, and Antigua under slavery, and their trade under freedom, the annual balance in favor of freedom will be found to have reached already FIFTEEN MILLIONS OF DOLLARS at the very lowest estimate.

This large increase in the trade of four out of the five principal West India colonies is sufficient, I think, to demonstrate (were there no other evidence at hand) that free labor, with which four have prospered, can not alone be held responsible for the decline of the fifth. The increase of sugar-production also demonstrates the improved industry of the islands to a very remarkable extent; for it must be remembered that the agricultural force now engaged in cane-cultivation is scarcely more than half of what it was in times of slavery, when the energies of the whole population were directed to this single end. One of the most natural and legitimate results of emancipation was to allow every man to do what seemed to him best—to achieve independence if he could—to pursue, in any case, the path of industry most agreeable to his tastes, and most conducive to his happiness. When we look at the vast political and social structure that has been demolished—the new and grander edifice that has been erected—the enemies that have been vanquished—the prejudices that have been uprooted—the education that has been sown broadcast, the ignorance that has been removed—the industry that has been trained and fostered—we can not pause to criticise defects, for we are amazed at the progress of so great a revolution within the brief space of twenty-five years. Those who have never lived in a slave country little know how the institution entwines itself round the vitals of society and poisons the sources of political life. The physical condition of the slave is lost in the contemplation of a more overwhelming argument. Looking at the question from a high national standpoint, it is, comparatively speaking, a matter of temporary interest and minor importance whether the bondsman is treated with kindness and humanity, as in America, or with short-sighted brutality, as in Cuba. It is the influence of the system upon the energies and the morality of a people that demands the calmest and most earnest consideration of patriots and statesmen. The present is, perhaps, not so much to be condemned as the future, from which all eyes are studiously averted, is to be dreaded. An act of the British Parliament, and a vote of twenty millions sterling, were sufficient to release 800,000 slaves; but no act of the British Parliament could thus summarily remove the curse that slavery had bequeathed to these islands, and had left to fester in their heart's core. Time only could do that; time has not done it yet.

I have endeavored to show—and I hope successfully—that the experiment of free labor in the West

Indies has established its superior economy, as well as its possibility. Not a single island fails to demonstrate that the Creoles of African descent, in all their avocations and in all their pursuits, work, under a free system, for proper remuneration, though their labor is often ignorantly wasted and misdirected. *That* arises from want of education, want of training, want of good example. I have not sought to justify the maudlin sympathy that the mere mention of these people seems to excite in certain quarters, nor have I advocated their interests to the detriment of any other interest whatever. I have simply maintained, from evidence before me, that the right of one class to enjoy the wages and fruits of their labor, does not and can not injuriously affect the rights of any other class, or damage, as some foolishly pretend, a country's prosperity. An ethnological issue, quite foreign to the subject, has been dragged into the argument. No one can deny that, up to the present time, the African, in intelligence, in industry, and in force of character, has been, and still is, the inferior of the European; but it is a tremendous mistake to suppose that his intelligence can ever be quickened, his industry sharpened, or his character strengthened under slavery; and it is worse than a mistake to consign him to slavery for defects that slavery itself engendered, or to condemn him because the cardinal virtues of civilization did not spring into life upon the instant that the heel of oppression was removed. With the destiny of the West Indies the welfare of these people is inseparably bound up, and it is as wrong to overlook their faults as to deny that they have progressed under freedom, or to doubt that, by the spread of education and under the dominion of an enlightened government, they will become still more elevated in the scale of civilization. Those who are not afraid of the confession will admit that the West Indian Creole has made a good fight. The act of emancipation virtually did no more than place liberty within his reach. Actual independence he had to achieve for himself. All untutored and undisciplined as he was, he had to contend against social prejudice, political power, and a gigantic interest, before he could enjoy the boon that the act nominally conferred upon him. The planter was bred to the belief that his business could only be conducted with serf labor, and he clung to the fallacy long after serf labor had been legally abolished. Witness the land tenure which still exists in a mitigated form throughout all the West Indies, and requires the tenant, on peril of summary ejection, to give his services exclusively to his landlord. The instinct of self-interest—the faintest desire for independence—would prompt any one to reject such a bondage. Yet this rejection is the sole accusation brought against the negro—this the only ground upon which he has been condemned. I have endeavored to point out the two paths that lay open to the West Indian Creole after the abolition of slavery. The one was to remain an estate serf and make sugar for the planter; the other was to rent or purchase land, and work for estates, if he pleased, but be socially independent of a master's control. I endeavored to follow these two classes of people in the paths they pursued—the majority, who have become independent, and the minority, who have remained estate laborers—and I have shown that the condition of the former is infinitely above the condition of the latter. Is this any where denied? Can any one say that it was not the lawful right of these people thus to seek, and, having found, to cherish their independence? Can any one say that, by doing so, they wronged themselves, the planters, or the government under which they lived? Can any one say that they are to blame if, by their successful attempts to elevate themselves above the necessitous and precarious career of labor for daily hire, the agricultural field force was weakened, and the production of sugar diminished? Yet this is the fairest case that can be made out for the oligarchies of these West India islands. They have denounced the negro for his defective industry; but what, we may ask, have they themselves done—in what have *they* given proof of their nobler civilization and higher intelligence? Surely a most important duty devolved upon them. They were the privileged aristocracy, the landed proprietors, the capitalists, the rulers of the colonies—as they still are. Their political power was supreme; yet what have they done, not for the permanent prosperity of the islands—for the question need not be asked—but in behalf of their own special interests? They arraigned the negro for deserting their estates and ruining their fortunes, when they themselves were absentees, and were paying the legitimate profits of their business to agents and overseers. They offered the independent peasant no pecuniary inducement, or its equivalent, to prefer their service; but they attempted to obtain his work for less remuneration than he could earn in any other employment. They never cared for the comfort or happiness of their tenants, or sought to inspire them with confidence and contentment. They made no effort to elevate labor above the degraded level at which slavery left it, and they never set an example to their inferiors of the industry that is still needed in the higher as well as in the lower classes of West Indian society. Enterprise never prompted them to encourage the introduction of labor-saving arts. Yet these were measures that demanded the action of an enlightened Legislature and the consideration of an influential proprietary long before scarcity of labor became a subject of complaint. Instead of averting the evil they dreaded, they hastened its consummation, and injured their cause still more deeply by the false and evasive plea that the idleness of the Creole was the cause of a commercial and agricultural depression that they had brought entirely on themselves. Is it any argument against the industry of the laboring classes of America that a large proportion annually become proprietors, and withdraw from service for daily hire? Yet this is precisely what the West India Creole has done; this is the charge on which he has been arraigned—this is the crime for which he has been condemned.

I do not think it can be doubted that a want of confidence between employer and employed, engendered altogether by the mistaken policy of the governing classes, contributed largely to the prolonged depression of the West Indies—a depression from which most of them, under the advantages of free labor, have greatly recovered within the last ten years. Many of the old sources of evil and complaint have been abolished; some still live. Absenteeism is prevalent, and hypothecation, in Jamaica more especially, weighs heavily upon the agricultural interest. But the West Indian planter now generally admits the superior advantages of free labor, and is careful to avoid the grosser errors into which his predecessors fell. Landed property is changing hands, and new men are building up, upon a broader and sounder basis than that of slavery, the most important interest of these islands. The storm of a great adversity has passed over. There is no longer a struggle to wring from an unwilling plantocracy an admission in favor of freedom. That belongs to the history of the battle of independence, which, in these colonies, was nobly fought and triumphantly won; and if I have recalled the contest to mind, it was not to revive old grievances, but to illustrate truth, and vindicate the policy of freedom. The mode by which those colonies that need labor are to be supplied with an intelligent and industrious population is the practical question of the day. It certainly would neither be wise nor just to oppose, by legislation or otherwise, the abstraction of labor from estates so rapidly going on. Nothing could be adduced to illustrate more forcibly the progress of the people. The abstraction did not commence until some years after emancipation—until those who had been able to save money began to purchase land and cultivate for themselves. This is the great West Indian problem. It has been so complicated and distorted that its most familiar acquaintances scarcely know what to believe; but, divested of such foreign incumbrances as "defects of African character," and other similar stuff and nonsense, it is simply a land question, with which race and color have nothing whatever to do. The same process goes on in the United States, in Canada, in Australia, and in all new countries where land is cheap and plentiful and the population sparse. The laborer soon becomes a proprietor; the ranks of the laboring force are rapidly thinned; and the capitalist is compelled to pay high, it may be extravagant wages. In the West Indies the capitalist refuses to pay high wages; he thinks that the control of the labor market is one of his rights. He imagines, and upon what ground I can not comprehend, that farming in these colonies should yield much larger profits than farming any where else. He calls it "planting," and fancies that there ought to be a wide social distinction between the man who grows cane or cotton and the man who grows potatoes and parsnips. God save the mark! Does any one dream that if West India planters stuck to their business like English farmers, and possessed one half of their practical ability and industry, the agricultural and commercial interests of the islands would have ever suffered from emancipation? The profits of sugar-cultivation, according to the planter's creed, must be large enough to yield the proprietor, though an absentee, a comfortable income, and pay large salaries besides to overseers and attorneys; otherwise estates are abandoned, and the sugar interest is "ruined." These expectations might have been realized in the days of the old monopoly; they certainly are not realized now, and never can be realized again, unless the British people recede from their principles of free trade and free labor. If labor in the West Indies is high—so high that sometimes the planter can not afford to pay the price demanded—he is not worse off than the capitalist in all new countries. His attempt to keep the people day laborers, and to check the development of a natural law, is foolish and wicked. There is but one remedy for this abstraction from estate-labor, and that remedy is immigration. It must be a constant immigration as long as land is cheap and plentiful, for the immigrants themselves—and notoriously the Portuguese, whose industry was once the theme of the planter's praise and exultation—forsake the laboring ranks, and become proprietors and tradesmen as soon as they are released from their contracts of service. It must be a colonizing immigration, or permanent prosperity can never be reaped. It must be a free immigration, violating in no points of theory and in no details of practice the grant of liberty conferred by the Act of Emancipation upon these islands and their populations forever. This immigration has been placed within the reach of all the colonies that required it, though the jealous fears of the British people have prompted them to withhold from the local governments its entire direction and control. By this immigration the planters of Trinidad and Guiana have greatly profited, while the planters of Jamaica, exceptional again, with languishing energies and paralyzed enterprise, have derived no more benefit from the labor they imported than from the Creole labor they profess to have lost, but which, in reality, they recklessly squandered.

Truth, we are told, will prevail, and freedom, we know, is truth. Howsoever people may differ on questions of political liberty, into which inequalities of birth, race, position, and intelligence are permitted to enter, modern civilization has recognized and ratified the inalienable right of men to the wages of their industry, to the happiness they have toiled for, and to the independence they have earned. Here is the true field of equality, where rank, or race, or intellect has no chartered precedence. From the day when this great principle was admitted throughout the British West Indies their true prosperity may be dated. For freedom knows no favoritism; her honors are not crowded upon a privileged class, her aid is not limited to a particular interest. The act of British emancipation has been widely abused; but its detractors must live among the people it disenthralled if they would learn the value at which it *can* be estimated. Time, which develops the freedom that act created, adds continually to its lustre; and long after England's highest achievements in arts or in arms shall have been forgotten, this grant of liberty shall testify to the grandeur of her power and to the magnanimity of her people. I have not assumed, in aught I have written, that the West Indian Creole is yet capable of self-government. I have simply endeavored to show that, under freedom, sources of industry and prosperity have been opened that, under slavery, would have remained closed forever. I have endeavored to show that, for the West Indies, freedom has been the best policy, though the moralist may condemn an argument that sets forth another motive for doing right than the sake of right itself. If emancipation did no more than relieve the West Indian slave from the supervision of a task-master I should have nothing left to say; for I admitted, at the outset, that the condition of the laboring classes was but one among many interests whose ruin, if personal liberty could ruin them, would make us disbelieve in truth itself. But freedom, when allowed fair play, injured the prosperity of none of these West Indian colonies. It saved them from a far deeper and more lasting depression than any they have yet known. It was a boon conferred upon all classes of society: upon planter and upon laborer; upon all interests: upon commerce and agriculture—upon industry and education—upon morality and religion. And if a perfect measure of success remains to be achieved, let not freedom be condemned; for the obstacles to overcome were great, and the workers were few and unwilling. Let it be remembered that a generation, born in the night of slavery, has not yet passed away, and that men who were taught to believe in that idol and its creations still control the destinies of these distant colonies. Reluctantly they learnt the lesson forced upon them; slowly their opposition yielded to the dawning of conviction; but, now that the meridian of truth has been reached, we may hope that light will dispel all the shadows of slavery, and confound the logic of its champions when they falsely assert that emancipation has ruined the British islands.

THE END.

HARPER'S WEEKLY.

A JOURNAL OF CIVILIZATION.

A First-class Illustrated Family Newspaper.

PRICE FIVE CENTS.

HARPER'S WEEKLY has now been in existence four years. During that period no effort has been spared to make it the best possible Family Paper for the American People, and it is the belief of the Proprietors that, in the peculiar field which it occupies, no existing Periodical can compare with it.

Every Number of HARPER'S WEEKLY contains all the News of the week, Domestic and Foreign. The completeness of this department is, it is believed, unrivaled in any other weekly publication. Every noteworthy event is profusely and accurately illustrated at the time of its occurrence. And while no expense is spared to procure Original Illustrations, care is taken to lay before the reader every foreign picture which appears to possess general interest. In a word, the Subscriber to HARPER'S WEEKLY may rely upon obtaining a Pictorial History of the times in which we live, compiled and illustrated in the most perfect and complete manner possible. It is believed that the Illustrated Biographies alone—of which about one hundred and fifty have already been published—are worth far more to the reader than the whole cost of his subscription.

The literary matter of HARPER'S WEEKLY is supplied by some of the ablest writers in the English language. Every Number contains an installment of a serial story by a first-class author—BULWER'S "*What will he do with It?*" has appeared entire in its columns; one or more short Stories, the best that can be purchased at home or abroad; the best Poetry of the day; instructive Essays on topics of general interest; Comments on the Events of the time, in the shape of Editorials and the Lounger's philosophic and amusing Gossip; searching but generous Literary Criticisms; a Chess Chronicle; and full and careful reports of the Money, Merchandise, and Produce Markets.

In fixing at so low a price as Five Cents the price of their paper, the Publishers were aware that nothing but an enormous sale could remunerate them. They are happy to say that the receipts have already realized their anticipations, and justify still further efforts to make HARPER'S WEEKLY an indispensable guest in every home throughout the country.

TERMS.—One Copy for Twenty Weeks, $1 00; One Copy for One Year, $2 50; One Copy for Two Years, $4 00; Five Copies for One Year, $9 00; Twelve Copies for One Year, $20 00; Twenty-five Copies for One Year, $40 00. *An Extra Copy will be allowed for every Club of* TWELVE *or* TWENTY-FIVE SUBSCRIBERS.

HILDRETH'S HISTORY OF THE UNITED STATES.

Written with candor, brevity, fidelity to facts, and simplicity of style and manner, and forms a welcome addition to the library of the nation.—*Prot. Churchman*.

Mr. Hildreth is a bold and copious writer. His work is valuable for the immense amount of material it embodies.—*De Bow's Review of the Southern and Western States.*

We may safely commend Mr. Hildreth's work as written in an excellent style, and containing a vast amount of valuable information.—*Albany Argus.*

His style is vigorously simple. It has the virtue of perspicuity. — *Zion's Herald.*

We value it on account of its impartiality. We have found nothing to indicate the least desire on the part of the author to exalt or debase any man or any party. His very patriotism, though high-principled and sincere, is sober and discriminate, and appears to be held in strong check by the controlling recollection that he is writing for posterity, and that if the facts which he publishes will not honor his country and his countrymen, fulsome adulation will not add to their glory.—*N. Y. Commercial Advertiser.*

We are confident that when the merits of this history come to be known and appreciated, it will be extensively regarded as decidedly superior to any thing that before existed on American history, and as a valuable contribution to American authorship. These stately volumes will be an ornament to any library, and no intelligent American can afford to be without the work. We have nobly patronized the great English history of the age, let us not fail to appreciate and patronize an American history so respectable and valuable as this certainly is.—*Biblical Repository (Bibliotheca Sacra).*

This work professes only to deal in *facts;* it is a book of *records;* it puts together clearly, consecutively, and, we believe, with strict impartiality, the events of American history. The work indicates patient, honest, and careful research, systematic arrangement, and lucid exposition.—*Home Journal.*

To exhibit the progress of the country from infancy to maturity; to show the actual state of the people, the real character of their laws and institutions, and the true designs of their leading men, at different periods, and to relate a sound, unvarnished tale of our early history, has been his design; and we are free to acknowledge that it has been executed with marked ability and triumphant success. Every lover of impartial history will accord to Mr. Hildreth his due meed of praise for the able and honest manner in which he has given the true history of the United States.—*Pennsylvanian.*

This work is full of detail, bears marks of care and research, and is written under the guidance of clear sight and good judgment rather than of theory, philosophical or historical, or of prejudice of any sort whatever. We trust that it will be widely read.—*N. Y. Courier and Enquirer.*

We pronounce it unsurpassed as a full, clear, and truthful history of our country so far. We rejoice that a work so important to our nation has been so ably performed.—*Literary American.*

Interesting, valuable, and very attractive. It is written in a style eminently clear and attractive, and presents the remarkable history which it records in a form of great simplicity and with graphic force. There is in it no attempt to palliate what is wrong, or to conceal what is true. It is a life-like and reliable history of the most remarkable series of events in the annals of the world.—*N. Y. Journal of Commerce.*

It is a valuable acquisition to American literature.—*Baltimore American.*

The history of our country with a scrupulous regard to truth.—*Buffalo Courier.*

We believe this to be a truthful, judicious, and valuable history, worthy of general acceptation.—*Philadelphia North American.*

The first complete history of our country.—*Chronotype.*

Published by HARPER & BROTHERS,
Franklin Square, New York.

*** HARPER & BROTHERS will send the above Work by Mail, postage paid (for any distance in the United States under 3000 miles), on receipt of the Money.

It is a work of real historical value, the result of accurate criticism, written in a liberal spirit, and from first to last deeply interesting.—*Athenæum.*

The style is excellent, clear, vivid, eloquent; and the industry with which original sources have been investigated, and through which new light has been shed over perplexed incidents and characters, entitles Mr. Motley to a high rank in the literature of an age peculiarly rich in history.—*North British Review.*

It abounds in new information, and, as a first work, commands a very cordial recognition, not merely of the promise it gives, but of the extent and importance of the labor actually performed on it.—*London Examiner.*

Mr. Motley's "History" is a work of which any country might be proud.—*Press* (London).

Mr. Motley's History will be a standard book of reference in historical literature.—*London Literary Gazette.*

Mr. Motley has searched the whole range of historical documents necessary to the composition of his work.—*London Leader.*

This is really a great work. It belongs to the class of books in which we range our Grotes, Milmans, Merivales, and Macaulays, as the glories of English literature in the department of history. * * * Mr. Motley's gifts as a historical writer are among the highest and rarest.—*Nonconformist* (London).

Mr. Motley's volumes will well repay perusal. * * * For his learning, his liberal tone, and his generous enthusiasm, we heartily commend him, and bid him good speed for the remainer of his interesting and heroic narrative.—*Saturday Review.*

The story is a noble one, and is worthily treated. * * * Mr. Motley has had the patience to unravel, with unfailing perseverance, the thousand intricate plots of the adversaries of the Prince of Orange; but the details and the literal extracts which he has derived from original documents, and transferred to his pages, give a truthful color and a picturesque effect, which are especially charming.—*London Daily News.*

M. Lothrop Motley dans son magnifique tableau de la formation de notre République.—G. Groen Van Prinsterer.

Our accomplished countryman, Mr. J. Lothrop Motley, who, during the last five years, for the better prosecution of his labors, has established his residence in the neighborhood of the scenes of his narrative. No one acquainted with the fine powers of mind possessed by this scholar, and the earnestness with which he has devoted himself to the task, can doubt that he will do full justice to his important but difficult subject.—W. H. Prescott.

The production of such a work as this astonishes, while it gratifies the pride of the American reader.—*N. Y. Observer.*

The "Rise of the Dutch Republic" at once, and by acclamation, takes its place by the "Decline and Fall of the Roman Empire," as a work which, whether for research, substance, or style, will never be superseded.—*N. Y. Albion.*

A work upon which all who read the English language may congratulate themselves.—*New Yorker Handels Zeitung.*

Mr. Motley's place is now (alluding to this book) with Hallam and Lord Mahon, Alison and Macaulay in the Old Country, and with Washington Irving, Prescott, and Bancroft in this.—*N. Y. Times.*

The authority, in the English tongue, for the history of the period and people to which it refers.—*N. Y. Courier and Enquirer.*

This work at once places the author on the list of American historians which has been so signally illustrated by the names of Irving, Prescott, Bancroft, and Hildreth.—*Boston Times.*

The work is a noble one, and a most desirable acquisition to our historical literature.—*Mobile Advertiser.*

Such a work is an honor to its author, to his country, and to the age in which it was written.—*Ohio Farmer.*

Published by HARPER & BROTHERS,
Franklin Square, New York.

Harper & Brothers will send the above Work by Mail (postage paid (for any distance in the United States under 3000 miles), on receipt of the Money.

www.ingramcontent.com/pod-product-compliance
Lightning Source LLC
LaVergne TN
LVHW020213110826
845151LV00003B/702

* 9 7 8 1 4 2 5 5 3 4 9 6 7 *